The Maximalist Novel

The Maximalist Novel

From Thomas Pynchon's *Gravity's Rainbow* to Roberto Bolaño's *2666*

Stefano Ercolino

Translated by Albert Sbragia

B L O O M S B U R Y
NEW YORK • LONDON • NEW DELHI • SYDNEY

Bloomsbury Academic
An imprint of Bloomsbury Publishing Inc

1385 Broadway
New York
NY 10018
USA

50 Bedford Square
London
WC1B 3DP
UK

www.bloomsbury.com

Bloomsbury is a registered trade mark of Bloomsbury Publishing Plc

First published 2014

Library of Congress Cataloging-in-Publication Data
A catalog record for this book is available from the Library of Congress.

ISBN: HB: 978-1-6235-6291-5
ePDF: 978-1-6235-6496-4
ePub: 978-1-6235-6190-1

Typeset by Deanta Global Publishing Services, Chennai, India
Printed and bound in the United States of America

To Massimo Fusillo

Contents

Part 2

List of Figures

Acknowledgments

I would like to thank Franco Moretti for the time he has dedicated to me and for his most valuable suggestions during the drafting of the manuscript. I would also like to thank Dorothy J. Hale for her intelligence and patience in commenting on the various versions of this work. I would like to thank the Department of Comparative Literature at the University of California, Berkeley, for hosting me during a rewarding research visit. Finally, I would like to thank my father, and Elvira, the only person who truly realizes everything that this project has cost me. Above all, I would like to thank Massimo Fusillo, without whom this book would not exist.

The Maximalist Novel

Gravity's Rainbow (Thomas Pynchon), *Infinite Jest* (David Foster Wallace), *Underworld* (Don DeLillo), *White Teeth* (Zadie Smith), *The Corrections* (Jonathan Franzen), *2666* (Roberto Bolaño), *2005 dopo Cristo* (Babette Factory)

The literary object I aim to define in this study is the *maximalist novel.* It is an aesthetically hybrid genre of the contemporary novel that develops in the second half of the twentieth century in the United States, then "emigrates" to Europe and Latin America at the threshold of the twenty-first. "Maximalist," for the multiform maximizing and hypertrophic tension of the narrative; "novel," because the texts I will discuss are indeed novels. The aim of this study is to stake out a new conceptual territory that will contribute to a reconfiguration of the traditional view of the postmodern as well as a rethinking of the development of the novel in the second half of the twentieth century. I will begin with the issue of periodization and with the textual corpus.

The principal texts on which the hypothesis of the maximalist novel was founded range, roughly, from the last quarter of the twentieth century to the present. To be precise, from Thomas Pynchon's *Gravity's Rainbow* (1973) to Babette Factory's *2005 dopo Cristo* (2005): a little more than 30 years. From 1973 to 2005. I will be looking at seven novels from this period: 1. *Gravity's Rainbow*, Thomas Pynchon (United States, 1973); 2. *Infinite Jest*, David Foster Wallace (United States, 1996); 3. *Underworld*, Don DeLillo (United States, 1997); 4. *White Teeth*, Zadie Smith (United Kingdom, 2000); 5. *The Corrections*, Jonathan Franzen (United States, 2001); 6. *2666*, Roberto Bolaño (Spain, 2004)[1]; 7. *2005 dopo Cristo*, Babette Factory (Italy, 2005).

Other texts could have been included. Novels such as Joseph McElroy's *Women and Men* (1987), William T. Vollmann's *You Bright and Risen Angels* (1988) and *Europe Central* (2005), William H. Gass's *The Tunnel* (1995), Thomas Pynchon's *Mason & Dixon* (1997) and *Against the Day* (2006) could

[1] The novel was published posthumously in 2004 in Spain, where Bolaño, a Chilean novelist and poet, lived from the 1970s until his death in 2003 in Barcelona.

have been discussed, albeit with certain distinctions, together with the seven selected texts. Not to mention just about the entire production of William Gaddis: from *The Recognitions* (1955) to *Agapē Agape* (2002), and including *J R* (1975) and *A Frolic of His Own* (1994). Besides the fact that sixteen novels—the nine just mentioned plus the seven analyzed in this study—would have been difficult to cover adequately, an important reason for excluding these other texts is that they are all American, while I am also interested in accounting for the supranational aspect of the maximalist novel, its transversal presence in Western literature. It is true that of the seven novels I will examine, four are American. This is in recognition of an American primacy, but it is a primacy that should not overshadow other important voices. Thus the insertion of the novel by Zadie Smith, an English author with Jamaican roots, that of Roberto Bolaño, a Chilean writer, and the novel by Babette Factory, a collective of Italian writers.

More difficult was the decision to leave out Gaddis; all the more difficult because of his (relative) chronological primacy, his first novel, *The Recognitions*, having been written in 1955. The decision to exclude him was motivated by the search for truly "paradigmatic" texts to serve as the basis for my analysis.[2] Pynchon's *Gravity's Rainbow* is very paradigmatic as regards American maximalist experiments, much more so than Gaddis's *The Recognitions*. So paradigmatic, in fact, that all maximalist novels which follow were either directly or indirectly influenced by it. It is hard to imagine a novel such as *Infinite Jest* without *Gravity's Rainbow* as a precedent. It is possible, to be sure, but problematic.

The idea of cutting into a *continuum*, arbitrarily selecting the objects to focus on, certainly not the only ones possible, presented some interesting theoretical implications. Literary genre theory is often obsessed by the problem of determining a beginning and an end, the appearance and the disappearance of a certain structure under analysis. This obsession frequently ends up obfuscating an important characteristic of every literary form, and of novel genres in particular: their intrinsic, greater or lesser, structural instability,

[2] In any case, it should be emphasized that Gaddis's influence on successive maximalist novelists is not lacking. To the contrary, it is rather apparent, especially in relation to the epistemological status of maximalist encyclopedism (see 33–5).

which derives from their constitutional osmotic opening toward the literary system as a whole. To say "it begins here" is a fairly binding affirmation, given that, as we shall see concerning the maximalist novel's strong ties to ancient epic, one can trace current literary phenomena to the origins of literature itself, if not even further to the shrouded mists of an oral culture in which those origins have their own roots. Therefore, it would be wiser perhaps to orient ourselves, in the ocean of literary forms, not by adhering to a genetic-eschatological approach, but to one that could be defined according to the double criterion of *concentration* and *salience*. We direct our attention to where we see the *concentration* of a certain number of common traits in a variety of literary objects, but we begin our analysis only at that place and time in which this *concentration* reaches high levels of *salience* in a given text, that is, when it becomes paradigmatic. This is precisely what occurs with *Gravity's Rainbow*, and that is why my analysis begins there.

Concerning the opposite limit point, the end, it is almost impossible, in speaking of contemporary literature, to say when something truly ends. The last maximalist novel to be considered here is from 2005, but there is at the very least one more that has appeared since, Pynchon's 2006 *Against the Day*. Why, for that matter, necessarily stop at the last exemplar, to date, of this contemporary novel genre, and not instead at the second to last, or the third to last? The word "end" is as restrictive as the word "beginning," so I will not speak here of beginnings or ends, but simply of a literary form that, at a certain point, became *observable, and thus definable*.

The maximalist novel possesses a very strong morphological and symbolic identity. There are ten elements that define it and as a genre of the contemporary novel:

1. Length
2. Encyclopedic mode
3. Dissonant chorality
4. Diegetic exuberance
5. Completeness
6. Narratorial omniscience
7. Paranoid imagination

8. Intersemioticity
9. Ethical commitment
10. Hybrid realism

These ten characteristics were chosen after intense close readings and syntheses of the seven novels in question, as will be amply documented. A comparative analysis of the textual corpus had initially yielded a grid of ten elements common to all of the novels, as well as eleven others shared by some of them: a jungle of categories and subcategories in which it became difficult to orient oneself. The features had to be compacted conceptually, so as to include hyponymous categories within hypernymous categories. For example, initially self-standing categories such as "genre mixing" and "polystylism," were subsequently incorporated into the category "encyclopedic mode," since both can be located within the voracious predisposition of the maximalist novel to merge genres and styles, one of the many forms assumed by its encyclopedism.

Not all ten features, of course, have the same importance in each of the texts examined, but all of them are decisive, insofar as they are systematically *co-present*, in determining that the text belongs to the maximalist novel as a genre. To imagine an absolute uniformity with relation to each feature would be to make one of those erroneous metatextual inferences typical of genre theory, by which the specificity of each text succumbs to the all-powerful exigency to create transversal virtual objects, each endowed with the greatest possible heuristic power. A necessary evil of theory perhaps, but one which should not make us forget how, beyond all efforts to typify, texts *always* maintain a certain margin of theoretical irreducibility, precisely because of their continual resemantization during their reading. The margin exists, to be sure, and it is what guarantees the vitality of the text through time, but it should not impede interpretive attempts that aim to circumscribe an imagery and a morphological makeup common to a plurality of texts. In the present case, we are talking about shared symbolic and formal structures that will allow us to speak of a genre of the contemporary novel with well-defined parameters, without neglecting the fact that the genre also provides for an ample variety of expressive solutions. Doing genre theory does not mean—or, better put, should not mean—disregarding the text's specificity. It simply means *choosing* a broader point of view in following as objectively as possible the intrinsically utopian nature of any theoretical effort, that is, *synthesizing the heterogeneous.* It is a suspect and highly ideologized operation, necessarily tending to abstraction.[3] Yet it also enables the creation of those hermeneutic frameworks necessary for understanding the relationships among the individual phenomena that occur within the literary system as well as the relationships instituted between them and the world.

Such is the case here. The varying treatment of the ten features that define the maximalist novel is often conditioned in a decisive way by the greater or lesser degree of experimentalism in the novels themselves. This degree of experimentalism is measured not across the totality of each novel, but at the level of single characteristics. As a result, we will have novels that are longer, novels that are more encyclopedic, novels that are more polyphonic, novels that are more digressive, novels that are more paranoid, novels that are more intersemiotic than others, but in all cases, there is the clearly identifiable presence of each feature in each novel. It is precisely on this common ground, on this intertextual *traceability* of a collective maximalist imagery, that the theoretical proposal of this study is based.

A note on methodology; rather than discussing each novel in relation to the ten common traits, I have opted for a thematic approach, which has the advantage of greater flexibility and transversality. The number of features is much less important than their *significance* and their individual *function.* Accordingly, my analysis will follow a double binary. On the one hand, I will focus on the theoretical, historical and aesthetic significance of each feature. On the other, I will discuss the function which each of them has in the internal dialectic of the genre. This will allow us at the end of the first part of the essay to speak of a *chaos function* and a *cosmos function* in relation to some of the features. What will emerge is a dialectic between centrifugal and centripetal forces within the narrative, in which traits such as "length," "encyclopedic mode," "dissonant chorality," and "diegetic exuberance"—in spite of their strong specificity and reciprocal irreducibility—will play a

[3] See Antoine Compagnon *Literature, Theory, and Common Sense* [1998], trans. Carol Cosman (Princeton: Princeton University Press, 2004), 1–14.

common role *against* traits such as "completeness," "narratorial omniscience," and "paranoia." In the second part of the study, we will see that even without having a particular role in the internal dialectic of the genre, the remaining three features, "intersemioticity," "ethical commitment," and "hybrid realism," will prove just as crucial as the other seven for understanding the ethical and aesthetic project of the maximalist novel.

The decalogue form, unfortunately, was unavoidable. The points in common were, in fact, ten, not one more, not one less. Be that as it may, I trust it will not prejudice the reader against getting acquainted with this new and fascinating literary object called the *maximalist novel.* But first, a bit of theory.

Introduction: Maximalist Paradigms

There are some precedents. Three other theoretical hypotheses, concerning narratives that, in a broad sense, could be called maximalist, exist: Tom LeClair's *systems novel*[1]; Franco Moretti's *world text* (*opera mondo*)[2]; and Frederick R. Karl's *Mega-Novel*[3]; "in a broad sense," because these theoretical proposals have few similarities with the genre of the maximalist novel discussed here. Nevertheless, it is important to take them into account, especially because we will be dealing with novels that LeClair and Karl have both examined, albeit in different ways, and because certain fundamental conceptual categories that Moretti uses for his world texts will appear more than once in my analyses, even if, depending on the case at hand, revised or, sometimes, even reversed.

These three theories are heuristically ambitious and often very sophisticated, in accordance with the complexity of the works they describe. They all have a common focus of investigation: long, superabundant, hypertrophic narratives, both in form and content. All aim at the description of a genre or a mode of literary representation. And all three, by some counts, are not suitable for describing the specific reality of the maximalist novel. But let us proceed step by step. Since all three have been influential for my own research hypothesis, and since I will often refer to them, I will expound on each one briefly and, as much as possible, neutrally. For the moment, I will limit myself to only a few considerations. These will prove to be useful, however, for a first approach in understanding the narrative universe and cultural context of the maximalist novel. I'll begin with the *systems novel*.

1 Tom LeClair, *The Art of Excess: Mastery in Contemporary American Fiction* (Urbana: University of Illinois Press, 1989).

2 Franco Moretti, *Modern Epic: The World System from Goethe to García Marquez* [1994], trans. Quintin Hoare (London: Verso, 1996).

3 Frederick R. Karl, *American Fictions: 1980-2000: Whose America Is It Anyway?* (Bloomington: Xlibris, 2001), 155–225.

1 "Art of excess": The systems novel

In *The Art of Excess*, Tom LeClair defines the *systems novel* primarily on the basis of two elements: the concept of "mastery," and systems theory.

Distancing "mastery" from any negative connotations, LeClair underlines its positive and paradoxically liberating potential. He argues that in order to challenge the logic of social and symbolic reproduction in the West, it is necessary and sufficient to establish a conceptual mastery of reality, one that operates a rhetorical control over the narrative processes by means of which that reality is represented. LeClair explains that the seven systems novels[4] he analyzes exercise three types of "mastery": (1) "of the world;" (2) "of narrative methods;" (3) "of the reader."[5] The first regards the conceptual-encyclopedic domination of the world; the second, the command of the rhetorical strategies of narrative representation; the third, the capacity of such novels to "transform" the reader, redirecting his interests "from the personal and individual to the common and global."[6] A triple mastery, therefore: semantic, rhetorical, and pragmatic.

The second component on which LeClair grounds his hypothesis is systems theory. The idea is that behind the appearance of the systems novel there is a paradigm shift that has occurred in the natural sciences—biology in particular—which has also implicated fiction, redefining its themes and methods. This paradigm shift is seen to involve the move from a mechanist approach based on physics, once prevalent in each branch of science, to systems theory,[7] at the heart of which lies the research of the Austrian biologist Ludwig von Bertalanffy, begun in the 1920s.[8] Totality, interconnection, organization, information exchange, and openness became the guidelines of a complex and transversal epistemological reorganization which took place more or less midway through the twentieth century

[4] *Gravity's Rainbow*, Thomas Pynchon; *Something Happened*, Joseph Heller; *J R*, William Gaddis; *The Public Burning*, Robert Coover; *Women and Men*, Joseph McElroy; *LETTERS*, John Barth; *Always Coming Home*, Ursula Le Guin.

[5] LeClair, *The Art of Excess*, 5.

[6] Ibid., 2–3.

[7] Ibid., 6–7.

[8] See Ludwig von Bertalanffy, *General Systems Theory: Foundations, Developments, Applications* (New York: G. Braziller, 1969).

and which redefined not only the field and methods of the mathematical, physical, and natural sciences but also our very way of life, not to mention its literary representation.[9] As LeClair himself recognizes,[10] systems theory is a "master code" for his analysis,[11] serving as a foundation for the vibrant utopia that permeates his entire essay. Only the encyclopedic knowledge and the awareness of the interconnection of all forms of learning expressed by systems novels, LeClair argues, can guarantee a solid conceptual grip on the world and possession of the intellectual means necessary to understand and challenge power, in addition to restoring to literature, together with a renewed capacity for social critique, its lost centrality in the system of the arts.[12]

Even from a strictly formal point of view, mastery and systems theory, for LeClair, shape the narrative processes of the systems novel. LeClair indicates, in this regard, five "aesthetic strategies" employed by the systems novelist: (1) the rhetorical transformation of text and reader; (2) the comic mode; (3) the narrator as "orchestrator"; (4) self-reference and the creation of imitative forms; and (5) the "Hermes" author as a parasite who enters into the mind of the reader and perturbs her thoughts, directing them toward the polemical objectives of the novel.[13] In brief, the first aesthetic strategy consists in continually soliciting and deconfirming the reader's expectations, resulting in the emergence of a questioning process capable of "transforming" her, enabling her to recognize that she is dealing with a representation that is critical to power and its instruments of control. The second involves a presentation of events and/or characters that is often comic in order to mitigate and eventually overcome the reader's resistance when faced with the harshness of systems novels. The third conceives of the narrator more as an arranger or orchestrator

9 Anthony Wilden [*System and Structure: Essays in Communication and Exchange* (New York: Tavistock, 1980), 241] defines this epistemological reorganization as being interdependent and traceable "to Freud, to Hegel, to Marx, to Clerk Maxwell, to von Bertalanffy, or to Szilard's solution of the problem of the Maxwell demon in 1929. Obviously, in such a complex epistemological reorganization as we are experiencing in this century, the new territory staked out by any one discipline, science, or movement cannot be comprehended except in relation to all the others." See LeClair, *The Art of Excess*, 7.

10 LeClair, *The Art of Excess*, 13.

11 Fredric Jameson, *The Political Unconsciousness: Narrative as a Socially Symbolic Act* (Ithaca: Cornell University Press, 1981), 10.

12 LeClair, *The Art of Excess*, 25–6.

13 Ibid., 21–5.

of the narrative materials, rather than as an inventor or artist.[14] The fourth strategy is composed of two distinct elements: self-reference and the creation of imitative forms. The first refers to the ability of systems novels to refer to themselves in terms of themselves, a manifestation of the self-referentiality of systems, a characteristic property of complex systems. The second—which will prove to be important for understanding the structural practices of the maximalist novel—consists in the creation of imitative forms or patterns, which rein in and give sense to the excess of data flowing through the "novels of excess." The fifth aesthetic strategy is the least firm and concrete of the five, more a metaphor than a true constituent principle. Borrowed by LeClair from Michel Serres's study, *The Parasite*,[15] it is at heart a variation on the theme of the first aesthetic strategy, based, as it is, on the maieutic image of the author as a Hermes-parasite, one who raises the reader's consciousness to partake in the exposure of power's mechanisms.

I will deal with the merits of the conceptual construct of the systems novel later. For now, I limit myself to a discussion of the presumed liberating power of the "novel of excess" which, according to LeClair, is guaranteed by mastery, that is to say, the control of narrative procedures and content. This conviction is present, even if in different forms, in all three of the theoretical hypotheses concerning maximalist narratives discussed in this introduction and, taken case by case, is not always so simple to justify. It can be misleading to attribute an excessively strong democratic vocation to the systems novel. It aspire to rival the world at large in breadth and complexity, but it does so in order to affirm its *own* complexity. The world is challenged with another world, reality with an extended and totalizing narrative. A battle between equal foes? Definitely not. Or perhaps it is. No novel, no matter how meandering and vast it might be, can ever provide more than a *synecdoche* of the world and of its uninterrupted informational

[14] "[T]he systems persona is a collector rather than a creator, an editor rather than an artist, an "orchestrator" (as Barth calls himself) rather than an inventor, a large-minded bricoleur rather than an engineer" (Ibid., 22–3). This idea is strongly inflected by Roland Barthes's concept of the "death of the author." In the course of my study, I will seek to show its extraneousness to the maximalist novel.

[15] Michel Serres, *The Parasite* [1997], trans. Lawrence R. Schehr, intro. Cary Wolfe (Minneaspolis: University of Minnesota Press, 2007).

flow.[16] And yet we see that in systems novels those synecdoches truly are extensive, certainly much more extensive than in any other narrative form. It is thus difficult to completely agree with LeClair when he affirms:

> Perhaps in the future some new word will replace "mastery," or perhaps writers, both male and female, will give up any attempt to understand and represent huge cultural realities. But now, in our time of massive mastering systems and small literary gestures, we need large-scale visions and powerful assertions. I think the masterwork's knowledge, imagination, and effect ultimately empower readers, illustrating what one mind, male or female, can do in one place. While manifesting an individual's intellectual interests and power, the masterwork also reminds readers that, whether our literary interests are primarily aesthetic (Barthesian pleasure or bliss) or political (economic, racial, or gender), all interests must exist within and recognize *the* master system—the global ecosystem—that is the ultimate subject of, frequent model for, and reason to write about the art of excess.[17]

A novel that empowers the reader and enables the realization that she belongs to the global ecosystem; one that reestablishes her harmony with the world in which she lives: a wonderful utopia indeed. But how can a novel with latent imperialist ambitions "liberate" and enlighten the reader? And can a reader truly have dazzling epiphanies reading a systems novel, that is to say, a novel that is torrential, chaotic, labyrinthine, long-winded, shrouded in obscure symbolisms, and structured by such rigid and often hard-to-unravel logic? It depends on the reader, of course. But perhaps the question is more complicated and takes us to the heart of the explicative possibilities of today's literature. It is an important question and one that I will try to address, albeit in a limited way, in the course of this study.

That being said, the critique of power and of grand narratives, so important in LeClair's analysis, is present in the systems novel, and it is present in a massive way. What seems questionable, instead, is how LeClair always has this

[16] LeClair points out that no writer masters the totality of the world or of information, since "[w]hat he masters is synecdoche, the illusion that the parts he has selected, structured, proportioned, and scaled are appropriate substitutes in context for what could be a much larger set of parts, which in turn would only suggest, not exhaust, the whole of discourse" (*The Art of Excess*, 18).

[17] Ibid., 31–2.

"deconstructive" moment followed by a "reconstructive" one. Such a thesis can, at most, be only partially true for a novel like *Gravity's Rainbow,* to take one example. Yes, Pynchon does ideally reassemble the chaos and destruction of wartime and postwar Europe in the hope of a new (re)integration and regeneration of all of humankind in the world system[18] but with tones and effects that are anything but liberating. Is it liberating to trade one system for another system, to trade one projection of mastery for another one? Can exchanging one narration with another, even if it is more "democratic" and critical, truly free anyone? Will it not be necessary to eventually jettison this new narrative as well when, sooner or later, it will prove insufficient and not complex enough *vis-à-vis* a world growing increasingly more complex? And yet the fact remains that the unmasking of the hypocrisies and false myths of the West is powerful and manifest in the systems novel. This being the case, rather than speak of a "novel of excess" as the vehicle for a counterpower endowed with a liberating and palingenetic potential, as LeClair does or, in contrast, as a novel genre with hegemonic ambitions, it would make more sense to speak of an *ambiguous* relationship between maximalist narrative forms and power.[19] And it is this very ambiguity which is the principal reason why the relationship between the maximalist novel and power, although not completely ignored, will receive only secondary attention in this essay.

Nonetheless, the fascination for this ambiguity remains. Extremely critical with regard to power and the West but, at the same time, unable to

18 Ibid., 36–68.

19 Franco Moretti, perhaps, alludes indirectly to this ambiguity when he writes, with reference to Goethe's *Faust*: "If the history so liberally dispensed by world texts were precisely the appropriate illusion for a Europe bent on conquering the globe? The 'walking encyclopaedias' mocked by Nietzsche as grotesque outcomes of a century sick with history—here they are: *Faust, Ulysses, Cantos, Waste Land*. . . . Thanks to them, the West has gained the breadth of vision consonant with its new world power—while keeping itself at a safe distance from crude geographical truth" (*Modern Epic*, 50). And when, on the other hand, we read with reference to *The Waste Land*: "So, yes: the totalitarian temptation is almost always present in the modernist world text, as a reaction to a complexity that has grown beyond every expectation. But it is just a temptation—which never becomes the dominant presence. And, let us be clear, it is not that literature cannot be fascist. It can very well be fascist, and indeed has been. But it is harder for that to happen *in the case of world texts*. Culturally impure, transnational, with no longer any sense of the 'enemy,' hypereducated, indulgent towards consumption, enamoured of eccentricities and experiments: hard to make reactionary works, with such ingredients" (Ibid., 228).

conceive of itself in a form that is not project-bound and tightly structured, the novel of excess reveals itself to be so saturated with the West that it is incapable of putting it into question without taking on its very project of mastery.

2 "A paradoxical form": The Mega-Novel

The third chapter of Frederick Karl's weighty *American Fictions: 1980-2000: Whose America is it Anyway*?[20] is dedicated to a novel genre which he calls the *Mega-Novel* and which appears in the second half of the twentieth century. Karl sees the Mega-Novel as the principal American narrative form after World War II and as the sole legacy it will leave to future generations,[21] and he immediately defines it as a paradoxical form:

> The so-called Mega-Novel is loaded with paradoxes: it *is* long but lacks any sense of completion; while it has no boundaries for an ending, of course it does end; it seems to defy clear organization—it seems decentered, unbalanced—yet has intense order; it is located outside traditional forms of narrative, but still employs some conventional modes. Its aim posits disorder, messiness, the chaos of our existence and by extension of our times; nevertheless, its length, complexity, and on-goingness make it a model of order.[22]

Karl condenses the principal characteristics of the Mega-Novel in a few lines: (1) length; (2) openness; (3) incompleteness; (4) chaos; (5) order; (6) traditionalism; and (7) experimentalism.[23] Each of these is discussed by Karl in relation to the

[20] A voluminous panorama of American narrative of the last two decades of the twentieth century, *American Fictions: 1980-2000* is a continuation of Karl's previous work, *American Fictions: 1940-1980: A Comprehensive History and Critical Evaluation* (New York: Harper and Row, 1983). It is an attempt to synthesize for a period of over 20 years the vast literary field of contemporary American narrative.

[21] Karl, *American Fictions: 1980-2000*, 162.

[22] Ibid., 155.

[23] There are evident points of contact between Karl's Mega-Novel and LeClair's systems novel. In *American Fictions: 1980-2000*, Karl himself points to a dialogue between the works of the two authors (495–6, n. 96).

novels he analyzes,[24] which do not, however, constitute all existing Mega-Novels, but only a small portion.[25] Karl maintains that the genre is born with William Gaddis's *The Recognitions* (1955) and develops very prolifically over the subsequent 40 plus years, up to Thomas Pynchon's *Mason & Dixon* (1997), the last exemplar, in chronological order, to be taken into consideration. As with LeClair's systems novel, I will touch on the merits of Karl's theoretical construction in the course of this study and will limit myself for the moment to just a few considerations.

Karl poses a very complex question: why did the Mega-Novel appear in the United States in the mid-1950s?[26] In a first instance, Karl responds that a constitutionally open-ended fiction is particularly well suited to the "American spirit."[27] He goes further though, remarking that, with the exception of the archetypal *The Recognitions*, the Mega-Novel truly begins to develop in the 1960s, and he suggests that it is the direct offspring of the culture of those years, that is to say, of

> the overwhelming sense we were on a frontier of knowledge; that we had glimpsed, however imperfectly, another kind of experience; and that this experience was open-ended, spatial, expansive, resolute but without resolution. Critical of the country and even negative as most of these novels are, they are profoundly American, intensely representative of the American spirit.[28]

The question is complex: Is it enough to evoke the "American spirit" and the spirit of the 1960s to justify the writing of a novel such as Pynchon's *Gravity's Rainbow* or David Foster Wallace's *Infinite Jest*? The reason why some of the most talented American writers of the second half of the twentieth century

[24] Joseph McElroy's *Women and Men*; Norman Mailer's *Harlot's Ghosts*; Harold Brodkey's *The Runaway Soul*; William Gaddis's *A Frolic of His Own*; and, in Chapter 6, dedicated to the 1990s, Don DeLillo's *Underworld*; David Foster Wallace's *Infinite Jest*; Thomas Pynchon's *Mason and Dixon*.

[25] To keep his analysis within the boundaries of 1980-2000, Karl, although he cites them, does not take into examination Mega-Novels written before 1980, some of which he had already discussed in *American Fictions: 1940-1980*.

[26] Karl, *American Fictions: 1980-2000*, 162.

[27] The Americanness of the Mega-Novel is for Karl a self-evident fact, and an important part of his theoretical hypothesis. LeClair too, for his part, speaks of the systems novel as a typically American phenomenon.

[28] Karl, *American Fictions: 1980-2000*, 162.

decided at a certain point to start writing monstrous novels, both in scope and ambition, novels that would end up consuming so many years of their lives, is something for which we can only provide relatively unsure conjectures. And it is also difficult to explain the proliferation of maximalist narratives from the 1950s until the present or the reason why the maximalist form ended up triumphant in the North American literary system, passing unscathed through the minimalist period of the 1980s, which had seemed destined to last indefinitely. Could one explanation be perhaps that a highly sophisticated literary form is the most suitable possible response to a hypercomplex world? Theoretically yes, perhaps, but at a practical-compositional level things are not so simple. Probably the answer to all of this should be searched for at the level of the cultural-literary imagery, beginning with the change in perception and aesthetic categories that took place toward the middle of the twentieth century with the advent of the postmodern and that then followed eccentric and unforeseen paths; paths which, for the moment, remain obscure and little explored by literary criticism.

Another thorny problem that LeClair had already raised,[29] and that Karl too raises in passing[30] is the minimal presence of women or minority writers in the systems novel or Mega-Novel canons. While Karl includes no women writers in the selection of novels he analyzes, and merely notes that Mega-Novels are written principally by white Protestant males,[31] LeClair, who does take into examination Ursula Le Guin's *Always Coming Home*, attempts to explain the phenomenon. He maintains that since women and minorities have often had to—and still have to—fight forcefully for the attainment of civil rights, they have not enjoyed the same privilege as white males to look at the entire country or the world from a position of full belonging. Focused so much and rightfully so on their status as individuals or groups and on their individual or collective relations with the dominant culture, women and minority authors, for LeClair, have not been able to fully "master" in their novels—even though they criticize it fiercely and often hypothesize alternatives to them—the power

[29] LeClair, *The Art of Excess*, 29–30.

[30] Karl, *American Fictions: 1980-2000*, 162.

[31] "While reviewers and critics have hooked on to categories of Jewish novelists, gays, black writers, female authors, another kind of novel has emerged: written mainly (not solely) by white Protestant males" (*American Fictions: 1980-2000*, 162).

systems of the great Western democracies, as the writers of systems novels do.[32] This can be debated of course, but it is probably true, and the reason could lie precisely in the fact that "these groups have certainly not had the white male's luxury of examining the whole of American or multinational culture from within, from the perspective of full membership."[33] It is not very refined as an analysis perhaps, but it does exemplify one type of the problems and answers that we will need to engage from time to time in the course of this study; problems that will be only broached, and answers only barely intimated, since it would require much more specialized expertise to propose truly satisfactory solutions. This study then should be taken as a first opening or platform from which to attempt to reflect from a different perspective on some of the most pressing questions of our time. Before beginning that process, however, we will conclude our theoretical excursus with Franco Moretti's *modern epic*.

3 "In the eyes of the world": The modern epic

> *Faust*, *Moby-Dick*, *The Nibelung's Ring*, *Ulysses*, *The Cantos*, *The Waste Land*, *The Man Without Qualities*, *One Hundred Years of Solitude*. These are not just any old books. They are monuments. Sacred texts that the modern West has subjected to a lengthy scrutiny, searching in them for its own secret. Literary history, though, is puzzled about what to do with them. It does not know how to classify them; it treats them instead as isolated phenomena: one-off cases, oddities, anomalies. Which, of course, is quite possible. But possible once or twice, not in every case. With so many and such prominent

[32] "I am aware that my criteria for mastery have allowed into *The Art of Excess* only one woman and no Afro-American writers. Are the criteria inherently prejudicial? Inasmuch as women and members of ethnic minorities have often been deprived of full participation in American life, the writers who have emerged from these groups have certainly not had the white male's luxury of examining the whole of American or multinational culture from within, from the perspective of full membership. Writing by women and members of ethnic minorities thus often concerns itself with definitions of the individual, her or his relation to the group, and the group's relation to American culture. The outsider's view is valuable to her or his group. When the view is far and wide, it offers not only a critique of the dominant culture but an alternative, the achievement of novels such as Leslie Silko's *Ceremony* or Ishmael Reed's *Mumbo Jumbo*. Although I include such books in my courses, I do not think they master the power systems of America as thoroughly or profoundly as the books included here." LeClair, *The Art of Excess*, 29–30.

[33] Ibid., 29.

> anomalies, it is far likelier there is something wrong with the initial taxonomy. So, rather than recording one exception after another, it would be better to change perspective, and postulate a different rule.
>
> The idea behind this book, therefore, is that the works just mentioned—along with others we shall encounter along the way—all belong to a single field that I shall term "modern epic." "Epic," because of the many structural similarities binding it to a distant past (something to which I shall naturally return, when the time comes for analysis). But "modern" epic, because there are certainly quite a few discontinuities: important enough, indeed, in one case—the supranational dimension of the represented space—to dictate the cognitive metaphor of the "world text" which, in what is not just a verbal calque, recalls the "world-economy" of Braudel and Wallerstein.[34]

Modern epic, then, and a truly extensive field of inquiry: from *Faust* to *Cien años de soledad*, almost 150 years of literary history. Why epic? Because, structurally, the appeal is to a "distant past." Why modern? Because the discontinuities with the epic tradition are nevertheless present, the most considerable of which is the supranational dimension of the representation. Whence, accordingly, "world texts." Let us begin with the decision to evoke the epic.

What immediately comes to mind is why "epic," and not other narrative forms such as the "novel?" Moretti provides a first response by paraphrasing Hans Blumenberg in regard to *Faust*[35]:

> . . . a modern epic came into being because it was an "inherited form." It was the form through which classical antiquity, Christianity and the feudal world had represented the basis of civilizations, their overall meaning, their destiny. In theory, modern literature could certainly have dispensed with that precedent, and contented itself with the far narrower space-time of the novel. But that would have been to admit its own inferiority with respect to the greatness of the past.[36]

It all seems clear, but in the above observation is hidden an extremely complex problem which involves, at a deep level, not only the relationship

34 Moretti, *Modern Epic*, 1–2.

35 Hans Blumenberg, *The Legitimacy of the Modern Age* [1966], trans. Robert M. Wallace (Cambridge, MA: MIT Press, 1983).

36 Moretti, *Modern Epic*, 36.

between the epic and the novel and the uncertain origins of the latter but also the thematic and formal structuring of the ancient and modern narrative universe.

Massimo Fusillo has shown how the bond between the epic and the novel has always been strong.[37] From the *Aethiopika* of Heliodorus to the nineteenth century, the novel has often looked to the epic, the canonical genre par excellence, adopting its motifs and formal procedures to legitimate its own spurious origins and to attempt to overcome its own age-old marginal status. But from the age of Goethe on, at which point the novel was anything but marginal and on its way instead to its lengthy and still unchallenged sway over the literary system, it has continued to look to the epic, no longer to legitimate itself, but rather to "expand and achieve new and increasingly totalizing forms."[38] For its part, the epic too, from the time of its origins, has not been extraneous to "novelistic" content and discursive strategies, so much so, that Fusillo, referring to a by now well-established tradition of study,[39] delineates how the timid and unsure beginnings of the novel can be located at the heart of the Homeric epic itself. This is not because the novel already existed in Homer's time but because certain traits considered typical of the novel were already present in the *Odyssey*,[40] if not in the *Iliad* as well.[41] A telling and precocious example of this type of "novelistic interference" in the epic can be found, for instance, in the *Argonautics* of Apollonius Rhodius, in which the erotic motif, sometimes intuitable but always on the background in the

[37] Massimo Fusillo, "Epic, Novel" [2002], trans. Michael F. Moore, in *The Novel*, ed. Franco Moretti (Princeton: Princeton University Press, 2006), vol. II, *Forms and Themes*, 32–63.

[38] Ibid., 41.

[39] See Uvo Hölscher, *Die "Odyssee": Epos zwischen Märchen und Roman* (Munich: C. H. Beck, 1988); Irene De Jong, *Narrators and Focalizers: The Presentation of the Story in the "Iliad"* (Amsterdam: Grüner, 1987); Robert J. Rabel, *Plot and Point of View in the "Iliad"* (Ann Arbor: University of Michigan Press, 1997).

[40] Gerard Genette finds in certain characteristic features of the *Odyssey*—such as the adventure theme, the almost exclusive focalization of the story on one hero only, and the presence of autodiegesis in books IX–XII—clear signs that it belongs to a genre which is different from that of the *Iliad*, or, in other words, clear signs of a movement from the epic sphere in the direction of the novel. See Genette, *Palimpsests: Literature in the Second Degree* [1982], trans. Channa Newmann and Claude Doubinsky, foreward by Gerald Prince (Lincoln: University of Nebraska Press, 1997), 179–92. See Fusillo, "Epic, Novel," 37–8.

[41] In this regard, Guido Paduano emphasizes that Achilles does not embody a collective spirit at all, but stands, to the contrary, in stark contrast with the world that surrounds him. He is not a hero who, with respect to the Western and, in particular, the Hegelian codification of the epic, incarnates the values and the behavioral codes of an entire community (or, at least, not completely), but is a more complex character, the bearer of marked anti-authoritarian traits. See "Le scelte di Achille," in Omero, *Iliade*, ed. Guido Paduano (Torino: Einaudi, 1997). See Fusillo, "Epic, Novel," 39.

Homeric epos, comes to the fore.[42] As it does later, of course, in Chretien de Troyes's Breton romances or in Ariosto's chivalric poem, where epic and novel are inextricably intertwined.

But let us return to that long-standing, self-legitimizing tendency of the novel to justify its content and form by referring to the epic, a lofty and prestigious genre in absolute; it is a tendency which conceals a core ideological defect which must be exposed. It was Hegel, codifying an age-old conviction, who baptized the epic as the original form par excellence and the novel as the "modern *bourgeois* epic," a derivative and secondary literary form at the antipodes of that "*primitive* poetic general situation" from which sprung the epic.[43] The Hegelian opposition between the epic and the novel closely echoes the opposition between the original and the derivative, the primary and the secondary[44]: two of those grand binarisms upon which modernity has erected its own symbolic order and which for some time now, under the long sway of poststructuralism, have been undermined. Thus, more than a question of the epic and the novel as a Scylla and a Charybdis situated at the opposite extremes of the system of narrative forms, with one brandishing the badge of originality and the other living in the shadow of the glory of the first, Fusillo proposes what we could call a *hybridization paradigm* between the two genres. As a matter of fact, the novel has always drunk at the formal and thematic well of the epic, at first to legitimize an unsure and perhaps still fragile identity, but later surpassing and devouring the epic in a totalizing aspiration in no way inferior to that of the ancient epic itself. It is this double movement of *making the novel epic* and *making the epic novelistic* that has shaped in a decisive, albeit not exclusive way, the narrative universe across the centuries.[45]

Let us now return to Moretti and, in light of what has been said, ask ourselves the following: even if it is true, as he argues, that between the eighteenth and

[42] Beginning with Chariton's *Chaereas and Callirhoe* (first century BC), the first of the extant Greek novels, eroticism is taken to be a key trait of the Greek, and later Roman, novel; on the Greek novel, see Massimo Fusillo, *Il romanzo greco: Polifonia ed Eros* (Venice: Marsilio, 1989). For this reason, but not only—in "Epic, Novel," 40, Fusillo notes the presence of other novelistic themes in Apollonius, such as travel, adventure and antiheroism—the *Argonautics* of Apollonius, in which the erotic motif appears in the ill-fated love of Medea for Jason, are seen to be a sort of proto-novel.

[43] Georg Wilhelm Friedrich Hegel, *Aesthetics* [1836–38], trans. T. M. Knox (Oxford: Clarendon Press, 1975), vol. II, 1092.

[44] Fusillo, "Epic, Novel," 32–3.

[45] Ibid., 41.

nineteenth centuries the modern epic had to emerge as an "inherited" form and as a more suitable means for expressing a yearning for grandeur that the literature of the age was unable to satisfy with the novel, why critically legitimate *today*, under the aegis of "modern epic," such an ideologically charged past yearning? The postmodern novel, whose galaxy includes the maximalist novel, has never known, for its part, those problems of legitimization that the novel encountered before affirming itself in the nineteenth century as an hegemonic form. In the same way that postmodernity is exempt from the problem of legitimization *tout court*, which was so decisive instead for the construction of the symbolic order of modernity. In this study, accordingly, we will not speak of epic, even a modern one, but of a novel structurally *hybridized* with the epic, of a novel that cannibalizes the epic to launch itself toward ever vaster and more totalizing horizons—just different names one could object, but that is not the case.

Let us try to reread Moretti bearing in mind Lukács's notion, also derived from Hegelian aesthetics, of the novel as a form dominated by the longing and the nostalgia for the totality of the epic but also aware of its impossibility.[46] What we see is the emergence of a Hegel-Lukács-Moretti train of thought that links the epic form to the ambition to a synthetic and totalizing representation of the world. That this representation of totality in world texts is only an attempt, and a substantially failed one at that,[47] does not count for much: the power and the universalizing dream of the ancient epic envelop the modern epic as well. A universalizing dream that in Moretti's analysis is evidenced in a fundamental characteristic of world texts: polyphony. The modern epic is a polyphonic epic, a form that aspires to a synthesis of the real through a strong embrace of dialogism. It is Lukács plus Bakhtin, or, more appropriately, a Hegelian-Lukácsian appropriation of Bakhtin. As is well known, the polyphonic literary form par excellence for

[46] "The novel is the epic of an age in which the extensive totality of life is no longer directly given, in which the immanence of meaning in life has become a problem, yet which still thinks in terms of totality." Georg Lukács, *The Theory of the Novel* [1919], trans. Anna Bostock (Cambridge, MA: MIT Press, 1971), 56.

[47] Moretti asserts repeatedly the notion of the "morphological imperfection" of world texts, a strong idea that drives a theory on the evolution of literary forms. See Moretti, *Modern Epic*, 17–22, and, in particular, Moretti, *Graphs, Maps and Trees: Abstract Models for Literary History*, afterword by Alberto Piazza (London: Verso, 2005).

Bakhtin is the novel, not the epic,[48] but Moretti has none of it: "*Pace* Bakhtin, in short, the polyphonic form of the modern West is not the novel, but if anything precisely the epic: which specializes in the heterogeneous space of the world-system, and must learn to provide a stage for its many different voices."[49]

It seems to be the same problem as before. Even when we leave aside Bakhtin's mechanical and mythicizing opposition between a monologic genre, the epic, and a polyphonic genre, the novel,[50] since, in the end, all literary forms engage to a greater or lesser extent in polyphony—and thus there is no absolute monologism, not even in lyric poetry—there still remains the Hegelian concept, tainted by the Western obsession for the original, that only the epic, as a form with its primitive "savagery,"[51] can aspire to offer a totalizing representation of the real. Yet it is possible, on the other hand, to see polyphony itself, as a decisive indicator that epic and novel have often intersected in the course of literary history and continue to do so today as well. To juxtapose a centrifugal and polyphonic epic to a centripetal and monologic novel[52] is the equivalent, in a manner of speaking, of considering literary genres to be smooth and impermeable, when instead they are highly karstic, porous, permeable. What I would like to propose then is the idea of a system of narrative genres constantly traversed by polyphonic and monologic tensions that cluster, in different historical moments, around either the epic or the novel, that is to say, a narrative system in which the epic and the novel continually *interfere*, defining each in relation to the other and insuring, in that way, their mutual *survival.* For just as the novel needed to recur to the legitimizing tradition of the epic, so today the epic, in a certain sense, needs the novel to continue to survive. The epic was, in fact, the first literary genre to come to light—Western literature is born with it—but it was

48 Mikhail Bakhtin, *The Dialogic Imagination*, ed. Michael Holquist, trans. Caryl Emerson and Michael Holquist (Austin: University of Texas Press, 1981).

49 Moretti, *Modern Epic*, 56–7.

50 Mark Sherman assumes a radical position in this respect, asserting that epic and novel have revealed themselves to be unproductive notions in literary praxis. See Mark A. Sherman, "Problems of Bakhtin's Epic: Capitalism and the Image of History," in *Bakhtin and Medieval Voices*, ed. Thomas J. Farrell (Gainesville: University Press of Florida, 1995), 180–95.

51 James Joyce, *The Critical Writings of James Joyce*, eds. Ellsworth Mason and Richard Ellmann (New York: Viking, 1964), 45.

52 Moretti refers in particular to the nineteenth-century novel that "pin[s] the story at the centre of the nation-state," *Modern Epic*, 56.

also a not very long-lived literary genre.[53] Milton's *Paradise Lost* is generally considered to be the last epic poem, and, if we except Derek Walcott's recent experimentation in a postcolonial epic with *Omeros*,[54] it becomes clear that the epic has endured over the centuries primarily in hybrid constructions, from the parodic and degraded form of the mock-heroic,[55] to Moretti's world texts. Today, it is the novel, and perhaps only the novel, that is able to take up the legacy of the epic and its universalizing dream. This is precisely what occurs in Mega-Novels, in systems novels, and in the maximalist novel. When the historical conditions which produced them disappear, and when the aesthetic framework in which they originally developed changes, literary forms die, but not always. It often, very often, happens that forms more resilient than others survive, "accommodated" in other forms. And so for the epic, which, in novels such as Don DeLillo's *Underworld* or Roberto Bolaño's *2666*, has returned to speak to us directly, transformed, to be sure, but preserving intact its utopian tension.[56]

All of the above serves to explain why I have chosen to use in this study the word "novel" and not "epic," even with Moretti's qualifier of "modern," to refer to those maximalist narratives, which I will attempt to set into a specific genre of the contemporary novel. Excessive zeal? Probably not, given the notable importance of Moretti's essay for this work. We will see, in fact, that some of his main points, such as the supranational dimension of the representation, namely the "strong" spatiality of world texts, will be very useful in clarifying certain aspects of my theoretical proposal.

But now, after these preliminaries, let us enter into the heart of our topic and let us begin to bring into focus our object of analysis. We will start therefore with the *material foundation* of the maximalist narrative project, *length*.

53 Fusillo, "Epic, Novel," 35.

54 On Walcott's *Omeros* and epic experiments in contemporary literature see *Epic Traditions in the Contemporary World: The Poetics of Community*, ed. Margaret Beissinger (Berkeley: University of California Press, 1999).

55 See Clotilde Bertoni, *Percorsi europei dell'eroicomico* (Pisa: Nistri Lischi, 1997).

56 See Fusillo, "Epic, Novel," 61–3.

Part One

1

Length

Gravity's Rainbow: 912 pages[1]; *Infinite Jest*: 1,079 pages[2]; *Underworld*: 827 pages[3]; *White Teeth*: 448 pages[4]; *The Corrections*: 672 pages[5]; *2666*: 1,105 pages[6]; *2005 dopo Cristo*: 401 pages.[7] From a minimum of 401 pages to a maximum of 1,105 pages. Long novels. In five cases, beyond long, very long. Why?

The length of maximalist novels is not a neutral material fact but something more. It is both a *possibility* and a potent *attraction*; a possibility, tied to the strongly innovative and experimental nature of maximalist novels as well as to their epic, totalizing ambition; an attraction, whose reasons instead lie in the advertising dynamics of the publishing market and in these novels' peculiar status as commodities.

As Viktor Shklovsky suggested, formal innovation is nothing other than the fruit of a slippage, of an accidental change. In literary texts, the old accumulates quantitatively on the new, and when the accumulated changes pass from being purely quantitative to being qualitative, a new form is born.[8] In *Modern Epic*, Moretti rereads this idea through the concept of bricolage, understood as the motor of literary evolution, and affirms that in moments of transition, the production of a new process cannot be planned, or rather, not always: "because

1 Thomas Pynchon, *Gravity's Rainbow* [1973] (New York: Vintage, 1998).
2 David Foster Wallace, *Infinite Jest* [1996], foreword by Dave Eggers (New York: Back Bay Books/ Little, 2006).
3 Don DeLillo, *Underworld* (New York: Scribner, 1997).
4 Zadie Smith, *White Teeth* (New York: Vintage, 2000).
5 Jonathan Franzen, *The Corrections* [2001] (New York: Harper Perennial, 2007).
6 Roberto Bolaño, *2666* [2004] (Barcelona: Anagrama, 2008); *2666*, English trans. Natasha Wimmer (New York: Farrar, Straus and Giroux, 2008).
7 Babette Factory, *2005 dopo Cristo* [*AD 2005*] (Turin: Einaudi, 2005).
8 Viktor Shlovsky, *Material i stil v romane L. N. Tolstogo "Vojna i mir"* (Moscow: Federatsiia, 1928), 232–7.

change is not planned: it is the fruit of the most irresponsible and free—the blindest—rhetorical experimentation."[9] He later concludes that

> if Shklovsky is right, and formal innovation proceeds "in a quantitative way"—then it will happen more easily in those texts that have *a larger quantity of space at their disposal*. I do not believe it accidental that Shklovsky should formulate his hypothesis while discussing *War and Peace* (or that it should find full confirmation in *Ulysses*). Large dimensions are probably favourable to formal innovation. They allow more time, more chances, greater freedom.
>
> And the epic form allows greater freedom for another reason, too—a structural one, this time. The epic, as we saw with *Faust*, is a form prone to digressions: full of episodes flanking the basic Action. Marginal episodes—and, for that very reason, favourable to experimentation. Because a truly innovative attempt usually begins in an uncertain, and perhaps even quite unpromising, fashion: if located in the foreground, it would be frozen by the immediate requirements of the plot. But if the experiment is at the margins of the text, the author is freer to play with the form. Even if things go as badly as can be (as in "Scylla and Charybdis", or "Sirens"), the catastrophe will have a limited effect, leaving the overall structure of the work intact. The textual periphery functions as a kind of protected space, where an innovation has time to develop, and consolidate its own peculiarities. Then, once it is ready, the new technique crystallizes: it rids itself of the old motivation, and it moves to the foreground.[10]

It could not be said better. A procedure, or a new genre, is born from a quantitative accumulation of details at the periphery of the text. They then move to its center when the innovation has become firmly consolidated. Length would represent the ideal condition for the unfolding of this process, insofar as it is possible that the more space that is available, the greater the accumulation of details, and hence, the greater the likelihood that a new form will be brought to light. Of course, both Shklovsky and Moretti point to single innovative processes which find, initially, a protected space at the periphery of the text where they can flourish, to then move to the textual foreground at the moment in which they have reached a certain

[9] Moretti, *Modern Epic*, 19.
[10] Ibid., 189.

expressive maturity. Moretti offers a brilliant example of this for stream of consciousness which, even though it had been used originally and notoriously by Édouard Dujardin, achieves the full extent of its formal potential only in *Ulysses*.[11] The case of the maximalist novel, instead, is a bit different. Its length is the necessary precondition for the radicalization of not just one aspect, but a multiplicity of procedures. As we shall see in the first part of this essay, the "morphosphere"[12] of the maximalist novel is defined by the constant and often extreme use—albeit within a certain spectrum of variability—of a series of rhetorical strategies. Except perhaps as regards the peculiar form of narratorial omniscience characteristic of some of the maximalist novels we will examine, these strategies do not contain in themselves features of strong innovation. It is rather their *copresence* and *interaction* which determine their unique formal contours. It is in this sense that length should be understood to be the indispensable material foundation of the maximalist narrative project: the container that has made and makes possible its existence as a highly experimental literary genre. It is difficult, if not impossible, to imagine a maximalist novel that is not long, and this is not only because of formal innovation. A text that aspires to rival the entire world cannot do so except by assuming the latter's amplitude. And some of the most important tools the maximalist novel employs to obtain that goal—encyclopedism, chorality, digressions, the polycentric multiplication of narrative threads—would not, in a restricted space, be able to fully express their potential as "world effects."[13] They require extensive dimensions to insure their full efficacy. But there is also more.

In a review of *Infinite Jest* for the *New York Times Magazine*, Frank Bruni quotes Amy Rhodes—head of marketing for the publishing house Little, Brown & Company, which released *Infinite Jest* in 1996—who stated that the publicity campaign for the promotion of the novel was orchestrated precisely

[11] Ibid., 173–81.

[12] Andrea Miconi derives this term from Yuri Lotman's celebrated concept of the "semiosphere," and he uses it to indicate "*the range of variations* and not the overall synthesis of structures of meanings" (Andrea Miconi, "Dal 'real meravilloso' al realismo magico: Approccio evolutivo alla formazione di un genere," *Paragrafo*, II (2006): 29 and n. 7).

[13] Recalling Roland Barthes's celebrated "reality effect," Moretti speaks of "world effects" in relation to the polyphonic scene of the "Walpurgis Night" in *Faust*: "devices that give the reader the impression of being truly in the presence of the world; that make the *text* look like the world—open, heterogeneous, incomplete." Moretti, *Modern Epic*, 59.

around its imposing dimensions, promoted as a clear sign of its importance.[14] Length became then a guarantee of worth and, in Rhodes's words, of "a certain undeniability" about it.[15] A careful marketing strategy was constructed around the novel's length in preparation for the release of *Infinite Jest*, a book which—the publishing house assured the 4,000 store owners, critics, and journalists to whom it had announced its imminent arrival in bookstores with an avalanche of elusive postcards—would give readers "infinite pleasure" with "infinite style."[16] An interesting or, at the very least, curious thing: a promotional campaign for a novel that revolves around a mere material fact, its length.

In the section "Grandville, or the World Exhibitions," of the opening "Exposé" of his *Arcades Project*, Walter Benjamin coined the suggestive expression of "the sex appeal of the inorganic" to describe the powerful and novel attraction exercised by commodities in the Paris of Baudelaire beset by modernity[17]:

> Fashion prescribes the ritual according to which the commodity fetish demands to be worshipped. . . . Fashion stands in opposition to the organic. It couples the living body to the inorganic world. To the living, it defends the rights of the corpse. The fetishism that succumbs to the sex appeal of the inorganic is its vital nerve. The cult of the commodity presses such fetishism into its service.[18]

The inorganic appeal and cult of the corpse: Benjamin establishes on Marxist grounds an extraordinary negative aesthetics of the commodity-object. Understood as the typical mode of the bourgeois gaze turned on consumer goods, a necrophilic gaze,[19] and a sort of dark side of the "theological niceties" of commodities,[20] fetishism is released from its traditional connotations

[14] Frank Bruni, "The Grunge American Novel," *New York Times Magazine*, 24 March 1996, 38–41.
[15] Ibid., 40.
[16] Ibid. See Stephen J. Burn, *David Foster Wallace's "Infinite Jest": A Reader's Guide* (New York-London: Continuum, 2003), 66–7.
[17] Walter Benjamin, "Paris, the Capital of the Nineteenth Century" [1935], in Benjamin, *The Arcades Project* [*Das Passagen-Werk* (1927-1940), ed. Rolf Tiedemann], trans. Howard Eiland and Kevin McLaughlin (Cambridge, MA: Belknap Press of Harvard University Press, 1999), 7–8.
[18] Ibid., 8.
[19] See Massimo Fusillo, *Feticci: Letteratura, cinema, arti visive* (Bologna: Il Mulino, 2012), 26.
[20] Karl Marx, *Capital: A Critical Analysis of Capitalist Production* [1867], intro. Ernest Mandel, trans. Ben Fowles (New York: Vintage, 1977), vol. I, 163.

of perversion and primitivism[21] and placed at the heart of a rich aesthetic category such as "the sex appeal of the inorganic." Mario Perniola has explored the category most efficaciously: analyzing heterogeneous phenomena such as cyberpunk, drugs, and metafiction, he has identified a new form of the contemporary cultural imaginary, as well as a way of living sexuality beyond traditional notions of desire and pleasure, as a death libido directed at the sphere of the inorganic.[22]

But let us return to the maximalist novel, and let us attempt to read the promotional campaign for *Infinite Jest* based on its notable length within the framework of the "sex appeal of the inorganic." Infinitization of quantity, and fetishistic fixation with the object of desire, length, in accordance with a substitution mechanism typical of fetishism,[23] becomes the tangible sign of something extremely precious and desirable. The maximalist novel would seem to be, from this point of view, one of the most refined literary products of late capitalism. Hundreds and hundreds of pages and some hefty weight, its status as a commodity is unequivocally confirmed at a *sensorial level.* It makes perfect sense. We find ourselves face to face with the quintessence of that progressive commodification of culture theorized by Fredric Jameson and fully revealed with the advancement of postmodernity and late capitalism.[24] Only in this kind of historico-economic context can the promotion of a book based on its dimensions make sense. That is to say, a publicity campaign that tries to make a novel desirable by treating it as an object endowed with its own sex appeal: a commodity item that takes up a good bit of shelf space in bookstores, which is impressive because of its physical size, and certainly not because it is a highly sophisticated literary product. It should not come as a surprise then that most maximalist novels in circulation have enjoyed

[21] Fusillo, *Feticci*, 25–7. The bibliography on so complex and ancient a cultural phenomenon is enormous, to say the least, especially if we take into consideration more or less recent contributions generated in the fields of cultural studies and, in particular, fashion studies. For an introduction, see Alfonso Maria Iacono, *Teorie del feticismo: Il problema filosofico e storico di un "immenso malinteso"* (Milan: Giuffré, 1985), and Stefano Mistura, *Figure del feticismo* (Turin: Einaudi, 2001).

[22] Mario Perniola, *The Sex Appeal of the Inorganic: Philsophies of Desire in the Modern World* [1994], trans. Massimo Verdicchio (New York: Bloomsbury, 2004). See Massimo Fusillo, *Estetica della letteratura* (Bologna: Il Mulino, 2009), 168–71.

[23] See Sigmund Freud, "The Fetish" [1927], in *The Standard Edition of the Complete Psychological Works of Sigmund Freud*, ed. and trans. James Strachey et al. (London: The Hogarth Press, 1961), vol. XXI, 152–7.

[24] Fredric Jameson, *Postmodernism, or the Cultural Logic of Late Capitalism* (Durham: Duke University Press, 1991), 1–66.

considerable editorial success. Suffice it to recall that *Infinite Jest, White Teeth*, and *The Corrections* were all bestsellers. The meager success of world texts with the reading public, lamented by Moretti, counterbalanced, however, by their academic cult status,[25] seems to be literally reversed in the case of maximalist novels. In order to understand the reasons why the maximalist novel has been so warmly embraced by the reading public while world texts were relatively unsuccessful in their brief time, we must probably look at that "sex appeal of the inorganic," under whose shadow modernity took root, and which was strongly accentuated beginning around the second half of the 1950s, on the heels of the epochal epistemological rupture of the postmodern. It is a phenomenon that was surely already present at an embryonic stage in Baudelaire's Paris or in Joyce's Dublin, but which fully unleashed its enormous power of enchantment only with the establishment and the boom of mass consumption society, drawing into its orbit ever new and diverse commodities. Today, more than ever, market globalization and the development of seductive and broadly accessible technologies seem to have considerably enlarged the domain of the fetishistic desire for the inorganic.[26] The high-tech and telecommunications industries, for instance, have demonstrated their ability to create new status symbols. Apple products, for example, are the reification of a certain way of thinking, of acting in the world, of doing politics; they are true and affordable *identity fetishes*, pure ideology. And in these times of dramatic existential uncertainties and ideological murkiness, who would not be willing to pay a price, and not a very high price at that, to secure an object endowed with such tremendous power?

Perhaps the same is true for the maximalist novel. To be sure, for a professional critic, the reason why one might feel drawn to a novel of large dimensions is, most likely, not so readily intuitable. That is, it is not at all simple to understand what the metaphysical substratum that underpins the mass appeal of large-dimensioned novels might be. One could conjecture that by buying a maximalist novel, the (common) reader believes he is entering

[25] Moretti, *Modern Epic*, 4–5.

[26] See Giovanni Anceschi, *Il progetto delle interfacce: Oggetti colloquiali e protesi virtuali* (Milan: Domus Academy, 1992); *La società degli oggetti: Problemi di intersoggettività*, eds. Eric Landowski and Gianfranco Marrone (Rome: Meltemi, 2002); Ernesto L. Francalanci, *Estetica degli oggetti* (Bologna: Il Mulino, 2006).

into possession of a rather full-bodied synecdoche of "Culture," of an identity fetish—a testimony to the appeal that the cultural universe still manages, perhaps, to exercise on the public at large. And it is clear that, in this case, it would be a question of the same logic adopted by the publishing house Little in the promotion of *Infinite Jest*, that is to say, the assumption that the dimensions of a book constitute an unequivocal sign, because it is a tangible one, of the book's importance. This is possibly a somewhat simplistic analysis, but a necessary one, given the close bond between the maximalist novel and the marketplace, as witnessed by its sales success. Especially if we consider that the appeal of books of large dimensions to a large reading public is a phenomenon that does not concern the maximalist novel alone but also a broad swath of so-called "popular literature," where the fascination with length is even more pronounced; suffice it to think of the immense publishing success of writers like Frederick Forsyth, John Grisham, and Dan Brown, all authors of long works of fiction.

Let us close, then, this chapter on length by underscoring the strong *Westernness* of the maximalist novel. Not sufficiently satisfied with making the West its exclusive object of representation, it constructs itself around its selfsame productive and symbolic obsessions, thereby asserting itself as the most representative literary product of our time.

2

Encyclopedic Mode

1 An "encyclopedic novel"?

Since Northrop Frye's classic discussion,[1] beginning in the 1970s, there have been several attempts toward a theory of encyclopedism, all in the direction of its identification as a novel genre or a mode, characteristic of literary modernity as such. In particular, I am referring to "encyclopedic narrative" and the "encyclopedic novel," theorized by Edward Mendelson and Stephen J. Burn, respectively. Let us begin with Burn.

A genre rooted in the origins and at the heart of modernity, a genre that begins its course with Flaubert's *Bouvard et Pécuchet*, passes through modernism and James Joyce's *Ulysses*, opens to the postmodern in the work of Gaddis, and culminates in the 1990s in the encyclopedic experiments of Wallace, Smith, Evan Dara, and Richard Powers. This is how Stephen Burn delineates the first steps of the "encyclopedic novel," which he considers to be a genre of the Western novel.[2]

In Flaubert's work, the famous dream of writing a book on nothing, which would stand solely on the strength and coherence of its very style,[3] coexists with one of the most impressive efforts made in Western literature to write a book, instead, on everything, *Bouvard et Pécuchet*, Flaubert's

[1] Northrop Frye, *Anatomy of Criticism: Four Essays* [1957], with a preface by Harold Bloom (Princeton-Oxford: Princeton University Press, 2000), 315–26.

[2] Stephen J. Burn, "The Collapse of Everything: William Gaddis and the Encyclopedic Novel," in *Paper Empire: William Gaddis and the World* System, eds. Joseph Tabbi and Rone Shavers, intro. Joseph Tabbi (Tuscaloosa: University of Alabama Press, 2007), 46–62.

[3] Thus, wrote Flaubert to Loiuse Colet in the celebrated letter of 16 January 1852: "What seems beautiful to me, what I should like to write, is a book about nothing, a book dependent on nothing external, which would be held together by the internal strength of its style, just as the earth, suspended in the void, depends on nothing external for its support; a book which would have almost no subject, or at least in which the subject would be almost invisible, if such a thing is possible." Gustave Flaubert, *The Letters of Gustave Flaubert (1830-1857)*, ed. and trans. Francis Steegmuller (Cambridge, MA and London: Belknap Press, 1979), 154.

final and unfinished novel project.[4] These two opposite inclinations have weighed heavily in the definition of modernist aesthetics. An aesthetics not so uniform and monocentric as it has often been maintained[5] but at the very least bipolar, if not polycentric, crisscrossed by radically opposite tensions. Italo Calvino pointed out how the desire to write encyclopedic novels was one of the strongest aspirations of modernism[6]: luminous examples being the works of James Joyce, Ezra Pound, Robert Musil, and John Dos Passos; an aspiration that often has been cast in the name of Flaubert's unfinished masterpiece[7] and has been seen, moreover, as so evident that many have defined it as the dominant tendency in literary modernism. Michael André Bernstein, for instance, refers to it in setting up an opposition between modernism and postmodernism, in which the encyclopedism of the great modernist masterpieces is seen as impossible within the landscape of postmodern culture, dominated by the Lyotardian waning of grand narratives and of any strong and totalizing worldview.[8] Nevertheless, Burn shows how the modernist encyclopedic afflatus has not weakened in the postmodern era but has acquired, instead, a hitherto unknown vigor and complexity in the works of Gaddis and in those of numerous contemporaneous North American writers. I will have occasion to pause repeatedly in the course of this study on the very interconnected and ambiguous relationship of the maximalist novel with the postmodern, and I will evidence different aspects of it in accordance with the topic under investigation. For the moment, I will limit myself to a small clarification concerning the well-known Lyotardian slogan of the "end of grand narratives."

Lyotard's "postmodern condition"[9] has often been evoked inappropriately with regard to the postmodern literary system. The end of some of the master

4 See Burn, "The Collapse of Everything," 47.

5 In *After the Great Divide: Modernism, Mass Culture, Postmodernism* [1986] (Basingstoke: Macmillan, 1988), 54, Andreas Huyssen maintains that Flaubert's ambition to write a book on nothing, standing solely on style, laid the foundations for literary modernism.

6 Italo Calvino, *Six Memos for the Next Millennium* (Cambridge, MA: Harvard University Press, 1988), 112–17.

7 Joyce himself explicitly pointed to Flaubert's project regarding his own *Finnegan's Wake*; see James Joyce, *Selected Letters of James Joyce*, ed. Richard Ellmann (London: Faber, 1975), 271.

8 Michael A. Bernstein, "Making Modernist Masterpieces," *Modernism/Modernity* 5, 3 (1998): 1–17. See Burn, "The Collapse of Everything," 48.

9 Jean-François Lyotard, *The Postmodern Condition: A Report on Knowledge* [1979], trans. Geoff Bennington and Brian Massumi, foreword by Fredric Jameson (Minneapolis: University of Minnesota Press, 1984).

metanarratives that have characterized modernity for a long time, and on the basis of which it has justified its project, has contributed in a decisive way to the postmodern epistemological turn and to the creation of a new sensibility,[10] but it certainly has not meant the disappearance of every sort of universalizing tension at the aesthetic level. To the contrary. After the World War II, when the ideological apparatus of modernity inexorably collapsed under the blows of history, a certain brand of postmodern literature remained stubbornly anchored to the encyclopedic and universalizing dream of modernism. A dream of utopian power, which seemed, and still seems, without limits. But it was not a question of merely reproposing rhetorical and cognitive strategies from the past, but rather of radically rethinking them. Let us try to give a brief account of this, starting, with the masterpiece of modernist encyclopedism: Joyce's *Ulysses*.

The encyclopedism of *Ulysses* is a commonly recognized fact.[11] It is based on the alienating and dramatic perception of the fragmentation, under way in Europe and Dublin during the first decades of the twentieth century, of the society and the urban fabric, in reaction to which, it casts itself as a partial, impossible, unifying attempt. Joyce himself, eloquently and half-ironically, summarized the meaning of the encyclopedic ambition of *Ulysses* when he declared that he wanted "to give a picture of Dublin so complete that if the city one day suddenly disappeared from the earth it could be reconstructed out of my book."[12]

An encyclopedism that is born then as a response to a threat of destruction that is as imminent as it is uncertain, an encyclopedism that offers itself as the last bulwark against the apocalypse: an immense *archive* able to preserve knowledge from possible catastrophes and to allow for the reconstruction of the world after a hypothetical cataclysm. The writing of an encyclopedic work, then, is not only possible, but posits itself as a veritable necessity, acquiring for itself strongly utopian connotations. A paradigmatic case in point is Bloom's library, composed of "several inverted volumes, improperly arranged and not in

[10] A new "structure of feelings"; see Raymond Williams, *Drama from Ibsen to Brecht* [1968] (Harmondsworth: Penguin, 1973), 9.

[11] See Burn, "The Collapse of Everything," 52–4.

[12] Quoted in Frank Budgen, *James Joyce and the Making of "Ulysses" and Other Writings* (London: Oxford University Press, 1972), 69.

the order of their common letters,"[13] that ranges from literature to philosophy, from theology to geography, from mathematics to history and biography:

> *Thom's Dublin Post Office Directory*. . . .
> Denis Florence M'Carthy's *Poetical Works*. . . .
> Shakespeare's *Works*. . . .
> *The Useful Ready Reckoner*. . . .
> *The Secret History of the Court of Charles II*. . . .
> *The Child's Guide*. . . .
> *When We Were Boys* by William O'Brien M. P. . . . .
> *Thoughts from Spinoza*. . . .
> *The Story Of The Heavens* by Sir Robert Ball. . . .
> Ellis's *Three Trips to Madagascar*. . . .
> *The Stark-Munro Letters* by A. Conan Doyle. . . .
> *Voyages in China* by "Viator". . . .
> *Philosophy of the Talmud*. . . .
> Lockhart's *Life of Napoleon*. . . .
> *Soll und Haben* by Gustav Freytag. . . .
> Hozier's *History of the Russo-Turkish War*. . . .
> *Laurence Bloomfield in Ireland* by William Allingham. . . .
> *A Handbook of Astronomy*. . . .
> *The Hidden Life of Christ*. . . .
> *In the Track of the Sun*. . . .
> *Physical Strength and How To Obtain It* by Eugen Sandow. . . .
> *Short but yet Plain Elements of Geometry* . . . by F. Ignat. Pardies. . . .[14]

A library composed of only 22 books, but whose variety and structural centrality in the overall architecture of *Ulysses* appears to be hinted at by the insertion of its description in the chapter "Ithaca," the penultimate of the novel's third part, which, according to Joyce's list of correspondences, was to constitute the "skeleton" of the work.[15]

In the postmodern, instead, things change considerably. The encyclopedic project explodes, crushed by its own weight. The enormous and amorphous mass of data that flows uninterruptedly from the multiple and pervasive

[13] James Joyce, *Ulysses* [1922], intro. Declan Kiberd (Harmondsworth: Penguin, 1992), 832.
[14] Joyce, *Ulysses*, 832–34.
[15] Burn, "The Collapse of Everything," 53.

channels of information established by the new media has rendered any attempt at encyclopedism titanic and destined intrinsically to fail. To possess the competence needed to master the immense quantity and quality of data in circulation has become definitively impossible.[16] And yet, encyclopedic works continue to be written.[17] Why?

Taking up Jean-Paul Sartre's notion of totalisation, linked to the project of the *Critique of Dialectical Reason* and against the current critico-philosophical gospel that sees an elevated ideological risk in any expression ascribable to the semantic field of totality (total, totalizing, universal, universalizing, etc.),[18] Fredric Jameson establishes a distinction between the concepts of "totality" and "totalization," often, in his opinion, inappropriately confused.[19] Whereas the word "totality" seems, to allude to a stable system of truth and to the establishment of a privileged point of observation of the real, the term "totalization," apart from the specific meaning it assumes in Sartre's philosophy,[20] is rooted conceptually in the assertion of their impossibility and undesirability. It refers, in fact, Jameson states, to a process of "summing-up" the existent, conducted from an intrinsically partial perspective and devoid of homogenizing pretentions.[21] A process that is all the more necessary, the more the individual finds herself fragile and the more the world reveals itself to be complex and impermeable to her needs and desires; a process that places itself at the heart of modernist and postmodern encyclopedism. Applying Jameson's distinction to our reflection on encyclopedic forms, we can see a crowd of oppositions (original/derivative, center/periphery, autocracy/democracy, etc.) thickening around the

[16] A veritable excess of information: that informative excess which, according to LeClair, is mastered in the systems novel by abundant synecdoches of the most disparate fields of knowledge. See LeClair, *The Art of Excess*, 15. Pynchon too, in his often cited essay "Is it O.K. to Be a Luddite?" (*New York Times Book Review*, 28 October 1984), speaks of the swirling flows of information in which we are immersed, and of the crucial importance to master the broadest swath of knowledge possible.

[17] It is important to note how the encyclopedic interests of certain maximalist novelists have often found expression in non-literary forms of writing. This is the case for David Foster Wallace, the author of a history of the mathematical concept of infinity: *Everything and More: A Compact History of Infinity* (New York: Norton, 2004). In this regard see Wallace's interview with Dave Eggers in *The Believer*, November 2003.

[18] Linda Hutcheon writes: "... 'to totalize' does not just mean to unify, but rather means to unify with an eye to power and control, and as such, this term points to the hidden power relations behind our humanist and positivist systems of unifying disparate materials, be they aesthetic or scientific." *A Poetics of Postmodernism: History, Theory, Fiction* (New York: Routledge, 1988), xi.

[19] Jameson, *Postmodernism*, 331–40.

[20] Ibid., 332–3. See Martin Jay, *Marxism and Totality: The Adventures of a Concept from Lukács to Habermas* (Berkeley-Los Angeles: University of California Press, 1984), 331–60.

[21] Jameson, *Postmodernism*, 332.

fundamental dyad totality/totalization, with the opposition closure/openness fixing the theoretical extremes of Western encyclopedism, and with Georg Lukács[22] and Sartre representing the paradoxical deities of the encyclopedism of the ancient epic and the encyclopedism of twentieth-century fiction, respectively. Such rationalization of a phenomenon of *longue durée* is intriguing but, unfortunately, suffers from theory's fatal attraction to the conceptual force of binary logic. That the twentieth-century attempts at encyclopedism, from *Ulysses* to *Infinite Jest*, do not aim at the definition or the celebration in absolute terms of a shared system of values and domains of knowledge, as was the case for the Homeric epic or for the didactic epic of Hesiod, certainly does not mean that they are devoid of the ideological risks inherent in any totalizing narrative project. However much one may wish to accentuate the process, dynamism, and partiality of the adopted point of view ("totalization"), rather than the finished product, that is, what is represented ("totality"), the fact remains that the goal of encyclopedic works is a synthetic representation of the *totality* of the real. The difference, then, between the encyclopedism of the ancient epic and that of the twentieth century does not lie in a change in its nature or function, but rather, as we will see further along, in the *multiplication* and the *differentiation* of the encyclopedic attempts. The ideological risks linked to the concept of "totality" appear then to noticeably diminish within the overall picture of the pluralistic ecology of contemporary encyclopedism. This, however, should not overshadow the fundamental reasons for the persistence of an encyclopedic tension over time, or for the symbolic proximity between the ancient epic and modernist and postmodern encyclopedic forms.

Commenting on the words of a character in *Doctor Zhivago*[23] and on a passage from "Evolution and Tinkering" by François Jacob,[24] Moretti

[22] On the concept of "totality" in Lukács' philosophy, see Jay, *Marxism and Totality*, 81–127.

[23] "[I] have understood why this stuff is so deadly, so insufferable and artificial even who you come across it in *Faust*. The whole thing is an affectation, no one is genuinely interested in it. Modern man has no need of it. When he is vexed by the mysteries of the universe he turns to physics, not to Hesiod's hexameters. Boris Pasternak, *Doctor Zhivago*, trans. Max Hayward and Manya Harari (London: HarperCollins, 1988), 10; quoted in Moretti, *Modern Epic*, 37.

[24] "The price to be paid for this [the scientific] outlook, however, turned out to be high. It was, and is perhaps more than ever, renouncing a unified world view. . . . Most other systems of explanation—mythic, magic, or religious—generally encompass everything. They apply to every domain. They answer any possible question . . . Science proceeds differently. . . . Actually, the beginning of modern science can be dated from the time when such general questions as, 'How was the universe created?' were replaced by such limited questions as, 'How does a stone fall? How does water flow in a tube?'" François Jacob, "Evolution and Tinkering," *Science* 196 (10 June 1977): 1161; quoted in Moretti, *Modern Epic*, 37.

writes: “physics will never replace Hesiod, *because it does not confront the same questions.* And vice versa: so long as the need is felt for ‘a unitary world-view,’ modern science will have to yield to those ‘systems which apply to everything . . . and answer all questions.’”[25] Encyclopedism responds to the desire to capture the world in one fell swoop. It gives body to the overwhelming desire for a conceptual mastery of reality which grows ever stronger and ever more impossible to the same degree that reality grows complex and evasive. A desire that is not born with *Bouvard et Pécuchet*, as Burn would have it, for his “encyclopedic novel,” but which is rooted in the ancient synthetic and totalizing ambition of the epic, reaching back to Homer and Hesiod. A desire science will never be able to fully satisfy because of its ever-increasing structural specialization. Just as the crisis of the great ideologies of modernity rendered the world ever more hypercomplex, multicentric, and elusive, so literature embraced in an ever more desperate fashion ambitious and unending encyclopedic projects, destined inevitably to remain incomplete. Homeric encyclopedism, in fact, seems rather narrow when compared with Joyce’s, just as, in its turn, the encyclopedism of *Ulysses* literally evaporates compared with those of *Gravity’s Rainbow* or *Infinite Jest*. The greater the complexity of the world, the greater the efforts to represent it and the domains of knowledge necessary to attempt its synthesis, but this has never at any point deterred the proliferation of encyclopedic endeavors in Western literature. Probably writers will never stop trying to write total works, because it is a praxis tied to a deep and ineradicable need and illusion of being able to order, and thus master, the chaos and madness of existence. Whatever Lyotard may have to say, not all grand narratives came to an end with the advent of the postmodern. Not at the aesthetic level, at least.

But let us return to Burn. We had just finished referencing very briefly the encyclopedic structure of *Ulysses* and were getting ready to pursue the development of the “encyclopedic novel” in the postmodern. Burn conducts his analysis principally with regard to the novels of William Gaddis, but

[25] Ibid., 38.

the conclusions he draws are extended to the overall relationship of the postmodern to encyclopedic forms. We will try to briefly reconstruct his intriguing reasoning.

In *The Recognitions*,[26] the proliferation of encyclopedic materials is accompanied by a profound reflection on them in order to assert the inconceivability, in the here and now, of a work able to envision the totality of human learning, thereby proclaiming the end of the medieval encyclopedic dream Richard Yeo has written about.[27] A dream possible in the Middle Ages only inasmuch as encyclopedias at that time were limited to the reflection of a reality preordained by God[28]; a reality which could be catalogued and known because it was observed within a stable theological framework which guaranteed its unity. Thus the word "speculum," often inserted in the titles of medieval encyclopedias, such as the *Speculum Maius* of Vincent de Beauvais. This view entered progressively into crisis when, beginning in the seventeenth century, an increasing specialization of the domains of knowledge took hold, especially in the field of science. The mastery of knowledge by a single person became increasingly more difficult from that moment on in a world that was appearing evermore complex. Unlike in the Middle Ages, encyclopedias ceased to have a sole author at that point and became the fruit of collaboration of more than one person: precisely what took place with the first encyclopedia of the modern age, the celebrated *Encyclopédie* of Denis Diderot and Jean-Baptiste Le Rond D'Alembert, born from the new understanding of the fragmentary nature of knowledge and of the impossibility of its organic synthesis by a single individual. And above all, an encyclopedia envisioned by D'Alembert as a "sanctuary" of knowledge, able to preserve it from the erosion of time and from political and social upheavals.[29] We also found the same intention at the core of the encyclopedism of *Ulysses*: a novel from which Dublin could

[26] William Gaddis, *The Recognitions* [1955], intro. William H. Gass (Harmondsworth: Penguin, 1993).

[27] Richard Yeo, *Encyclopaedic Visions: Scientific Dictionaries and Enlightenment Culture* (Cambridge: Cambridge University Press, 2001), 5.

[28] See William N. West, *Theatres and Encyclopedias in Early Modern Europe* (Cambridge: Cambridge University Press, 2002), 22.

[29] Jean-Baptiste Le Rond D'Alembert, *Preliminary Discourse to the Encyclopedia of Diderot* [1751], trans. Richard N. Schwab and Walter E. Rex, intro. Schwab (Indianapolis: Bobbs-Sams, 1963), 121. See Burn, "The Collapse of Everything," 51–5.

have been reconstructed if one day it were to be destroyed. From its origins, in fact, the writing of an encyclopedic work has been firmly anchored to a sense of impending catastrophe, in reaction to which and because of which, it is written. Albeit it comes with the necessary qualifiers pertaining to the different nature of the two works, for both the *Encyclopédie* and *Ulysses*, the value and the utility of an encyclopedic work are indisputable: encyclopedism is useful and is necessary because it safeguards the centuries-old patrimony of human knowledge. I will return to the powerful apocalyptic sensation which pervades the maximalist novel. For the moment, we will look at it as linked in two complementary ways to the encyclopedic project: a sensation which, at an initial stage, enveloped the Enlightenment encyclopedia and later modernist encyclopedism and then burst open in the postmodern cultural perspective, paradigmatically putting into question, in the works of Gaddis, the very foundations of encyclopedic ambition.

In *The Recognitions*, the juxtaposition and the tension between the medieval model and the Enlightenment model of the encyclopedia develop across the span of the entire narration in the shadow of a progressive and creeping sense of collapse, framed emblematically within the incipit and conclusion of the novel. The epigraph, "Nihil cavum [vacuum] neque sine signo apud Deum," a distorted citation taken from the *Adversus haereses* of Irenaeus, as well as the ancient archetypal and alchemical symbol of the Uroboros on the title page (a serpent biting its tail, symbolizing the cyclical and interconnected nature of matter), seem to promise a novel adhering to the circularity and completeness of knowledge incarnated in the medieval model of the encyclopedia.[30] This promise, however, is progressively ignored during the course of the narrative and is radically overturned, at its end with Stanley's death, in the collapse of the church of Fenestrula, an eloquent symbol of the implosion of the cultural system under its own weight. Stanley's new musical composition, which turned out to be unbearable for the architecture of the building, and the inability of Stanley himself, an expert in musical composition and history, to comprehend the priest's warnings, reveal how the vertiginous increase of cultural entropy and the extreme specialization of knowledge have rendered impossible, once

[30] See Burn, "The Collapse of Everything," 56–7.

and for all, the encyclopedic mastery of human learning on the part of a single human being[31]:

> There [Stanley] explained he had come early, to play through this one part he would play later, explained as best as he could, that is, with his hands, the pages, pointing to the organ, to himself (the red necktie), for this priest understood no English, and spoke to him in Italian, a continuous stream of it as he conducted Stanley to the keyboard, leading him with a hand on his arm, then on his shoulder, and Stanley came on head bowed, closely attending the words he did not understand. . . . Prego, fare attenzione, non usi troppo i bassi, le note basse. La chiesa è così vecchia che le vibrazioni, capisce, potrebbero essere pericolose. Per favore non bassi . . . e non strane combinazioni di note, capisce . . .
>
> When he was left alone, when he had pulled out one stop after another (for the work required it), Stanley straightened himself on the seat, tightened the knot of the red necktie, and struck. The music soared around him. . . . The walls quivered, still he did not hesitate. Everything moved, and even falling, soared in atonement.
>
> He was the only person caught in the collapse, and afterward, most of his work was recovered too, and it is still spoken of, when it is noted, with high regard, though seldom played.[32]

We are at the antipodes of the Enlightenment encyclopedic dream and of *Ulysses*. Encyclopedic fiction collapses: crushed by the ungovernable mass of data it contains, it does not escape catastrophe. This collapse will be more explicit still in Gaddis's final and posthumous novel, *Agapē Agape*,[33] whose central topic is the futile and unfinished attempt of a terminally ill writer to order the observations and encyclopedic notes he has accumulated over the course of a lifetime.[34]

Burn delineates then a genre that is defined essentially on the basis of two characteristics: (1) encyclopedism and (2) meta-encyclopedism, that is a reflection on encyclopedism itself—a fairly self-referential and narrow narrative genre. Certainly not because there are no other narrative forms in the

[31] Burn, "The Collapse of Everything," 57.
[32] Gaddis, *The Recognitions*, 955–6.
[33] William Gaddis, *Agapē Agape*, intro. Joseph Tabbi (New York: Viking, 2002).
[34] Burn, "The Collapse of Everything," 58.

modern or postmodern literary sphere that are strongly self-referential and of limited thematic breadth—one need only think of metafiction[35]—but because Burn's inclusion of the fiction of maximalist authors such as Pynchon, DeLillo, Wallace, and Smith within the cramped category of the "encyclopedic novel" is problematic. As we will see, in the novels of these authors, there is *much more* than mere encyclopedism. Not to mention, the meta-encyclopedic component, with the exception of just a few examples,[36] is practically marginal. Nevertheless, Burn's analysis is noteworthy for having identified a rich seam of modern encyclopedic thought: from the Enlightenment *Encyclopédie* to Richard Power's *Galatea 2.2* and *The Gold Bug Variations*. These last two novels in particular engage in a restoration of the encyclopedic project, after its apocalyptic collapse in the works of Gaddis. In *Galatea 2.2*, a re-writing of the myth of Pygmalion, it is augured the writing of an encyclopedia of the "Information Age."[37] It is an encyclopedia which, in *The Gold Bug Variations* (as in *Ulysses*), is embodied in the image of a library. The library is taken once again as the symbol of encyclopedic storage, even if no longer in the fixity of the catalogue form of Bloom's book inventory (which expressed Joyce's belief with regard to the possibility of producing and mastering a synthetic-totalizing knowledge of the real). Power's library "is constantly being invaded by the world: by people bringing music into [it] (Todd enters, humming Bach) and by suggestions from its question board. Rather than a private store, it is an open, evolving archive."[38] The idea of encyclopedic knowledge, which *The Gold Bug Variations* assumes, preserves the utopian charge it possessed in modernism, insofar as the encyclopedia

35 See Patricia Waugh, *Metafiction: The Theory and Practice of Self-Conscious Fiction* (London-New York: Routledge, 1984), 21–62.

36 In *Gravity's Rainbow*, for example, as Slothrop wanders in the Zone—as postwar Germany is called in the novel—in search of the mysterious S-Gerät, he turns to a spy, Semyavin, whom he engages in the following dialogue:

> "But do you know what?"
> "Let me guess."
> A tragic sight. "Information. What's wrong with dope and women? Is it any wonder the world's gone insane, with information come to be the only real medium of exchange?" (*Gravity's Rainbow*, 307)

It is an interesting dialogue to be sure, and it demonstrates Pynchon's attentiveness to information and its control, but it is marginal in the narrative. After this episode, the argument will not be broached again. See John Johnston, *Information Multiplicity: American Fiction in the Age of Media Saturation* (Baltimore-London: The Johns Hopkins University Press, 1998), 61–96.

37 Richard Powers, *Galatea 2.2* (New York: Farrar, 1995), 215.

38 Burn, "The Collapse of Everything," 61.

configures itself as an osmotic space of exchange, becoming constitutively *open*, interactive, and programmatically incomplete. It is an encyclopedia which, under the flag of flexibility, would seem capable of sustaining the blast of the increasing complexification of the real. I will return briefly to Burn and his "encyclopedic novel" in the third section of this chapter, but first let us take a look at "encyclopedic narrative" as defined by Edward Mendelson.

2 An encyclopedic "genre"?

Edward Mendelson considers "encyclopedic narrative" to be the most important and exclusive genre of Western literature, and he establishes a series of criteria on the basis of which a given narrative can be seen to be encyclopedic. It should offer an ample synecdoche of the learning produced by a given culture and provide a summary of at least one science or one technology; it should include a multiplicity of literary genres and styles; it should refer to arts other than literature; it should make a history of language; but, above all, it should occupy a central position in the literary system to which it belongs.[39] Mendelson's classificatory schema has enjoyed great fortune in the theoretical definition of literary encyclopedism: it can be found at the origin of Moretti's definition of the "world text,"[40] and it is also a polemical target in Burn's definition of the "encyclopedic novel."[41]

There are two principal problems with Mendelson's formulation of an encyclopedic narrative understood as a genre: (1) the rigidity of his theoretical proposal; (2) the requirement of cultural centrality for encyclopedic works. Accepting the breadth of the synecdochal representation of a given culture, there remains the problem that, to be called encyclopedic, a novel should not necessarily provide a history of language, refer to an art different than literature, speak of a specific science or technology, and employ a multiplicity of styles.

[39] Edward Mendelson, "Encyclopedic Narrative: From Dante to Pynchon," *Modern Language Notes* 91 (1976): 1267–75.

[40] Moretti himself recognizes this: Moretti, *Modern Epic*, 4.

[41] Burn, "The Collapse of Everything," 49–52. Mendelson's idea of "encyclopedic narrative" is also discussed by Hillary Clark at the beginning of her work on the encyclopedic form: *The Fictional Encyclopaedia: Joyce, Pound, Sollers* (New York: Garland, 1990).

Nor must it be central within the literary culture which produced it. In fact, Mendelson's notion that a given culture, in becoming aware of itself and its means, should generate at a certain point an encyclopedic author, whose work is considered to be a sort of "sacred text"[42] and, as such, is the object of a never-ending and maniacal exegesis, is more problematic than it might seem.[43] Even if the first six examples of encyclopedic narratives given by Mendelson—Dante's *Divina Commedia*, Cervantes's *Don Quijote*, Rabelais's *Gargantua et Pantagruel*, Goethe's *Faust*, Melville's *Moby Dick*, and Joyce's *Ulysses*—might enjoy perhaps a certain cultural centrality and an uninterrupted attention by critics, a "routinization of charisma,"[44] things become much more complicated instead in regard to the final work Mendelson discusses, Pynchon's *Gravity's Rainbow*.[45] Without taking anything away from Pynchon's novel, which, apart from personal preferences, is undeniably one of the most representative novels of Western literature of the second half of the twentieth century and which surely merits an important place in the postmodern literary canon, it is objectively difficult to profess its centrality in the contemporary literary system. It is a thorny question. First off, because the aesthetic and cultural reference system should be clarified: if *Gravity's Rainbow* is a novel that can be labeled as "postmodernist," are we certain that is also the case for its most immediate rivals for "cultural centrality," *Underworld* and *Infinite Jest*? One could raise more than one doubt as to the matter, or, at the very least, there should be agreement on what is exactly meant by "postmodern," given that it is a complex phenomenon with multiple souls, which is the case. Not to mention that the exegesis of Pynchon's novel pales in comparison to that of the *Commedia*, *Faust*, or even *Ulysses*. It is only a question of time, one could object. But it is not so; there is something else. One sole maximalist novel would have a difficult time aspiring to the centrality which the works of Dante, Goethe, or Melville enjoy in their respective literary systems because *there are too many* maximalist novels. *Gravity's Rainbow* does not tower unchallenged

42 Moretti, *Modern Epic*, 4.

43 Mendelson, "Encyclopedic Narrative," 1268.

44 Max Weber, *Economy and Society: An Outline of Interpretive Sociology* [1922], eds. Geunther Roth and Claus Wittich, trans. Ephraim Fischoff et al. (Berkeley-Los Angeles: University of California Press, 1978), vol. I, 246–9.

45 See also Edward Mendelson, "Gravity's Encyclopedia," in *Mindful Pleasures: Essays on Thomas Pynchon*, eds. George Levine and David Leverence (Boston: Little, 1976), 161–95.

over decades and decades of literary history: one has, before and after, the novels of Gaddis, *Infinite Jest* and *Underworld*, which can contest it for dominance. And that is, if we limit ourselves to North American literature. The contemporary literary sphere is too fragmented to be able to speak of a center. It is instead more of a polycentric and fluctuating space, within which maximalist tensions are particularly pronounced. As such, a single novel can no longer aspire to being the "sacred text" for a given culture because there are lots of aspiring sacred texts, so many that by now almost nothing remains that is sacred.[46] More than at the level of individual literary texts, one could maintain, at most, that the maximalist novel does aspire to a central position in the contemporary literary canon but *as a genre*. We do not have then a single star but a constellation at the center of the extremely mobile universe of present-day fiction. This, at least, is a view which seems to be more consistent with the structure of the postmodern literary space.

3 The encyclopedic mode

It is not possible to establish a series of traits on the basis of which a novel could be considered to be or not be encyclopedic because encyclopedism is *not* identifiable with an existing literary genre, nor is it conceptually assimilable to one. With regard to either Mendelson's "encyclopedic narrative" or Burn's "encyclopedic novel," it is not a question of genres, but of a specific *modality* of representation. That is to say, we are dealing with an *encyclopedic mode*, definable as a particular aesthetic and cognitive attitude, consisting of a more or less heightened and totalizing narrative tension in the synthetic representation of heterogeneous realities and domains of knowledge, ascribable, in essence, to the powerful hybridization of maximalist narratives with the ancient epic. This hybridization was already present in masterpieces of literary modernism such as Joyce's *Ulysses* and Robert Musil's *Der Mann ohne Eigenschaften*, two texts, which can be taken to be among the most immediate modernist novelistic forerunners to the encyclopedic experimentalism discussed in this study. To sum up, encyclopedism is not the goal of maximalist fiction,

[46] See Burn, "The Collapse of Everything," 50.

as Burn would seem to have it, but is instead a *tool*—and not the only one, as we will see—in attempting to satisfy its synthetic ambition. How this tension is manifested and articulated in individual works counts for relatively little in the determination of its presence. Certainly, the traits Mendelson uses to define "encyclopedic narrative"—an ample synecdoche of knowledge produced by a given culture with reference to a science or a technology; an account of arts other than literature; a sampling of genres and styles; a history of language; cultural centrality—if they were to be all present in a given work, would undeniably define it as encyclopedic. But this is not always the case. If you think of Dante's *Commedia*, Goethe's *Faust*, or Melville's *Moby Dick*, the claim, with a bit of coaxing, could perhaps be made.[47] But what would happen, instead, if we took into consideration Roberto Bolaño's *2666*, for example? Bolaño's novel offers an ample representation of multiple social, historical, and cultural realities. It continually refers to painting and, to a lesser degree, cinema. It evokes marine biology through the fixation of the young Hans Reiter—the future and legendary writer Benno von Arcimboldi—with seaweed. It covers a gamma of highly varied literary styles, from the suggestive and fabulating "The Part about Amalfitano" to the dry, chronicle-like register of "The Part About the Crimes." It moves freely among heterogeneous literary genres—from magical realism to nonfiction. But it does not offer any history of language, nor does it occupy a central place in Chilean culture or, at least, not yet. Does this mean that *2666* should not be considered an encyclopedic novel? Of course not. Or let us take DeLillo's *Underworld*. We find in it half a century of American history, a sinister technological obsession with nuclear weapons, a vast spectrum of literary genres—from the historical novel to the *Bildungsroman* and to the social novel—pervasive references to painting, to cinema, and to visual culture in a broad sense, but here too, even if not totally absent, the reflection on language is not crucial, a reflection which is extensive instead in *Gravity's Rainbow* and in *Infinite Jest*, for example.[48] Nor can it be

[47] Let it be clear, the claim might also work in relation to the Western literary canon as consecrated by *today's* literary criticism, but, even in this case, there would be objections. It seems almost superfluous to remember that Dante's *Commedia*, for instance, did not enjoy even minimally for centuries the least amount of cultural centrality in Italian literature.

[48] On the importance of linguistic reflection in the works of Wallace, and, in particular, in the short stories of *Oblivion* [2004] (New York: Back Bay Books, 2005), see James Wood, *How Fiction Works* (New York: Farrar, 2008), 30–5.

argued that *Underworld* enjoys more or less centrality than Pynchon's novel in the American literary canon of the second half of the twentieth century.[49] Or let us consider *2005 dopo Cristo* by Babette Factory, which is not especially varied stylistically and is anything but central in Italian literature, even of the last few years, but which is steeped in archaic myths, visual imagery, cinema, pop culture and aesthetics, as perhaps only *Infinite Jest* can be said to be among the seven novels under discussion. Or Franzen's *The Corrections*, it is too fairly uniform stylistically and not too open to nonliterary intertexts yet very profound in identifying the mechanisms of reproduction of American society borne of the post-World War II era, and rich in its deep understanding of macroeconomics and neurobiology.

The essence of maximalist encyclopedism resides in the clear perception on the part of the reader of a strong narrative tension directed toward the construction of vast and heterogeneous cross sections of specific socioeconomic and cognitive contexts. It is not sufficient, in fact, that a novel concerns itself with a particular science or technique to qualify as encyclopedic. For instance, in Philip Roth's *American Pastoral*,[50] the narrator indulges repeatedly and at length on extremely technical details of the women's glove industry. From the tanning of leather to distribution, the reader is minutely apprised of each stage of the production process of a glove; but *American Pastoral* cannot be considered to be an encyclopedic work. Yet there are not one but two important ingredients: the detailed description of a technique, as well as the representation of a broad cross section of society—and specifically American society of the second half of the twentieth century, seen in the light of the advent of the postindustrial economy and of the dramatic oppositions caused by the war in Vietnam with its tragic consequences on the life of the Swede, the protagonist of the novel. But *American Pastoral* seems to be more a *fresco* of an era, even if it is a grand one, rather than an encyclopedic novel. Two important features characteristic of any fiction with an encyclopedic vocation

[49] We should specify perhaps "recently," since DeLillo has taken much longer than Pynchon to finally become considered a pivotal author of American literature of the second half of the twentieth century, if Wallace's definition of him as a longstanding underestimated novelist is true. This was in 1990 and DeLillo had already published *White Noise*. See David Foster Wallace, "E Unibus Pluram: Television and U.S. Fiction" [1990], in Wallace, *A Supposedly Fun Thing I'll Never Do Again: Essays and Arguments* (Boston: Little, 1997), 21–82, specific reference to page 47.

[50] Philip Roth, *American Pastoral* [1997] (New York: Vintage, 1998).

are in fact missing: *syntheticity* and *heterogeneity*. Encyclopedic knowledge is by definition a heterogeneous knowledge. An encyclopedia is comprised of many entries, and many fields of knowledge are taken into consideration, which in and of itself implies a certain syntheticity of treatment. Hans's taxonomical obsession with seaweed in *2666* is an excellent example. Since it is not a scientific study, it is obviously unthinkable for an encyclopedic novel to give an account of all aspects of a discipline. What gets represented is a partial synthesis, a synecdoche regarding one specific aspect, as in the case of *2666*, in which the description of the alga *Letathesia difformis* indicates a *synecdochal relationship* with marine biology in its overall sense as a natural science. It seems, indeed, that literary encyclopedism has a sort of *fetishistic* character. The detail is taken for the greater system, and it becomes the substitute for an intensely desired totality, but one that is understood as being impossible to represent. And this is precisely what is missing in *American Pastoral*. After having read Roth's novel, the reader will know (presumably) *everything* there is to know about the production of a women's glove: the information acquired is not synthetic but rather exhaustive. Nor, moreover, does Roth's novel offer an ample heterogeneity of learning: apart from the glove industry, one does not find domains of knowledge that depart markedly from those traditionally found in a novel. Quite the opposite in both the maximalist novel as a genre and in its individual representatives, in which the encyclopedic tension targets considerably variegated domains of knowledge. Let us look at a few examples:

> *Gravity's Rainbow*, statistics:
>
> When it does happen, we are content to call it "chance." Or we have been persuaded. There do exist levels where chance is hardly recognized at all. But to the likes of employees such as Roger Mexico it is music, not without its majesty, this power series $Ne^{-m}(1+m+m^2/2!+m^3/3!+\cdots+m^{n-1}/(n-1)!)$, terms numbered according to rocketfalls per square, the Poisson dispensation ruling not only these annihilations no man can run from, but also cavalry accidents, blood counts, radioactive decay, number of wars per year. . . . (165–6)
>
> *Infinite Jest*, toxicology:
>
> The organopsychedelic muscimole, an isoxazole-alkaloid derived from *Amanita muscaria*, a.k.a. the fly agaric mushroom—by no means, Michael

Pemulis emphasizes, to be confused with *phalloides* or *verna* or certain other kill-you-dead species of North America's *Amanita* genus, as the little kids sit there Indian-style on the Viewing Room floor, glassy-eyed and trying not to yawn—goes by the structural moniker 5-aminomethyl-3-isoxazolol, requires about like maybe ten to twenty oral mg. per ingestion, making it two to three times as potent as psilocybin, and frequently results in the following alterations in consciousness (not reading or referring to notes in any way): a kind of semi-sleep-like trance with visions, elation, sensations of physical lightness and increased strength, heightened sensual perceptions, synesthesia, and favorable distortions in body-image. (66)

Underworld, painting:

Edgar reads the copy block in the matching page. This is a sixteenth-century work done by a Flemish master, Pieter Bruegel, and it is called *The Triumph of Death*. . . .

He studies the tumbrel filled with skulls. He stands in the aisle and looks at the naked man pursued by dogs. He looks at the gaunt dog nibbling the baby in the dead woman's arms. These are long gaunt starveling hounds, they are war dogs, hell dogs, boneyard hounds beset by parasitic mites, by dog tumors and dog cancers. . . .

He finds a second dead woman in the middle ground, straddled by a skeleton. The positioning is sexual, unquestionably. But is Edgar sure it's a woman bestraddled or could it be a man? He stands in the aisle and they are all around him cheering and he has the pages in his face. The paint has an instancy that he finds striking. Yes, the dead fall upon the living. But he begins to see that the living are sinners. The cardplayers, the lovers who dally, he sees the king in an ermine cloak with his fortune stashed in hogshead drums. The dead have come to empty out the wine gourds, to serve a skull on a platter to gentlefolk at their meal. He sees gluttony, lust and greed. (50)

White Teeth, genetics:

A two-week-old FutureMouse© is to be out in display at the Perret Institute in London on December 31, 1992. There it will remain on public display until December 31, 1999. This mouse is genetically normal except for a select group of novel genes that are added to the genome. A DNA clone of these genes is injected into the fertilized mouse egg, thus linking them to the chromosomal DNA in the zygote, which is subsequently inherited by cells of the resulting embryo. Before injection into the germ line, these genes are custom-designed so they can be "turned on" and expressed only in specific mouse tissue and along a predictable timetable. The mouse will be the site for an experiment into the aging of cells, the progression of cancer within cells, and a few other matters that will serve as surprises along the way! (356–7)

The Corrections, chemistry:

Tonight something unusual was happening in the ferroacetate gel. His conductivity readings varied wildly, depending on where exactly he stuck the ammeter's probe. Thinking the probe might be dirty, he switched to a narrow needle with which he again poked the gel. He got a reading of not conductivity at all. Then he stuck the gel in a different place and got a high reading.

What was going on?

The question absorbed and comforted him and held the taskmaster at bay until, at ten o'clock, he extinguished the microscope's illuminator and wrote in his notebook: STAIN BLU CHROMATE 2%. VERY VERY INTERESTING. (313–14)

2666, marine biology:

Por esa época comenzó a dibujar en un cuaderno todo tipo de algas. Dibujó la *Chorda filum*, que es un alga compuesta por largos cordones delgados que pueden, sin embargo, llegar a alcanzar los ocho metros de longitud. Carecen de ramas y su apariencia es delicada, pero en realidad son muy fuertes. Crecen por debajo de la marca de la marea baja. Dibujó tambien la *Leathesia difformis*, que es un alga compuesta por bulbos redondeados de color marrón oliváceo, que crece en la rocas y sobra otras algas. Su aspecto es estraño. Nunca vio ninguna, pero soñó muchas veces con ellas. (800)

[Around this time he began to draw all kinds of seaweed in a notebook. He drew *Chorda filum*, made up of thin strands that could nevertheless grow to be twenty-five feet long. It had no branches and looked delicate but was really very strong. It grew below the low-tide mark. He also drew *Leathesia difformis*, rounded bulbs of olive brown that grew on rocks and other seaweed. A strange-looking plant. He never saw it, but he often dreamt about it.] (641)

2005 dopo Cristo, myth:

> —Sa cosa succedeva nelle comunità primitive quando veniva ucciso il re? Passata la fase di partecipazione orgiastica all'evento, *qualcuno* faceva sempre in modo che le cose riprendessero il loro corso naturale. Ma quale corso? C'è bisogno che *qualcuno* riporti l'ordine, dal caos al cosmos—. La voce si trasforma in un incomprensibile bzz bzzz. Poi dice:—Capisce cosa vogliamo dire, se diciamo che l'Italia ha bisogno di un santo? (162)
>
> ["Do you know what happened in primitive communities when the king was killed? After the period of orgiastic participation in the event, *somebody* always found a way to get things to resume their natural course. But what course? There is a need that *someone* reestablishes order, from chaos to cosmos." The voice mutates into an incomprehensible bzz bzzz. Then it says: "Do you know what we mean, if we say that Italy needs a saint?"] (162)

And statistics, toxicology, painting, genetics, organic chemistry, marine biology, myth are certainly not the only encyclopedic breaches present, respectively, in these maximalist novels: they represent only a *part* of the fields of knowledge they take into consideration. For *Gravity's Rainbow*, we must add rocketry, systems theory, and behavioral psychology. For *Infinite Jest*, psychopharmacology, computer sciences, mathematics, philosophy of mind and philosophy of language, sport, cinema. For *White Teeth*, botany and religion. For *The Corrections*, neurobiology and macroeconomics. And even if we were to proceed in this way, we would not capture in any case the extraordinary complexity and variety of the fabric of maximalist encyclopedism. From myth to science, from religion to philosophy, to the entire sphere of the arts, it is human learning in its totality which appears to be susceptible to the varying encyclopedic interests of maximalist authors. There is, in fact, not just one form of encyclopedism, there are instead *multiple* forms.

In an essay on the fiction of Powers, Vollmann, and Wallace,[51] LeClair asks about the specificity of the scientific knowledge so abundant in the pages of these authors. He finds a preponderance of the life sciences (biology, genetics, medicine, etc.) and of ecology over physics and mathematics, very present,

[51] Tom LeClair, "The Prodigious Fiction of Richard Powers, William Vollmann, and David Foster Wallace," *Critique* 38, 1 (1996): 12–37.

instead, in *Gravity's Rainbow* by Pynchon, held LeClair to have been the American writer to have first looked at the mathematical and physical sciences as privileged interlocutors for literary discourse.[52] The emphasis on how, thanks to Pynchon, scientific knowledge burst forth in a massive way into American literature in the postwar period is fundamental for understanding the role of innovator that he played in the making of the postmodern literary canon. And LeClair seems to be perfectly cognizant of this, showing, how even those authors who belong to the same generation as Pynchon have been deeply and directly influenced by his use of radically nonliterary intertexts, from DeLillo in *Ratner's Star* to Coover in *The Public Burning* and to Barth in *LETTERS*.[53] Nevertheless, even if LeClair's thesis seems suitable for Power's *The Gold Bug Variations* and Vollmann's *You Bright and Risen Angels*, to make generalizations for a novel like *Infinite Jest*, which contains a boundless encyclopedic knowledge not reducible to the life sciences alone, can be misleading. Not because a systematic mapping of maximalist encyclopedism is not useful—it would, in fact, be very desirable—but because to exhaust its significance in the choice, based on supposedly different epistemological premises, by a certain author to engage in one scientific field instead of another, risks being reductive. Emphasizing, for example, the massive presence of psychopathology and psychopharmacology in the pages of *Infinite Jest* bears witness, on the one hand and correctly, to a longstanding and dramatic obsession consistently present in Wallace's fiction,[54] and on the other, it obscures the overall sense of the embrace of encyclopedism by *Infinite Jest*, which we know resides in the characteristic ambition of the maximalist novel to construct a totalizing narrative. But there is yet another aspect, which, at times, joins together the different variants of maximalist encyclopedism.

Frye has claimed that the Western encyclopedic tradition has found historical continuity in the forms of satire and irony.[55] This thesis finds a certain resonance in the maximalist novel as well since encyclopedism is often exposed to histrionic ridicule in its pages: from the study of the erection of Slothrop's

[52] Ibid., 13.

[53] Ibid.

[54] Themes already at the heart of Wallace's first published short story, "The Planet Trillaphon As It Stands in Relation to the Bad Thing," in *The Amherst Review* (1987).

[55] Frye, *Anatomy of Criticism*, 322.

penis in the experiments in behavioral psychology devised by Doctor Jamf in *Gravity's Rainbow* to the imaginary branch of mathematical analysis called "extra-linear dynamics" in *Infinite Jest*, to the grotesque and ironic promotion of the revolutionary neurobiological therapy *Corecktall* to combat degenerative diseases of the nervous system in *The Corrections*. Moretti has argued that it has been irony which has kept encyclopedism alive, but not much more than having kept it alive, which is the point:

> Turning the encyclopaedia into farce is a way of avoiding failure, rather than the beginning of a new form. It is a sign of great intelligence—but of an unfree intelligence, which has given itself an impossible task, and labours under the tremendous pressure of history. In this respect, the mocking epithet that has followed *Faust* and all the rest like a shadow is fully justified. Masterpieces, to be sure. But flawed masterpieces.[56]

An encyclopedism derided perhaps and a bit farcical sometimes but encyclopedism none the less. It is not very important in the end whether it is possible or not possible to write an encyclopedic work: it gets written in any case. And this is the case because, as we know well, the encyclopedic strain encapsulates the longstanding aesthetic utopia and the synthetic necessity to represent the *totality* of the real, a strain which probably will never cease to exercise its immense fascination on Western literature. Mockery is certainly a consequence, as Moretti writes, of the "tremendous pressure of history," and of the awareness of living in an era in which a total knowledge of the world is absolutely out of reach. And yet the irresistible need to try has remained, and it is precisely in the maximalist novel that it appears to be more urgent than ever. Paraphrasing Eugenio Montale, we can affirm that the encyclopedic dream of Western man is not finished.[57]

56 Moretti, *Modern Epic*, 36–7.

57 Eugenio Montale, "Il sogno del prigioniero" [The dream of the prisoner], in Montale, *Tutte le poesie* (Milan: Mondadori, 1984), 277.

3

Dissonant Chorality

We have seen how Moretti closely links the totalizing desire of world texts to Bakhtin's category of polyphony and defines the modern epic as a "polyphonic epic," that is to say, as a literary form that aspires to totality through a strong dialogic opening.

We saw in the preceding chapter that, in the maximalist novel, this ambition takes the shape of an encyclopedic surge in the narration arrangement, and now we will see how it unfolds at the morphological level in a peculiar structuring of plot and organization of narrative dynamics. I will label this process *dissonant chorality*, definable as an inextricable web of *chorality* and *polyphony*. Let us begin with chorality.

1 Chorality

"Chorality" in the sense that in the maximalist novel the narration is advanced by a greater or lesser multiplicity of voices, which does not allow for the affirmation of a dominant narrative locus. It would be rather difficult to maintain that *Gravity's Rainbow* pivots wholly around lieutenant Slothrop and his quest for the S-Gerät, while he flees from a team of mad Pavlovian scientists. Mexico, Jessica, Blicero, Katije, Enzian, and Tchitcherin, for example, are figures of notable weight in the novel, without whom it would lose the bulk of its elements of interest. Likewise, it would be problematic to assert that in *Infinite Jest* Hal Incandenza is a more central character than Don Gately in relation to the two principal narrative branches around which the endless diegetic material of the novel articulates itself; just as it would be to claim that the stories clustered around the members of the Enfield Tennis

Academy are more significant or occupy more space than those clustered around the members of the Ennet House rehabilitation community. Similarly, can one claim that in *Underworld*, Nick Shay is without a shadow of doubt the protagonist of the novel? One is compelled to ask: what about Klara Sax? And Manx Martin? But, most of all, what about the baseball?

And this is to mention only three of the novels in the textual corpus under consideration here, for which doubts could be raised concerning the absence of dominant individual characters and/or narrative threads. For the remaining four, instead, this absence is so evident that no particular clarifications are necessary in supporting the hypothesis of their choral structure. Thus, a choral impulse shapes these works in accordance with their tendency to eschew the imposition of primary protagonists or stories. But let us try now to understand how it formally extrinsicate itself. We thus penetrate into the morphosphere of the maximalist novel and speak of the *fragment*.

In all of the seven under analysis, the narration is systematically noncontinuous and proceeds instead by means of diegetic units that are more or less independent and self-contained in meaning. That is to say, we do not encounter a compact narrative *continuum*, but rather its segmentation: fragments, to be precise. Fragments of variable length, of course—sometimes fairly long, as in Franzen's *The Corrections*, or brief, if not very brief, in Bolaño's *2666*—but always and in all cases fragments, separated one from the other by a typographical spacing.

At the level of the organization of narrative information, the use of the fragment in the maximalist novel tends generally to exist side by side with the traditional subdivision of the narrative into parts and chapters. In *White Teeth*, we have five parts, each formed by five chapters, each of these in turn fractured into fragments. The same thing occurs in *2005 dopo Cristo*, with the distribution of the narrative across three sections, each divided into numbered fragments, some only a few lines long and without the mediation of a macrotextual structure such as the chapter. Not to mention *Infinite Jest*, in which the classic setup of the novel form organized according to immediately recognizable textual partitions shatters completely. The fragment here is elevated to a system with the segmentation of the abundant narrative flow via the simple use of shorter or longer fragments, albeit often having a title, and the consequent abolition of any paratextual or intratextual grid to which the reader can refer.

Whatever its dosage—measured in *The Corrections*, a novel with a more traditional narrative structure; extreme, instead, in *Infinite Jest*—the fragment is the privileged bearer of maximalist narrative information, while the more usual divisions of the narrative into parts and chapters seem to behave more as conventional structural criteria, although they have sometimes a specific function, as we will see. The fragment is the textual segment responsible for the production of meaning, the semantic entity in which the conflicting perspectives of author, narrator, characters, and readers are played out, the place in which geographic space and time are disassembled and recombined by the voracious storytelling frenzy of the maximalist narrator.[1]

It is in the typographic space that separates one fragment from another that a gamma of *morphological potentialities* is arranged to be actualized in accordance with narrative contingencies. In the maximalist novel, typographical space is always the signal of a *change of scene*—in Genette's sense of the term[2]—occurring in the transition from one fragment to another fragment. A change of scene orchestrated in accordance with a precise rhetoric and traceable in essence to three typologies: (1) *variation of point of view*; (2) *transition in time or in space* (even within a single segment of the story); (3) *introduction or resumption of a narrative thread.*

In the section entitled "The Failure" in *The Corrections,* we read about the brief reunion of the Lamberts in Chip's apartment in New York, prior to Alfred and Enid's departure for a cruise in Nova Scotia. After entreating his sister Denise to stay with their parents, Chip sets off on the trail of his (ex-)lover Julia, who had just broken up with him on his doorstep, and engages at the same time in a battle against time to prevent Eden Procuro, a movie producer (Julia is her personal assistant), from reading the screenplay which he had sent to her. From Chip's Manhattan apartment to the streets of New York, to Eden's office, and within the framework of an overall solidly omniscient narratorial perspective, the narrator engages in a sweeping and alternated use

1 These aspects will be investigated in depth in the chapters dedicated to diegetic exuberance and narratorial omniscience.

2 See Gerard Genette, *Narrative Discourse: An Essay in Method* [1972], trans. Jane E. Lewin, foreward by Jonathan Culler (Ithaca: Cornell University Press, 1980), 109–12.

of restricted points of view, moving freely from Chip to Denise, to Enid and Alfred. The organization of the section into fragments contributes to singling out the individual points of view concerning the story, to facilitating their interaction, and to guaranteeing contrastive effects. Let us take a passage such as the following:

> He touched the hundreds.
>
> "Why don't I get online and make plane reservations for you both," Eden said. "You can leave right away!"
>
> "So, you gonna do this thing?" Gitanas asked. "It's a lot of work, lot of fun. Pretty low risk. No such things as no risk, though. Not where there's money."
>
> "I understand," Chip said, touching the hundreds.
>
> In the pageantry of weddings Enid reliably experienced the paroxysmal love of *place*—of the Midwest in general and suburban St. Jude in particular—that for her was the only true patriotism and the only viable spirituality. Living under presidents as crooked as Nixon and stupid as Reagan and disgusting as Clinton, she'd lost interest in American flag-waving, and not one of the miracles she'd ever prayed to God for had come to pass; but at a Saturday wedding in the lilac season, from a pew of the Paradise Valley Presbyterian Church, she could look around and see two hundred nice people and not a single bad one. (*The Corrections*, 134–5)

Having reached Eden's office, Chip finds Gitanas, Julia's husband and a Lithuanian, who offers him an improbable and not very transparent job in Lithuania which Chip ends up accepting. The end of the first fragment closes with Chip touching the hundred dollar bills Gitanas has offered to him as an advance and with the sense of fascination that the money, the illegality, and the prospects of cheap sex hold over him. This fascination contrasts markedly with the following fragment, which opens, instead, with Enid's love of weddings, provincial St Jude, and its obtuse inhabitants and closes with an allusion to the mother's prim and proper incomprehension of Denise's divorce and Chip's life. Two different and irreconcilable perspectives on the world are contained here in two consecutive fragments, separated by a typographical space that becomes the bearer of a notable change in point of view.

In the first part of *2666*, "The Part About the Critics," typographical spacing often indicates a spatial movement. From fragment to fragment, across the cities in which Espinoza, Pelletier, and Liz Norton live, and those in which the Arcimboldi conventions take place, the narrative traverses different geographical regions. Here, typographical space almost acquires the connotations of a territorial borderland: a graphic void able to frame the happenings of the characters within the confines of a nation-state. It is the visual signal of a spatial and existential distance covered by the critic-protagonists in this section of the novel in order to meet up in the great European capitals. In this sense, the white space becomes the indicator of a trip. Just as we can see in the three consecutive fragments below, in which we go from London—with Pelletier about to return to Paris and Liz, who resumes her academic routine after a night of lovemaking with him—to Madrid, where Espinoza invites Liz Norton, starting up, in his turn, an amorous relationship with her:

> Por las mañanas, después de llamar un taxi, Pelletier se vestía sin hacer ruido para no despertarla y se marchaba al aeropuerto. Antes de salir la miraba, durante unos segundos, abandonada entre las sábanas, y a veces se sentía tan lleno de amor que se hubiera puesto a llorar allí mismo.
>
> Una ora después el despertador de Liz Norton se ponía a sonar y ésta se levantaba de un salto. . . . Si tenía reunión con los colegas de su departamento, iba a la reunión, si no tenía reunión se encerraba en la biblioteca, a trabajar o a leer, hasta que llegaba la hora de su próxima clase.
>
> Un sábado Espinoza le dijo que tenía que ir a Madrid, que él la invitaba, que Madrid en aquella época del año era la ciudad más hermosa del mundo y que además había una retrospectiva de Bacon que no se podía perder.
>
> —Voy mañana—le dijo Norton, algo que Espinoza no esperaba, ciertamente, pues su invitacíon había obedecido más a un deseo que a la posibilidad real de que ella aceptara. (*2666*, 51–2)
>
> [In the mornings, after he called a cab, Pelletier slipped soundlessly into his clothes so as not to wake her and headed for the airport. Before he left he would spend a few seconds watching her, sprawled on the sheets, and sometimes he felt so full of love he could have burst into tears.
>
> *
>
> An hour later, Liz Norton's alarm would sound and she'd jump out of bed. . . . If she had a meeting with her department colleagues, she would go

> to the meeting, and if she didn't have a meeting she would shut herself up in the library to work or read until it was time for class.
>
> *
>
> One Saturday Espinoza told her that she must come to Madrid, she would be his guest. Madrid at this time of year was the most beautiful city in the world, and there was a Bacon retrospective on, too, which wasn't to be missed.
>
> "I'll be there tomorrow," said Norton, which caught Espinoza off guard, since what his invitation had expressed was more a wish than any real hope that she might accept.] (*2666*, 32–3)

In the same way, the change can also occur in time, within an individual narrative segment or in an analeptic-explicative regime. In the fifth chapter of the second part of *Underworld*, the discussion between Nick Shay, his brother Matt, and their mother Rosemary is cadenced by the subdivision of the narrative into fragments. In particular, the change from one fragment to the next is analogous to an ellipsis between scenes; it disassembles the story into narratively autonomous familiar frames,[3] which are, however, always locatable within the same narrative sequence, that is to say, within the ongoing discussion between the two brothers across the span of the entire chapter on the opportuneness of a hypothetical move by Rosemary from the Bronx to Phoenix, the city where Nick lives and works. Let us take a look at how the successive moments from supper to after supper, when Nick and Matt are now finally free to contend over their mother's old age, are separated by a typographic spacing that cadences the moments of intimacy and family conflict, allowing the narrative to advance through discrete units:

> "He wants you to sit on his patio, Mama. Bright stars above. Cactus outlined in the moonlight."
>
> "Imagine me and cactus."
>
> "No noise in the street. They arrest people for noise out there. If your front yard isn't neat and clean, your neighbor's kids won't talk to your kids." . . .
>
> One of the cats rubbed against his ankle, the orange tom his mother had found in the street. He shook it off and poured coffee all around.

[3] Ibid., 106–9.

> They sat at the table talking in low tones.
>
> Rosemary was in the bedroom and they talked across the dishes and cups and the flick of split milk.
>
> "Where do you sleep?"
>
> "I make up the sofa," Matt said. "Where do you sleep?"
>
> "Park Avenue South. The Doral. You drove down?"
>
> "Took the shuttle. Tell me in all seriousness. Do you really want to take her out there?"
>
> "More than ever." (*Underworld*, 201–2)

But the temporal change usually occurs most frequently across distant chronological levels. So in the first chapter of the first part of *White Teeth*, a narratorial analepsis recuperates an antecedent important for understanding Clara's reasons for accepting Archie's courtship of her, that is to say, her grotesque adolescent relationship with Ryan Topps. Typographical spacing, a structuring strategy used systematically by Zadie Smith, prepares us for a temporal leap, intended to recapture Clara's immediate past, with the intention of shedding new light on her encounter with Archie:

> And Clara might never have run into the arms of Archie Jones if she hadn't been running, quite as fast as she could, away from Ryan Topps.
>
> Poor Ryan Topps. He was a mass of unfortunate physical characteristics. . . .
>
> Ryan's unpopularity at St. Jude's was equaled only by Clara's. On her first day at the school her mother had explained to her she was about to enter the devil's lair, filled her satchel with two hundred copies of the *Watchtower*, and instructed her to go and do the Lord's work. (*White Teeth*, 23–4)

Finally, typographical spacing can precede a fragment in which a new character is introduced or it can facilitate the resumption of a narrative thread even at the removal of numerous pages, similarly to the procedure of *entrelacement*. This practice is widespread in *Infinite Jest*, in which, for example, we find ourselves asking at length what has happened to Ken Erdedy, the marijuana-addicted advertising executive we meet in the opening pages of the novel, only to meet up with him hundreds of pages later among the patients at the Ennet House. Also very common is the introduction of a character by means of a narrative fragment to that effect, as in the case of Don Gately who, even though already mentioned ambiguously by Hal in his delirium on the occasion of his admission interview at the University of Arizona, is introduced more fully to the reader only later, after a brief fragment on Mario Incandenza's function as a video cameraman at the Enfield Tennis Academy:

> Eighteen in May, Mario Incandenza's designated function around Enfield Tennis Academy is filmic: sometimes during A.M. drills or P.M. matches he'll be assigned by Coach Schtitt et al. to set up an old camcorder or whatever video stuff's to hand on a tripod and record a certain area of court, videotaping different kids' strokes, footwork, certain tics and hitches in serves or running volleys, so the staff can show the tapes to the kids instructionally, letting the kids see on the screen exactly what a coach or prorector's talking about. The reason being it's a lot easier to fix something if you can see it.
>
> AUTUMN — YEAR OF DAIRY PRODUCTS FROM THE AMERICAN HEARTLAND
>
> Drug addicts driven to crime to finance their drug addiction are not often inclined toward violent crime. Violence requires all different kinds of energy, and most drug addicts like to expend their energy not on their professional crime but on what their professional crime lets them afford. Drug addicts are often burglars, therefore. One reason why the home of someone whose home has been burglarized feels violated and unclean is that there have probably been drug addicts in there. Don Gately was a twenty-seven-year-old oral narcotics addict (favoring Demerol and Talwin), and a more or less professional burglar; and he was, himself, unclean and violated. (*Infinite Jest*, 54–5)

Now, leaving aside the inevitable schematic nature of the taxonomy just proposed, a schematicity that does not do full justice to the wealth of nuances of maximalist narrative organization, and bearing in mind how the three typologies are almost always contemporaneously present in the same novel, it seems legitimate to see in the maximalist use of typographical spacing a graphic indicator of *multiplicity*: a verbal void capable of generating meaning; a *polyfunctional* void enabling the expansion of the narrative representation by means of juxtaposed, heterogeneous fragments.

The fragmentation of the story into discrete narrative units is systematic in the maximalist novel, the principal organizational criterion of the diegesis.

Here, the fragment does not indicate by any means a "loss" of the system to the detriment of a conventional intratextual organization and of a strong, modeling vision of the real,[4] but rather is itself *the* system. A system which is open and fractal. An indefinitely expandable system but, as we will see governed by peremptory ordering criteria. It is the only textual system possible for a literature of global aspirations; the only textual system possible for a novel that dares to challenge the complexity of the world. In this sense, the fragment is the morphological counterpart of the *rhizomatic* cognitive structure of the maximalist novel. And it suggests that the only way available to contemporary narrative to construct a totalizing literary representation lies in the creation of a horizontal and mobile approach to the real and to the narrative material.[5]

The reasons behind the decision to organize the narration in fragments now begin to emerge clearly. But the maximalist use of the fragment corresponds to other exigencies as well, linked to *internal genre dynamics*, *genre/literary system bonds*, and the *mimetic relationship* between *literary representation* and the real. It is a rather thorny question, but it can be articulated in terms of four basic elements, each related to a formal aspect of the maximalist novel, and each responsible for the systematic use of the fragment as a structuring principle: (1) the choral set up of the maximalist novel; (2) the heavy formal debt to the epic; (3) polyphony; (4) providing an effective propulsive motor to the narration. Let us put aside the fourth element for the moment—which we will discuss in relation to the diegetic exuberance of the maximalist novel, a feature inseparable from dissonant chorality—and begin with the first: the choral construction.

The organization of the diegesis into fragments constitutes an ideal morphological platform for the grafting and development of a choral narration because it is *neutral*: a narrative segment which is mechanically assigned each time to

[4] On the opposition of detail and fragment, in which the first term is used to indicate the emergence of an element in its autonomy following the *disappearance* of the system and the second is used instead to evoke a *loss* of the system and a rupture of totality—a totality still present, although negatively—see Denis Boisseau, "De l'"inexistance' du détail," in *Le detail*, ed. Liliane Louvel (Poitiers: la Licorne, 1999), 15–33.

[5] See Gilles Deleuze and Félix Guattari, *Anti-Oedipus: Capitalism and Schizophrenia* [1980], preface by Michel Foucault, trans. Robert Hurley et al. (Minneapolis: University of Minnesota Press, 1983).

an individual character or to a single story, avoids the emergence of a privileged discursive center, and the diverse narrative units come to arrange themselves along a single hierarchical plane. It is a multilinear diegetic organization, which clearly demonstrates that what counts in the maximalist novel is not the individual character or the single story, but rather a *collectivity* of characters and a *plurality* of stories.[6] It is a technique that configures the maximalist novel as a genre of contemporary fiction which is highly decentered in relation both to its own diegetic material and to its own system of characters, or rather as a genre which is able to reach the reader *simultaneously* from several sides.[7] This is a textual strategy that seems to come from far away.

The epic form, from its inception, has been strongly tied to the idea and practice of a pronounced autonomy of the individual parts that make up the narrative, primarily on account of its digressive nature.[8] This practice has been later ignored to varying degrees through the centuries: first by the theorizations and, to a lesser degree, by the epic experiments of Aristotelian stamp, in the name of a unity of action, far removed from the Homeric epos. In the wake of the Latin translation of the *Poetics* of Aristotle completed by Alessandro de' Pazzi in 1536, Francesco Robortello, in his *In librum Aristotelis de arte poetica explicationes* (1548), extended for the first time the famous Aristotelian unities of time, place, and action, originally prescribed for tragedy, to the epic as well. These three unities were then, in accordance with the dictates of the Counter-Reformation, rigidly codified by Vicenzo Maggi—who was, among other things, in fierce polemic with Robortello himself and with secular Aristolelianism—in his *In Aristotelis librum "De Poetica" communes explanationes* (1550), which

6 On multilinear narratives in modernism, see Kathleen L. Komar, *Pattern and Chaos: Multilinear Novels by Dos Passos, Faulkner, Döblin, and Koeppen* (Columbia: Camden House, 1983). See also *Chaos and Order: Complex Dynamics in Literature and Science*, ed. Katherine N. Hayles (Chicago: University of Chicago Press, 1991), and Gordon E. Slethaug, *Beautiful Chaos: Chaos Theory and Metachaotics in Recent American Fiction* (Albany: State University of New York Press, 2000).

7 Regarding Joseph McElroy's *Women and Men*, Karl writes: "Often we do not know the derivation of the voices; and while this is temporarily disturbing, it serves a longer-range function of developing a novel whose languages seek their own definition. Words take on an unworldly aspect. McElroy is the master of this dimension of novel-writing: that ability to come at the reader from all sides simultaneously, to subvert linear narrative without recourse to streams of consciousness, to provide a freely-associated context without going completely inside. All is disguise, veils, mists, even deceptions. The aim is not only to disorient, but, ultimately, to reorient the reader in a different context of reality; to break the thread of the realistic novel even while including realistic scenes and events." Karl, *American Fictions: 1980-2000*, 169.

8 See Fusillo, "Epic, Novel," 50–1.

had a great influence on Anglo-Saxon theorizations of the epic from the second half of the seventeenth to the early part of the eighteenth century.[9] Only in the Romantic period would the autonomy of its parts come again to be recognized as one of the distinctive features of the epic, beginning with Schiller, who, in April of 1797, wrote to Goethe that "the independence of its parts is a main characteristic of the epic poem,"[10] while Goethe, disputed the Aristotelian principle of the unity of action, arguing that it was completely extraneous to the Homeric epos:

> Because the epic poem cannot have dramatic unity, and because one cannot really prove such an absolute unity in the *Iliad* and the *Odyssey* (rather, according to recent ideas, they look even more cut up than they actually are), the epic poem is not supposed to demand any kind of unity. In my view, that means it should stop being considered a poem. These are meant to be pure principles, and if one pays close attention to experience, it clearly contradicts them. The *Iliad* and the *Odyssey*, even if they had gone through the hands of thousands of poets and editors, still show the powerful tendency towards unity of a poetic and critical mind.[11]

In a few decades this debate would spill over into the noted debate on the unity of *Faust*, in which Eckermann would define the principal scenes of Goethe's poem as "so many little independent worlds, each complete in itself."[12]

Leaving aside the critical dispute on the reception of Aristotle's *Poetics*—an epochal *querelle* here mentioned only in passing—it is important to underscore that the autonomy of the parts is a procedure that finds a fundamental *raison d'être* in the epic desire for a narrative synthesis of the world. A synthesis that is possible at the formal level because of the tentacular nature of a narration which proceeds through fragments and which enables the representation of a large quantity of objects without excessive worries as to the coherence of the narrative whole. Thus, it is not at all surprising that the maximalist

[9] See Hugh Thomas Swedenberg Jr., *The Theory of the Epic in England: 1650-1800* (Berkeley-Los Angeles: University of California Press, 1944); Moretti, *Modern Epic*, 43–9.

[10] Johann Wolfgang von Goethe and Friedrich Schiller, *Correspondence between Goethe and Schiller 1794-1805*, trans. Liselotte Dieckmann (New York: Peter Lang, 1994), 182.

[11] Ibid., 188.

[12] Quoted in Moretti, *Modern Epic*, 44.

novel, heir to the totalizing ambition of the ancient epic, should have made its own and brought to a point of paroxysm (as is the case likewise for almost every formal procedure it inherits from the past) the so-called "autonomy of the parts." This autonomy has been institutionalized and radicalized in the important textual strategy of the systematic use of the fragment, as we have seen, and, in continuity moreover, it must be highlighted, with some of the pivotal literary texts of modernism from Joyce's *Ulysses* to Dos Passos's *Manhattan Transfer*. Clearly however, it is not the procedure in itself which counts, but rather the result it permits the text to attain. A narrative which proceeds through fragments lends itself well to the representation, as Moretti suggests in relation to *The Waste Land*,[13] of the great plurality of voices and experiences which comprise the chaos of the contemporary world. T. S. Eliot writes: "The ordinary man's experience is chaotic, irregular, fragmentary. The latter falls in love, or reads Spinoza, and these two experiences have nothing to do with each other, or with the noise of the typewriter or the smell of cooking. . . ."[14]

A total novel, such as the maximalist novel, would not be able not to take all of this into account. And it is precisely its extraordinary embrace of *polyphony* which lends to maximalist chorality its particular attribute of being "dissonant."

2 Polyphony

The maximalist novel is strongly polyphonic.[15] Languages, registers, styles, genres, fields of knowledge, and character voices accumulate paroxistically in it, forging a dialogic complexity and richness without precedents. Underscoring one more time that a "naturally" polyphonic genre does not

13 Moretti considers the use of the fragment to be Eliot's version of polyphony; a polyphony which in *Ulysses* operates instead through stream of consciousness. See Moretti, *Modern Epic*, 186–7.

14 T. S. Eliot, "The Metaphysical Poets" [1921], in Eliot, *Selected Prose* (Harmondsworth: Penguin, 1951), 110; quoted in Moretti, *Modern Epic*, 186.

15 An interesting approach to one of the most complex, if not the most complex of the maximalist novels taken into consideration here, *Infinite Jest*, is an essay by Catherine Nichols which evidences well the strong dialogic opening and carnivalesque euphoria of Wallace's novel. See Catherine Nichols, "Dialogizing Postmodern Carnival: David Foster Wallace's *Infinite Jest*," *Critique* 43 (2001): 3–16.

exist, it has to be noted that in the maximalist novel polyphony nevertheless attains dizzying heights. It is so varied and pervasive that not even the most attentive reader can take it all in. A first and purely material reason for this exceptional swarming of voices lies without doubt in the length of the novels in question. It is fairly evident, even if certainly not automatic, that the greater the number of pages available, the greater and more heterogeneous will be the narrative material. The maximalist novel's elevated number of pages allows, in fact, for an undoubtedly more extensive diffusion of voices than would be the case in a short or moderately long novel. A second and very important reason for the swarming of voices arises instead as the direct consequence of the encyclopedism of the maximalist novel. The representation of a wide-ranging gamut of knowledge and languages entails, by necessity, a polyphonic narrative framework, analogous to the large diversity and multidisciplinarity of entries which make up an encyclopedia. But there is a third, more subtle reason which should be evidenced: the calling into question by the maximalist novel of some of the anthropocentric contrivances of the traditional novel. Let us begin once again with *Ulysses*.

In relation to the stream of consciousness in *Ulysses*, Moretti has spoken of a polyphony free from any anthropocentric frame or motives. A technique that has cast off the fetters of bourgeois realism and offers itself exclusively for what it is: a narrative device. A movement in the direction of the emancipation of form from mimesis, the initial symptoms of which can be found already in the eighteenth century, beginning with Diderot's *Le Neveu de Rameau*, in which Rameau constitutes "the first figure of the modern—who embarks on the great venture of 'self-estrangement', nourishing his own individuality upon the countless forms of modern culture."[16] It is a phenomenon previously theorized by Viktor Shlovsky in relation to Laurence Sterne's *Tristram Shandy*: "Sterne was a radical revolutionary as far as form is concerned. It was typical of him to lay bare the device. The aesthetic form is presented without any motivation whatsoever."[17]

A device, then, which frees itself from the mimetic and anthropocentric encumbrances of realistic representation and offers itself in its quality as pure

[16] Moretti, *Modern Epic*, 193.
[17] Viktor Shlovsky, *Theory of Prose* [1929] (Elmwood Park: Dalkey Archive Press, 1990), 147.

technique or, rather, as pure form, containing exclusively within itself its own purpose. Moretti writes eloquently:

> The emancipation of polyphony from anthropocentric motivation is, to be sure, a development of literary technique: but a formal development that *duplicates a general tendency of modern capitalism.* If the languages of Joycean polyphony seem to "speak of their own accord," no longer relying on concrete subjects, it is because *they have all become institutional languages*, and follow "the purely objective norms" of Church, School, Journalism, Nation, Advertising. . . . Try making a map of *Ulysses*, and comparing it with the one Pierre Bourdieu once made for *Sentimental Education*. One thing leaps to the eye immediately: Flaubert's Paris is made up of private houses. Joyce's Dublin of public places. Collective spaces, or institutional ones. And *spaces that talk.* "A cultural object comes into existence which as a total unit is *without a producer*," writes Simmel again. True, and these new objects are precisely the protagonists of the second *Ulysses.*[18]

The process just described reaches full fruition only in the first decades of the twentieth century, even if we can already espy it in embryonic form in the eighteenth century. And it was delayed in reaching that full fruition, according to Moretti, because of the ascent of the novel in the eighteenth century and, later, of realism. Freed from the fetters of the latter, polyphony burst forth in *Ulysses* with all of its explosive force and took the form of stream of consciousness: both as a tendency of modern capitalism (as the receptacle of the multiplicity of languages and of the innumerable material seductions that bombard Bloom in his wanderings through Dublin) and as a mosaic of institutional languages (publicity, journalism, etc.), which, as Simmel suggests, no longer have any single producer because they are generated by the homologating force of capitalism and of its promotional logic.[19] Something similar occurs in the maximalist novel, in which polyphony is not manifested in the Joycean stream of consciousness, to be sure—not as a rule, at least, although its use is not infrequent or unusual within the broad gamut of techniques employed—but lends itself, and especially well, to the expression of a series of important necessities.

[18] Moretti, *Modern Epic*, 196.

[19] See Georg Simmel, "On the Concept and Tragedy of Culture" [1911], in Simmel, *The Conflict in Modern Culture and Other Essays*, trans. and intro. K. Peter Etzkorn (New York: Teachers College Press, 1968), 27–46.

Reserving a specific analysis of the peculiar status of maximalist realism for the final chapter of this essay, for the moment, I will limit my comments to noting how a strong polyphony contributes, together with chorality, to the systematic placement of all individual or individualizing needs in a subordinate position. As it has already been shown, in each of the seven novels constituting our textual corpus, the narration is never wholly entrusted to a single character, or linked to a single narrative thread, but is comprised instead of a greater or lesser number of intertwining stories and characters. In this sense, it is interesting to observe how, in relation to the system of characters, polyphony in the maximalist novel always has a certain *organization*, a certain uniformity of treatment. Within our set of texts under consideration, at least two distinct forms of polyphony seem to take shape, by means of which the numerous voices of the characters either *group* around one or more narrative nucleuses, or are left *free*.

The first case is exemplified well by the novels *White Teeth* and *The Corrections*. In *White Teeth*, the characters either are the components of or gather mainly around three families that operate as ordering foci: the Jones, the Iqbals, and the Chalfens. In *The Corrections* instead, there is only one center, the Lambert family. We could call this means of arrangement of the system of the characters *nuclear*, in contrast instead to the second means, adopted by *Gravity's Rainbow*, *Infinite Jest*, *Underworld*, *2666*, and *2005 dopo Cristo*, which we could call instead *free*, because it does not provide narrative pivots for the mass of characters which populate these novels to rotate around. And this is certainly not because they are lacking stability poles in the narration, quite the contrary. But rather because these poles do not operate as gravitational centers capable of attracting and organizing the system of characters. As a result, we have a more mobile polyphony, freer to expand. Even if, to be sure, it is never a question of complete freedom, but if anything of a "guarded freedom," since polyphony never degenerates into chaos in the maximalist novel. There will always be ordering criteria to the story—criteria we will deal with shortly—which serve to contain the rich maximalist polyphony within sustainable and "audible" limits, thereby preventing deflagration and anarchy.

Whereas detachment from anthropocentric procedures characteristic of nineteenth-century realist novel—locates the maximalist novel at the endpoint of an evolutionary line begun by Sterne and Diderot in the eighteenth century and culminating in with modernism in the works of Joyce and Dos Passos, a crisis in bourgeois individualism, traditionally linked to the ascent of the modern novel,[20] has been identified by LeClair and Karl in their systems novels and Mega-Novels as well. While Karl notes in passing how the Mega-Novel refutes any sort of individualization of experience—something which occurs frequently, he argues, in ethnic, gay, and women's literary practices—because Mega-Novelists are prone to sensing America "as a whole,"[21] LeClair lingers on the anti-individualism of the systems novel repeatedly, and in a rather particular manner:

> I will argue that the novels included here are masterworks because they flexibly employ postmodern methods to displace the priority of the individual and to deform the conventions of realism which encode an ideology of the local. Anticipating or written during the Age of Narcissism, the masterworks controvert it and what I think is one of narcissism's primary expressions, literary minimalism, the work of the local self.[22]

And further along:

> In fiction, the experimental energies of the early 1970s were damped by late '70s neo-realists and moral fictionists. In the 1980s the novella and the short story have become increasingly popular. . . . In both genres, the current fashion is carved-down minimalism. John Barth, self-described as a "maximalist," makes the best possible case for minimalism in his essay "A Few Words about Minimalism," but the mode's inherent weakness is expressed by one of its most influential practitioners, Donald Barthelme: "In earlier times people could attempt to explain everything. Today there is too much to explain. The effort would be fruitless. So you have to try and do something else. For me it's more attempting to deal with parts instead of attempting to deal with the whole." . . .

20 See Ian Watt, *The Rise of the Novel: Studies in Defoe, Richardson, and Fielding* [1957], afterword by W. B. Carnochan (Berkeley-Los Angeles: University of California Press, 2001), 9–34.

21 "In the main, the Mega-Novelists have avoided the individualization of ethnic, gay, or female experience and sensed the country as a whole; that in itself insures length, volume, vastitude, oceanic experience. Now that most postwar energies are being exhausted, it is clear that the Mega-Novel almost alone remains as a reflection of the final decades of the century." Karl, *American Fictions: 1980-2000*, 164.

22 LeClair, *The Art of Excess*, 2–3.

> I think the art of excess is the serious author's response to this environment, for excess is a strategy that first meets and then transforms conventional, even popularly engineered expectations to have an impact on the reader.[23]

LeClair interprets the writing of systems novels as the reaction to a literary scene dominated by minimalism, the expression of the most exasperated individualism and narcissism and of a complete civic disengagement. Systems novels versus minimalism, then. The question merits some exploration.

[23] Ibid., 25–6.

Minimalism/Maximalism

In "A Few Words about Minimalism," one of the most lucid reflections on the American minimalist literary moment, John Barth looks at minimalism and maximalism as two opposite metahistorical attitudes of language related to the internal dynamics of the system of the arts.[1] From the cryptic responses of the Delphic oracle to the Homeric poems, from Bauhaus to postmodern architecture, from Samuel Beckett to Pynchon, minimal and maximal expression have become the standard-bearers over the centuries of divergent artistic and speculative impulses which could be synthesized respectively by the well-known slogans "less is more"[2] and "less is a bore."[3] Barth writes:

> The medieval Roman Catholic Church recognized two opposite roads to grace: the *via negativa* of the monk's cell and the hermit's cave, and the *via affirmativa* of immersion in human affairs, of being in the world whether or not one is of it. Critics have aptly borrowed those terms to characterize the difference between Mr. Beckett, for example, and his erstwhile master James Joyce, himself a maximalist except in his early works.

Specifically, the minimalism, which in the 1980s animated the season of the New American Short Story, is seen in part by the American writer and essayist as a reaction against the baroque and neurotic prose of postmodern authors such as Pynchon, Coover, Elkin, Heller, Barthelme, and Barth himself, who belong to a preceding generation with respect to the post-Carver minimalist authors. A reaction whose elements of novelty are put into a historical perspective by Barth and contextualized within the compass of those *cyclical*

[1] John Barth, "A Few Words about Minimalism," *The New York Times*, 26 December 1986.

[2] A motto coined by Christoph Martin Wieland and taken up again by Robert Browning in the dramatic monologue *Andrea del Sarto*, but known above all thanks to Ludwig Mies van der Rohe's use of it in reference to his functional conception of living space.

[3] An expression thought up by the postmodern architect Robert Venturi in his polemic with the "International Style" and architectural modernism. See *Learning from Las Vegas: The Forgotten Symbolism of Architectural Form* [1972], eds. Robert Venturi et al. (Cambridge, MA: MIT Press, 2001), 93–103.

corrections of excess operating in the history of literature and the arts from their inception, and in that of cultural history in a broader sense:

> The functionalism of the Bauhaus was inspired in part by admiration for machine technology, in part by revulsion against the fancy clutter of the gilded Age, in language as well as elsewhere. The sinking of the elegant Titanic has come to symbolize the end of that age, as the sight of some workmen crushed by a falling Victorian cornice symbolized for young Frank Lloyd Wright the dead weight of functionless architectural decoration. Flaubert raged against the plague of bourgeois speech, bureaucratic speech in particular; his passion for the *mot juste* involved far more subtraction than addition. The baroque inspires its opposite: after the excesses of scholasticism comes Descartes's radical reductionism—let us doubt and discard everything not self-evident and see whether anything indubitable remains upon which to rebuild. And among the scholastics themselves, three centuries before Descartes, William of Ockham honed his celebrated razor: *Entia non sunt multiplicanda* ("Entities are not to be multiplied"). In short, less is more. Beyond their individual and historically local impulses, then, the more or less minimalist authors of the New American Short Story are re-enacting a cyclical correction in the history (and the microhistories) of literature and of art in general: a cycle to be found as well, with longer rhythms, in the history of philosophy, the history of the culture. Renaissances beget Reformations, which then beget Counter-Reformations; the seven fat years are succeeded by seven lean, after which we, no less than the people of Genesis, may look forward to the recorrection.[4]

Barth's analysis has an undeniable merit. It locates the minimalism/maximalism dialectic in a historical framework extended in time, distancing itself from those theorizations which saw, and still see, minimalism as a contingent phenomenon, born in opposition to postmodernism in general,[5] and understand with the term "postmodernism" those literary practices dominated by a playful, nihilistic, and self-conscious conception of the artistic act: literary practices exemplified in quintessential fashion by the works of Pynchon. These theorizations are as diffused as they are exceptionally reductive, and,

4 Barth, *A Few Words about Minimalism*.

5 See Robert Rebein, *Hicks, Tribes, & Dirty Realists: American Fiction after Postmodernism* (Lexington, The University Press of Kentucky, 2001), 22–40; Zoltan Abadi-Nàgy, "Minimalism vs. Postmodernism in Contemporary American Fiction," *Nohelicon* 28, 1 (2001): 129–44.

in addition to flattening postmodern literature to the compliant stereotype of a frivolous and self-validating literature, they do not take into consideration the continual interferences between the two phenomena. It is Barth, again, who points out how in the production of a master of the short form, Donald Barthelme—variously considered together with Raymond Carver to be the heir to the modern American short story tradition, according to a genealogy that begins with Poe and extends all the way to Hemingway—the predilection for short fictional genres does not have much to do with that "terse, oblique, realistic or hyperrealistic, slightly plotted, extrospective, cool-surfaced fiction"[6] characteristic of authors like Bobbie Ann Manson, James Robinson, Ann Beattie, Tobias Wolff, and others, who, together with Carver, are generally defined as minimalist. Excellent examples include the extreme experimentalism of the short story "Sentence," consisting of a single sentence seven pages long,[7] or the icy intellectualism of "Kierkegaard Unfair to Schlegel."[8] And yet the perception that minimalism was a reaction against the baroque excesses of postmodernism must have been shared to a good extent if Carver himself, the acknowledged and tirelessly imitated father of the New American Short Story, tended to think of his fiction as something radically opposite to postmodern experimentalism and of Barth's writing, in particular.

Making a distinction between the concepts of "communication" and "expression," where the first necessarily implies the idea of an audience, while the second is connoted instead by a greater disinterest and privateness, Carver, in a 1986 interview with William L. Stull, asserts that the experimental writers of his times failed in essence as communicators, having lost sight of the reading public, and he defines the postmodern as "an odd time in the literary history of the country," as an interruption in the course of realism.[9] But 5 years prior, Carver had been even more clear-cut. In his essay "On Writing," which appeared in *The New York Times Book Review* in February 1981 as a response to Barth's complaints in the same publication about a presumed

6 Barth, *A Few Words about Minimalism*.

7 Donald Barthelme, "Sentence" [1970], in Barthelme, *Forty Stories*, intro. Dave Eggers (New York: Penguin, 2005), 147–53.

8 Donald Barthelme, "Kierkegaard Unfair to Schlegel" [1970], in Barthelme, *Sixty Stories*, intro. David Gates (New York: Penguin, 2003), 154–62.

9 Marshall Bruce Gentry and William L. Stull, *Conversations with Raymond Carver* (Jackson: University of Mississippi Press, 1990), 183–4. See Rebein, *Hicks, Tribes & Dirty Realists*, 26.

experimental lassitude in the fictional production of students in the 1980s as compared with those in the 1960s and 1970s,[10] Carver expressed himself very unambiguously on the dangers of formal innovation in literature:

> Too often "experimentation" is a license to be careless, silly or imitative in the writing. Even worse, a license to try to brutalize or alienate the reader. Too often such writing gives us no news of the world, or else describes a desert landscape and that's all—a few dunes and lizards here and there, but no people; a place uninhabited by anything recognizably human, a place of interest only to a few scientific specialists.[11]

"Alienate the reader," "no news of the world," "a place of interest only to a few scientific specialists": if we refer all this to the maximalist novel, the experimental character of which is extremely marked, one wants to ask what is it Carver is talking about or how the maximalist novel could somehow be adapted to fit this type of definition. Carver probably had a particular sort of fiction in mind, a fiction ideally represented by John Barth's experimental masterpiece, *Lost in the Funhouse*—an expression of only *one* of the multiple souls of the postmodern, that of *postmodernism* in its restricted sense, as it has been defined by Jameson in his celebrated essay of the same name—in which the real objects of the discourse tend to succumb under the claustrophobic pressure of a narration that is acrobatic and hyperconscious. But in distancing himself from this sort of fiction, Carver engages in a dangerous generalization, extending his criticism to every experimental literary work, indirectly involving Pynchon as well, and, as a consequence, the maximalist novel. Paradoxically no less, since it is precisely minimalism that has been criticized by LeClair for its meager ability to engage the reader intellectually, and which he finds guilty of having nourished a renunciatory and narcissistic concept of literature.

Nevertheless, Carver's line must have seemed a winning one also to Frederick Barthelme, the younger brother of Donald, who tried to free himself from the heavy burden of being seen as epigones which affected the reception of the minimalist authors of the "second generation"[12]—among whom he himself

10 Raymond Carver, "On Writing" [1981], in Carver, *Fires: Essays, Poems, Stories* (New York: Vintage, 1989), 22–7. See Rebein, *Hicks, Tribes & Dirty Realists*, 25–6.

11 Carver, "On Writing," 23–4.

12 See Madison Smartt Bell, "Less is Less: The Dwindling of the American Short Story," *Harper's*, April 1986, 64–9; Rebein, *Hicks, Tribes & Dirty Realists*, 34.

and Amy Hempel, for example—often liquidated in the name of a natural continuity with Beckett, Hemingway, and Carver, without any elements of substantial novelty having been acknowledged in their works.[13] Frederick Barthelme maintained that post-Carver minimalism was as different from postmodernism as from the traditional realism against which postmodern literature had rebelled in its own stead. It was a minimalism able to take the best from those two traditions, while, at the same time, discarding their most conventional and artificial aspects. An operation that was anything but simple to realize, however, and with debatable results, as Robert Rebein has shown.[14]

To conclude, it is not completely mistaken to think of a "maximalism" in opposition to a "minimalism," but only if the two terms are regarded within a long-term perspective. Presented otherwise, the entire question becomes a false problem. The copresence of both minimalist and maximalist practices within the same span of time, from the 1980s through the 1990s more or less, could certainly be misleading, of course. However, maximalism was not born as a reaction to American literary minimalism because it has *always* been present in the postmodern system of novel genres, already beginning with Gaddis's *The Recognitions*. A presence that, we now understand, is the sign of a strong continuity with modernism and, even before that, a strong continuity with the epic. As a result, the reasons for maximalism should not be sought out exclusively in very recent times and in response, moreover, to a specific and unique literary phenomenon, North American minimalism. It is also true, however, that the choices a writer makes relate directly and principally to the literary sphere of the times to which she belongs and in whose orbit her work is conceived and, in a first moment, welcomed. Thus, from a certain point of view, it makes sense to speak of a maximalist literary praxis which is hypercomplex in form and engaged in grand ideas in juxtaposition to minimalist-type writings which are lean and saturated with solipsism, since two contrary and contemporaneous phenomena demand almost automatically to be interpreted, the one with respect to the other. But an analysis of this sort lays bare a short-term literary memory. Be it with LeClair's thesis of

[13] Frederick Barthelme, "On Being Wrong: Convicted Minimalist Spills Beans," *The New York Times*, 3 April 1988.

[14] Rebein, *Hicks, Tribes & Dirty Realists*, 36–40.

"maximalism" understood as a critical and engaged response to "minimalism" or in Barth's opposite view of "minimalism" born as a reaction to the excesses of "maximalism" or Carver's notion of a stereotyped postmodern. The case of the maximalist novel is, in fact, a perfect example of how absolutely fundamental it is, in the analysis of literary forms, to reason from a *longue durée* perspective[15] since it is impossible to fully comprehend its significance if one does not take into consideration literary history as a whole.[16] Thus, rather than seeing minimalism as a "cyclical correction" of maximalism as Barth does, the two phenomena can be understood as being *dialectically coexistent*: two elementary possibilities of human expression which have always existed side by side (as in the 1980s and 1990s for example) or alternated (between the twentieth and twenty-first centuries) in determining the aesthetic horizon of a given literary system. A dialectical coexistence in which both tendencies have undergone *phases of dormancy* and *acute phases*, without one or the other, however, ever disappearing completely. And this thanks to that astonishing subterranean survival of forms, capable of resisting for centuries in unthought-of cultural spaces, to then resurface, often so changed as to appear almost unrecognizable. As it happens with the maximalist novel, the reader of which, to reach its morphological and symbolic heart, has to retrace the course of time all the way to the dark and remote night of the ancient epic.

[15] See Fernand Braudel, "History and the Social Sciences: The *Longue Durée*" [1958], in Braudel, *On History*, trans. Sarah Matthews (Chicago: University of Chicago Press, 1980), 25–54.

[16] Joseph Tabbi made an interesting attempt pointing at this direction in his essay "American World-Fiction in the Longue Durée," in *American Studies/Shifting Gears*, eds. Birte Christ et al. (Heidelberg: Universitätverlag Winter, 2010), 117–42. See also Joseph Tabbi, "William Gaddis and the Autopoiesis of American Fiction," in *Paper Empire*, eds. Tabbi and Shavers, 90–117.

4

Diegetic Exuberance

The maximalist novel abounds in diegetic material. Its narration is hypertrophic and ultra-dense; the stories and characters that populate it are innumerable, as are its digressions and themes. One finds oneself face to face with something similar to that "inflation of discourse" of which Charles Newman has spoken in relation to Pynchon's *Gravity's Rainbow*[1]: a discursive excess that causes the maximalist novel to appear to be an overflowing river, the narrative substance of which seems to proliferate almost spontaneously, rather than being the fruit of a well-planned creative operation.[2] The key word is *inclusion*: not to leave anything out, to bring the entire world into the novel. Karl writes in relation to *Infinite Jest*:

> It is clear that even as we dismiss some hijinks Wallace's paradigm was one of inclusion. Exclusion would mean selection, and while of course, he is selecting, he must give the appearance of all-ness, in a postmodern version of Thomas Wolfe's obsession with consuming everything by way of words. . . . Since [Wallace] cannot forgo the opportunity to tell a story, *Infinite*

1 Newman is not far off the mark when he asserts that the inflation of discourse in *Gravity's Rainbow* leads to an "aesthetic absolutism," since Pynchon tends to write for "an audience which not only does not exist, but *cannot* exist unless it progresses with the same utopian technical advancement of expertise, the same accelerating value, which informs the verbal dynamics of the novels written for them." Charles Newman, *The Post-Modern Aura: The Act of Fiction in an Age of Inflation* (Evanston: Northwestern University Press, 1985), 92. One could use this idea to plumb more deeply the strong authorial narcissism which pervades maximalist narratives, consisting in the exhibition on the part of the author of his own knowledge and his own technical capabilities. It is a complex question which would leave maximalism not too far removed from that narcissism of the "local self" which, according to LeClair, characterizes minimalism. At the very least, I feel that it is indeed a question of two different forms of narcissism: a more traditional, Freudian one (withdrawal of the ego and its libidinal cathexis) in the case of minimalism; and a post-Freudian, and specifically Grunberger-inflected narcissism, in relation to the maximalist novel (omnipotence of thoughts, play). It is a suggestion which cannot, however, be expanded upon here.

2 "Because the materials of systems novels often seem to grow, rather than to be built, the noise, gaps, and gratuitousness in the texts imply an open and natural system rather than a closed and artificial ordering." LeClair, *The Art of Excess*, 23.

> *Jest* can be viewed less as a "novel"—however defined—than as a sequence of short stories or riffs, or unleashed verbal segments. These stories attempt, like Wolfe, to encompass America, particularly its underside and its more horrific failures. . . . America is kaleidoscopic, impenetrable, indescribable, divisible into miniscule elements, segmented and hierarchical. *Infinite Jest* reflects everything America tries to disguise in its presentation of itself as the world's supreme victor. The world's greatest, here, is imploding into segments which do not mesh, do not function, do not cohere, and which, each in its way, is a form of disease (from tennis to heroin).[3]

Karl points out very effectively a fundamental aspect not only of *Infinite Jest* but of the maximalist novel in general: its tendency to incorporate a very broad and extremely heterogeneous range of narrative materials in the diegesis, as if it were desirous of "consuming everything by way of words." It is a praxis which at the formal level finds once again a necessary point of support in the versatile maximalist use of the fragment.

A fragmentary narrative lends itself quite well to the insertion of multiple and diversified diegetic materials since it allows for ample freedom in their arrangement, without excessive worries either to the coherence of the whole or to overbearing structural constraints. In the maximalist novel, the fragment not only serves as the basic morphological unit located at the core of its peculiar narrative organization, resulting as we know from an inextricable intermingling of chorality and polyphony, but it is also the tool which enables the deployment of the novel's extraordinary diegetic exuberance. The fragment is, in fact, a textual device able to assume a surprising array of functions in the maximalist novel, one among which is that of providing a support structure for the propulsive system of the diegesis. The exclusive goal of this propulsive mechanism, based on *digression*, is to enable extensive representations of the real.

Digression is the principal means by which the diegetic exuberance of the maximalist novel manifests itself. It is an ancient procedure, deriving from the epic, and one we will, therefore, examine in relation to it. As Alessandro Portelli writes, digression makes it possible to "contain all the world within

[3] Karl, *American Fictions: 1980-2000*, 477–8.

one text."[4] It is an age-old ambition of the epic, and, as we now well know, a very recent ambition of the maximalist novel. It would be difficult indeed to imagine a narrative technique more adept than digression to assist in the maximalist poetics of inclusion, precisely because of its constitutive and practically unlimited extendibility. In the maximalist novel, there is virtually no limit to the insertion of digressions into the narrative, since that of "limit" is a concept that is totally extraneous to the very notion of digression, if we view the latter, in the light of what Moretti argues for *Faust* and for world texts in general, as a "mechanical form," a form centered on a purely *additive* principle. We read in *Modern Epic*:

> A form that may be cut at will. Above all, one that may be *added to* at will. To which may be added a section experimenting with polyphony: then another about money and allegory; and yet another on the growth of the world-system. . . . A form in continuous growth: one "that wouldn't exclude something merely because it didn't fit" (Ezra Pound). A form "distending itself for centuries, like pythons swallowing sheep" (Frye), and thus becoming the "incommensurable whole" of which Goethe speaks a year before his death. All definitions dictated by pride in a form that dares to contend in breadth with the entire world.[5]

The additive nature of the epic has been roundly underscored by critics of very different orientations and has generally been considered to be one of its constitutive traits. Emil Staiger had noted in his time that, "The principle of composition most truly epic in character is that of simple addition. On a small as well as on a large scale epic brings independent elements together."[6] Frye too, later, spoke of the epic as an "encyclopedic aggregate,"[7] while Daniel Madelenat has demonstrated how the principle of addition in the epic allows for a continual growth in the text through collage, montage, and the juxtaposition of the individual parts of which it is composed.[8]

4 Alessandro Portelli, *The Text and the Voice: Writing, Speaking and Democracy in American Literature* [1992] (New York: Columbia University Press, 1994), 100.

5 Moretti, *Modern Epic*, 96.

6 Emil Staiger, *Basic Concepts of Poetics* [1946], trans. Janette C. Hudson and Luanne T. Frank (University Park: The Pennsylvania State University Press, 1991), 122.

7 Northrop Frye, *Anatomy of Criticism*, 55–61.

8 Daniel Madelenat, *L'Épopée* (Paris: Presses Universitaires de France, 1986), 72. See Moretti, *Modern Epic*, 96.

Addition, collage, montage, parataxis-all ingredients of the epic form which transmigrate *en masse* into the maximalist novel, and which qualify it as an eminently digressive narrative genre made of endless and heterogeneous diegetic materials. Almost as if, as Moretti writes, digression becomes the very purpose of the representation:

> A unified world is not necessarily a *closed* world: and if *Faust* is made up almost entirely of digressions, that does not mean that it lacks any unitary Action—but that *the digressions have themselves become the main purpose of the epic Action.*
>
> Digressions—indeed, their very proliferation—as substance and purpose of the Action.[9]

It is a fascinating idea, and not far removed from maximalist narrative practices. Let us take a closer look.

Digression can normally be defined as a deviation from the principal argument of the discourse. This is a definition which becomes rather problematic in reference to the maximalist novel, given that it is truly difficult to unequivocally isolate within it a central narrative subject. In this sense, a few apparently banal questions raise, whose answers, however, are anything but simple. What, in the end, do *Gravity's Rainbow*, *Infinite Jest*, *Underworld*, *White Teeth*, *The Corrections*, *2666*, and *2005 dopo Cristo* speak about? What do the digressions so abundant in these novels "deviate" from, with respect, that is, to what privileged object of the discourse? If, in the Homeric epic, there always remains a principal action from which the individual digressions branch off, albeit in a markedly autonomous manner, in the maximalist novel, the idea of a unitary and unifying narrative action explodes into a thousand pieces, flooding into a large number of stories. This does not, in any way, imply the return to a certain type of modernist fiction dominated by a weak propensity for storytelling, but, rather, precisely the opposite. The deflagration of the unity of plot here is not due to an exasperated and absolutist formal experimentalism, but to the desire to include in the diegesis enough fictional material to fill at least three or four novels. It is not a question of a want of narrativity, but, rather of its vertiginous *excess*. If, in a certain sense, maximalist discourse can be

[9] Moretti, *Modern Epic*, 48–9.

incorporated into the "return to storytelling" variously theorized in relation to postmodern fiction,[10] it takes that tendency to such an extreme as to generate a lethal narrative short circuit responsible for the detonation and the dispersion of plot. Whether it is modernism or maximalist novel, the result is the same, one could say, the plot breaks apart. Yes, it is true, the result is the same, but what is important is how one arrives there. For novels such as *Ulysses*, Virginia Woolf's *The Waves*, and Dos Passos's *Manhattan Transfer*, it was a question of taking in the valuable experimental legacy of the avant-gardes and turning it against some of the conventional elements of the novel (plot and character above all),[11] animated as they were by a utopian tension intent on a refounding of narrative language. For the maximalist novel, instead, it should have been about reacting against the excesses of modernist experimentation and against the barrenness of its storytelling. This, at least, is what the postmodern *Zeitgeist* demanded. And it is a reaction which did occur, but so intense that it produced the opposite of the desired effect. Different from what takes place, for instance, with the encyclopedic mode, I am inclined not to see any continuity between the maximalist novel and modernism in the dismantlement of plot, but rather a strong discontinuity which paradoxically came up with the same outcome.

But to return to digression, if it is not possible to identify with certainty a principal narrative thread in the maximalist novel, can we still speak of digressions? The answer to this question is yes, but it requires a small clarification with respect to the nature of digression in the maximalist novel. More than a distancing of the narration from the central focus of the representation, maximalist digression should be understood as an extended and constant *turbulence* produced by the omnivorous and encyclopedic *élan* of the story. It is a turbulence governed by the tension created between the polyphonic openness of the maximalist novel and the necessity, instead, to give form and order to that which otherwise would be an ungovernable

10 See Anders Stephanson, "Regarding Postmodernism: A Conversation with Fredric Jameson" [1986], in *Postmodernism. Jameson. Critique*, ed. Douglas Kellner (Washington: Maisonneuve Press, 1989), 43–74.

11 See Giacomo Debenedetti, *Commemorazione provvisoria del personaggio-uomo* [1965], in Debenedetti, *Saggi*, ed. Alfonso Berardinelli (Milan: Mondadori, 1999), 1280–322; Mario Lavagetto, *Lavorare con piccoli indizi* (Turin: Bollati Boringhieri, 2003), 279–97.

narrative chaos. One could think of the narrative space of the maximalist novel as a sort of electrostatic field, traversed by powerful and uninterrupted charges—the digressions—which do not, however, gather around or move away from a stabile narrative pole, but freely crisscross the entire field. Freely, yes, but always within its confines. We can say, then, that the object of maximalist diegesis is this sort of narrative field considered in its entirety and completely devoid of a unifying narrative action.

We have alluded repeatedly, in this study, to textual strategies capable of reining in maximalist polyphony and digressions, countering their centrifugal impulses. These textual strategies possess a fundamental *ordering function* which we will look at more closely in the next chapter.

5

Completeness

A warhorse in Karl's definition of the Mega-Novel is the conviction that it is a chaotic mass of narrative materials: ". . . the Mega-Novel has forsaken inclusivity for indeterminacy. Its aims are the decentering or deconstruction of elements rather than gathering in. It is *more mass than content*."[1]

Decentering, deconstruction, and chaotic narrative mass in the Mega-Novel novel. LeClair writes:

> Systems novelists employ multiple framing devices and metafictional pointers both to represent the wholes-within-wholes nature of systems and to help guide the reader through their masses of data. Self-reference, a device that often seems mere decadence in much postmodern experimentation is, in natural systems and in systems novels, an enabling, necessary procedure. Both framing and self-reference contribute to the systems novelists' fundamental artistic accomplishment: the creation of imitative forms. . . . These imitative forms are ways of structuring novelistic information so that it reflects the density, homologous structure, and scale of information in life.[2]

The existence of "imitative forms" in systems novels which structure the narrative information. We are at the opposite extreme from Karl, there *chaos*, here *cosmos*. Let us try to understand.

At first, the superabundance of narrative material in a maximalist novel can certainly appear chaotic. It is understandable, after all, that novels which are very long, encyclopedic, choral, and digressive in form, might produce a sense of disorientation in the reader and give the impression of a high degree of disorder. It is not by chance, in fact, that there is general agreement that in novels such as *Gravity's Rainbow* or *Infinite Jest,* disorder reigns uncontested.

1 Karl, *American Fictions: 1980-2000*, 157.
2 LeClair, *The Art of Excess*, 23–4.

To quote Karl, once again, on *Infinite Jest*: "Wallace's method is not to bring order to disorder, but to reveal disorder so broad that even the novelist's efforts to achieve some order cannot prevail. . . . [H]is disorder is of such a magnitude that any effort to harness, by the author or by an outside force, is futile."[3]

This appraisal, as we shall see, is not only debatable with regard to *Infinite Jest*, but also in relation to the maximalist novel in general, since the latter *always* resorts to sturdy structuring devices which guarantee the tightness and unity of the whole. The enormous number of digressions might lead a reader astray and give the impression of an immense chaos, but there is order, and grasping its peremptoriness is fundamental for understanding the maximalist project. It is necessary to definitively dispense with the idea, which probably has arisen precisely because of the coexistence of chorality and digressions in these texts, that maximalist novelists abandon themselves to the wildest associations of ideas and to the most unpredictable meanderings in an out-of-control narrative delirium. Nothing excludes, in fact, that the abundance of character voices and diegetic material in maximalist fiction can be lodged within a *container*, a structure able to give form to the diegesis and to establish its confines. And this is precisely what occurs in our novels.

1 Structural practices of the maximalist novel

LeClair's insight that *systems novels* develop "imitative forms" through which their excess of information is structured and reined in is, perhaps, his most important contribution to the theory of maximalist narrative forms, and it is a very important one to bear in mind in attempting to define one of the most characteristic features of the maximalist novel, *completeness*. Let us start, then, with the essence of completeness, with order, and with the various forms in which it manifests itself.

We have spoken of the existence of structures that are able to exercise a function of control over the narrative. There are three types of these structures: *geometric*, *temporal*, and *conceptual*. Let us begin with the first type, in an attempt to outline a taxonomy of the structural practices of the maximalist novel.

[3] Karl, *American Fictions: 1980-2000*, 473.

1.1 Circular geometries

Infinite Jest, *Underworld*, and *2666* are constructed on the basis of a pronounced *circular* geometry.

Infinite Jest begins in November of the Year of Glad, with Hal Incandenza who falls prey to a sort of delirium/epileptic attack/illness, during an interview with the admissions committee of the University of Arizona. It ends on 20 November of the Year of the Depend Adult Undergarment (YDAU), with Don Gately immobile in his hospital bed—dazed by the atrocious pain of a shoulder wound from a gunshot—and moving continually between states of consciousness and unconsciousness, between memories and/or hallucinations caused perhaps by the administration of pain relievers, despite his protests (having been a drug addict, he explicitly asks to not receive treatment with narcotic drugs, even though the pain from his wound is terrible). Adhering to the distinctive chronology of the novel, that of Subsidized Time,[4] the Year of Glad, during which the novel begins, is the year immediately following the YDAU, in which the novel ends. The beginning of *Infinite Jest* would be absolutely incomprehensible if one does not take into account everything that happens throughout the course of the entire narration and which culminates in the events of the YDAU, even if many doubts nevertheless remain. Does Hal most likely fall prey to delirium because he has ingested the very potent DMZ, a drug he and his companions, Pemulis and Axford, had agreed to take on 20–21 November of the YDAU? Or is it because he has incidentally, or voluntarily, seen the dangerous and sought out "Entertainment," *Infinite Jest*, created by his father? This viewing must have taken place after 20 November of the YDAU, the moment at which the novel ends and in which Gately is in the hospital because up to that point Hal had not been in possession of the film and because, while he is in the emergency room where he was taken after the epileptic/delirious attack/illness which struck him during his interview for admission to the University of Arizona with which the novel opens, he remembers when he and Gately, characters who do not have any

[4] Subsidized Time is the ironic temporal organization at play in the novel. Adopted at a certain point by the ONAN (Organization of North American Nations), a territorial entity which has "integrated" the single North and Central American nation-states into a sole confederation comprising the United States, Canada, and Mexico (within which the first holds leadership while the other two are in a subordinate position), it consists in the assignation of a sponsor to each calendar year, from which the latter take their name.

sort of direct relationship over the course of the entire narrative, were digging to unearth the head of his father James (while John Wayne was the lookout), probably because in the grave of James Incandenza was hidden the original, and therefore duplicable, cartridge of *Infinite Jest*.[5] A circular ending, then.

After the "Prologue," which takes place during the baseball game in which Bobby Thomson hits his famous homerun which clinched the victory and the National League championship for the 1951 Giants, the first part of *Underworld*, "Long Tall Sally," opens in the spring-summer of 1992 with Nick Shay driving in the desert being directed to Klara Sax, by then an old and celebrated artist who had once been his lover. We then proceed backwards in time, section after section until we reach the "Epilogue," "Das Kapital," in which we engage in a type of return to the future, with the narration that picks up from 1992 and with Nick who is in Kazakhstan for some nuclear tests. Once again, a circular ending. And if we take into account the fact that the "Prologue" takes place on 3 October 1951, during the famous game between the Giants and the Dodgers, and that the sixth and last part of the novel returns us—after having gone back through fifty years of American history—to the fall of 1951, we find ourselves with another circular ending. As such, we can speak of, in the case of *Underworld*, a double circular ending.

Finally, the closing section of the first part of *2666*, "The Part of the Critics," consists of the trip of the three literary critics and university professors, Pelletier, Espinoza, and Norton, to Mexico (Morini, the fourth, disabled and in poor health, remains in Turin, the city in which he lives and teaches), on the trail of the mysterious writer Arcimboldi, whose work is the exclusive object of their academic interests. The fifth and last part of the novel, "The Part of Arcimboldi," ends up with the elderly Arcimboldi who leaves for Mexico to bring help to his nephew, in custody and faced with the terrible accusation of being the serial killer of Santa Teresa.[6] One more time, the linear sequence of

5 The objective of the *Assassins des Fauteuils Rollents* (A.F.R.), an extremist and grotesque fringe of Québecois separatism, to flood the United States with an avalanche of copies of the lethal *Infinite Jest*, can be achieved only by getting hold of the master cartridge of the film. As such, Burn's hypothesis of a forced participation of Hal in the A.F.R. would seem to find confirmation in Hal's recollection, and in the missing year between the end and the beginning of the novel. See Burn, *David Foster Wallace's "Infinite Jest,"* 37–8.

6 Bolaño transfers to the urban and suburban areas of Santa Teresa the locales of the serial murders of young women which for years have bloodied Ciudad Juárez, a city in the Chihuahuan Desert of Mexico.

events is turned on its head. One more time, a circular closure: we set off from Mexico and we return to Mexico.

Circularity: to begin with what chronologically happens at the end. It seems to be exactly what occurs, according to Mario Vargas Llosa, in *Cien años de soledad*, the final world text that Moretti discusses:

> 1. At the start of an episode, the main fact in the narrative unit is mentioned: it is usually the last, in chronological terms. In other words, the episode begins with a leap towards the future . . . "Many years later, as he faced the firing squad . . ." . . .
>
> 2. The narrative then jumps to the remotest past of the fact mentioned, whence it follows a linear chronological account of events, until it reaches the future fact that has been displaced and reported at the start of the episode: in this way the circle is closed, and *the episode ends where it began, just as it had begun where it would end.*[7]

A practice which, according to Moretti, lends an epic feel to the narrative:

> Future, past, future. It is an interplay of prolepsis and flashback that endows the novel with its peculiarly unforgettable quality: announcing a fact long before it takes place, and then recalling it long afterwards—like the *Leitmotiv* in the *Ring*, or in *Ulysses*—endows it with a truly epic grandeur.[8]

True, as it is also true that the web of circular plots in these three novels constitutes a first, and an important, textual strategy put into play in the attempt to order their narrative chaos.

1.2 Temporal architectures

Underworld and *White Teeth* have a rigorous temporal order, a rigid framework within which the various narrative threads of these novels unfold.

As mentioned earlier, *Underworld* begins with a "Prologue," "The Triumph of Death," which takes place on 3 October 1951. This is followed by "Part 1," "Long Tall Sally," spring–summer 1992; "Part 2," "Elegy for Left

[7] Mario Vargas Llosa, *García Márquez: Historia de un deicidio* (Barcelona: Barral Editores, 1971), 549; quoted and translated in Moretti, *Modern Epic*, 242.

[8] Ibid., 242.

Hand Alone," mid-1980s–early 1990s; "Part 3," "The Cloud of Unknowing," spring 1978; "Part 4," "Cocksucker Blues," summer 1974; "Part 5," "Better Things for Better Living Through Chemistry," 1950s and 1960s; and "Part 6," "Arrangement in Gray and Black," fall 1951–summer 1952. It all closes with an "Epilogue" that returns the narrative to 1992. All of this is punctuated by three interludes devoted to Manx Martin—"Manx Martin 1," between "Part 1" and "Part 2"; "Manx Martin 2," between "Part 3" and "Part 4"; and "Manx Martin 3," between "Part 5" and "Part 6"—and to his attempts to sell Thomson's homerun baseball (bought by his son Cotter during the game and stolen by his father while he was asleep), beginning on the very same evening of the game, that is to say, between 3 and 4 October 1951, in an ideal temporal succession with the "Prologue." To recapitulate: we begin in 1951; we then jump forward to 1992, we then move backwards until we return to the fall of 1951 and are subjected once more to a temporal move forward which, at the end, brings us back to 1992. And in this chronological inversion are located the three temporal segments centered on 1951 and Manx Martin's attempt to sell the baseball. The temporal order is contorted but implacably rigid at the same time. As if the only way to cover half a century of American history and to lay bare its contradictions is to do it in reverse, moving back through history against its current, in an attempt to trace the contours of that "counterhistory" of which DeLillo himself speaks in "The Power of History."[9] Besides having an important structural function, the manipulation of time also acquires thematic implications in that the revelation of the darker aspects of recent American history is the principal objective of *Underworld*. An objective which, moreover, perfectly and brilliantly hits the mark.

White Teeth, on the other hand is divided into four sections, in each of which the narrated facts take place within the span of time between the two dates referred to in the title of each section. Proceeding in order: "Archie 1974, 1945"; "Samad 1984, 1857"; "Irie 1990, 1907"; "Magid, Millat and Marcus 1992, 1999." In the first three sections, there is a movement from the narrative present in which each one opens to the past, and, in the last, a movement from the

[9] Don DeLillo, "The Power of History," *New York Times Magazine*, 7 September 1997.

present to the future. Therefore, a double movement; first backwards, stretching toward the past, a past understood as a recovery of the roots that ground the identity of the novel's characters; and then forward, projected toward the future, a future which is possible only if constructed on the awareness of one's own origins. Through this present-past/present-future double movement, time is bended to the objective of the representation to impart order to the narrative material and to convey at a structural level the idea running throughout the entire novel that the future resides in one's roots, however much these roots may often constitute an oppressive burden.[10]

These cases, just seen in *Underworld* and *White Teeth*, in addition to illustrating a peculiar structural practice of the maximalist novel, highlight another characteristic feature often present in the texts under examination: the *omnivorous* relationship with time. We have repeatedly made reference to the synthetic-totalizing desire of the maximalist novel, which we have seen enacted in a multiplicity of aesthetic choices and formal solutions. And if that totalizing tension is so pervasive, why should time be left out of it? Like *Underworld* and *White Teeth*, *Gravity's Rainbow*, through history,[11] and *Infinite Jest* and *2005 dopo Cristo*, through myth, establish an omnivorous relationship with time, consisting in an attempt to contemplate it in its unlimited extension. It is an attempt, to be sure, that is intrinsically partial, synecdochal. In this regard, Jameson's well-known idea that the postmodern cultural horizon is dominated by spatiality, while that of high modernism by time, should perhaps be revisited.[12] Jameson's formulation appears to be crafted almost exclusively on the postmodernist developments in American

[10] This is the meaning of the final denouement which has Irie return to Jamaica, the land of her mother and her grandmother, to raise the son she has had by Magid, or by Millat—which of the two remains a mystery—and has the latter, twins separated at a tender age by an ocean of diffidence and difference, finally reconcile.

[11] An example is the reference, during the course of the novel, set in World War II Europe, to the bloody wars of extermination by Germany against the Herero people between 1904 and 1907. Another is the insertion of lengthy episodes on central Asian myth and folklore.

[12] "We have often been told, however, that we now inhabit the synchronic rather than the diachronic, and I think it is at least empirically arguable that our daily life, our psychic experience, our cultural languages, are today dominated by categories of space, rather than by categories of time, as in the preceding period of high modernism" (Jameson, *Postmodernism*, 16). Likewise: "The crisis in historicity now dictates a return, in a new way, to the question of temporal organization in general in the postmodern force field, and indeed, to the problem of the form that time, temporality, and the syntagmatic will be able to take in a culture increasingly dominated by space and spatial logic" (Ibid., 25). Or see the entire sixth chapter dedicated to space: "Utopianism After the End of Utopia" (Ibid., 154–80).

architecture and urbanistics, as well as on a crisis of historicity in the postmodern that probably needs to be more thoroughly assessed. But, above all, it bespeaks the anxiety of determining what is the aesthetic equivalent of a phenomenon which is primarily economic, that is to say, that late capitalism pointed out in Jameson's study as the mode of production at the core of the cultural logic of postmodernism. The omnivorous relationship of the maximalist novel to time is, in fact, a clear example of how the category of time is fundamental not only in modernism,[13] and that binary oppositions cannot do justice to the complexity of the vastness of the broad postmodern cultural horizon, of which the maximalist novel is the most mature and controversial fruition.

That being said, spatiality certainly has a strong role in maximalist narratives, and *2666* is an excellent example. Bolaño's novel is a very particular case of the maximalist novel in that it is not tied to a single geographic and socio-cultural context. For *Gravity's Rainbow*, we have the Europe of the World War II; for *Underworld*, *Infinite Jest*, and *The Corrections*, the United States of the second half of the twentieth century (with the partial semi-futuristic exception of *Infinite Jest*); for *White Teeth*, the multiethnic London of post-decolonization; and for *2005 dopo Cristo*, Berlusconi's Italy. Bolaño's novel, instead, unfolds under the sway of a conspicuous transversality: from the major European metropolises of our day to the Sonoran desert in Mexico; from New York to prewar, wartime, and postwar Germany; to return once again to Mexico. The geography of *2666* is extremely complex and varied, as is its cultural identity; Chilean, because Bolaño was Chilean? Spanish, given that he lived in Spain for almost 30 years? Mexican, because Mexican society is perhaps the one best represented among those traversed by the protagonists of the novel, or because all of the principal narrative threads seem to mysteriously converge in Mexico? Probably none or all of the three. *2666* is, in fact, a fascinating example of a stateless narrative that seems to

[13] See Ronald Schleifer, *Modernism and Time: The Logic of Abundance in Literature, Science, and Culture, 1880-1930* (Cambridge: Cambridge University Press, 2000). On the changes in the perception and representation of the spatio-temporal continuum from modernism to postmodernism, see Gerhard Hoffmann, *From Modernism to Postmodernism: Concepts and Strategies of Postmodern American Fiction* (Amsterdam-New York: Rodopi, 2005), ch. 6. On the peculiar narrative perception of time in postmodern fiction, see Ursula K. Heise, *Chronoschisms: Time, Narrative, and Postmodernism* (Cambridge: Cambridge University Press, 1997).

speak directly to the world, without regard to any particular national context of belonging. The preeminence of the spatial dimension in *2666* is an isolated example however, since this is not a prescribed dominant in the maximalist novel. In *Underworld*, for example, is the geographical range really so broad? The United States is considered in its entire territorial extension, and at the end, there is even a brief episode in Kazakhstan, but nothing beyond this. Time is much more important than space for understanding DeLillo's novel. Thus, rather than engaging in misleading simplifications, we will limit ourselves to the observation that spatiality and temporality are *both* important in the maximalist novel, each being, case by case, of greater or lesser consequence in the representation. The postmodern scene is in fact too vast and still largely unexplored to allow for excessively generalized observations concerning it. It would probably be more appropriate to recognize a *plurality* of tendencies within it, either *dominant* or *emerging*,[14] and perhaps even in opposition with one another, rather than to yield to the temptation to establish overarching polarities which, in the end, almost always prove inadequate.

1.3 Conceptual structures

There are basically three types of conceptual structures in the maximalist novel for giving order to the narrative material: *leitmotiv*,[15] *myth*, and *intertextual forms*. Let us begin with the first.

1.3.1 Leitmotiv

One of the most significant leitmotivs we find in the textual corpus under examination here, and one that acts as the exclusive ordering principle in Franzen's *The Corrections*, is the leitmotiv of "correction." A correction of any behavior deviating from that which is "right," acting in the name of middle-class false consciousness and the pettiness of provincial Midwest America; a correction which is the absolute moral principle governing the lives of Enid

[14] See Steven Best, "Jameson, Totality, and the Poststructuralist Critique," in *Postmodernism. Jameson. Critique*, ed. Kellner, 333–68.

[15] In *Modern Epic*, Moretti speaks of leitmotiv in relation to Richard Wagner's *Ring of the Nibelungen* and Joyce's stream of consciousness, and emphasizes its ordering function. See Moretti, *Modern Epic*, 156–9.

and Alfred and a source of supreme unhappiness in those of their three children:

> The correction, when it finally came, was not an overnight bursting of a bubble but a much more gentle letdown, a year-long leakage of value from key financial markets, a contradiction too gradual to generate headlines and too predictable to seriously hurt anybody but fools and the working poor.
>
> It seemed to Enid that current events in general were more muted or insipid nowadays than they'd been in her youth. She had memories of the 1930s, she'd seen firsthand what could happen to a country when the world economy took its gloves off; she'd helped her mother pass out leftovers to homeless men in the alley behind their rooming house. But disaster of this magnitude no longer seemed to befall the United States. Safety features had been put in place, like the squares of rubber that every modern playground was paved with, to soften impacts.
>
> Nevertheless, the markets did collapse, and Enid, who hadn't dreamed that she would ever be *glad* that Alfred had locked their assets up in annuities and T-bills, weathered the downturn with less anxiety than her high-flying friends. (*The Corrections*, 647)

At the end of the novel, we find Enid relieved that she has not suffered from the downturn in the financial markets, unlike the friends she had envied all of her life; in the end, her husband had been right to be prudent. But it is in the hoped-for and consoling correction brought by the markets to a life spent in the illusion of making money through amateurish stock operations that Enid's middle-class wretchedness is to be found. Alfred, terminally ill, is shut away in a nursing home; Gary continues to be morbidly attached to money; and Denise seems to be waiting for no one knows what. The only one who might appear to have achieved some modicum of stability is Chip, who marries a seven-month pregnant woman to the complete disapproval of Enid, although we are soon informed that his sole preoccupation is the umpteenth revision of his script *The Academy Purple*. More corrections, then: Chip remains the prisoner of his failures until the end. The "correction," as a leitmotiv, keeps the otherwise fairly detached stories of the five members of the Lambert family united, while it functions as an efficacious ordering strategy in the novel, condensing within a single recurring word, correction, the anxieties of an entire nation.

Another significant leitmotiv, one which recurs in *Gravity's Rainbow*,[16] is that of the "child separated from home," defined by LeClair as "the Hansel and Gretel story,"[17] a fairytale that is referred to more than once and in various ways in course of the novel, especially in the tale of the frightful and prolonged imprisonment of Katje and Gottfried by Blicero.[18] All the ingredients are there more or less. A lonely place in the woods:

> Brother [Gottfried] in play, in slavery . . . she had never seen him before coming to the requisitioned house near the firing sites, hidden in the woods and parkland of this settled tongue of small farms and estates that reaches eastward from the royal city, between two expanses of polder, toward Wassenaar. . . . (*Gravity's Rainbow*, 112)

Captivity and fattening up:

> But did Blicero also cut her hair? She can't remember now. She knows she wore Gottfried's uniforms once or twice (pushing her hair, yes, up under his forage cap), looking easily his double, spending these nights "in the cage," as Blicero has set the rules, while Gottfried must wear her silk stockings, her lace apron and cup, all her satin and her ribboned organdy. But afterward he must always go back again to the cage. That's how it is. Their Captain allows no doubt as to which, brother or sister, really is maidservant, and which fattening goose. (Ibid., 113)

Killing the evil witch: "It is she [Katje] who, at some indefinite future moment, must push the Witch into the Oven intended for Gottfried" (Ibid., 114). And, a Pynchon addition, a desire for self-annihilation:

> Yet he [Blicero] cares, more than he should and puzzled that he does, about the children—about their motives. He gathers it is their freedom they look for, yearningly as he for the Oven, and such perversity haunts and depresses him . . . he returns again and again to the waste and senseless image of what was a house in the forest, reduced now to crumbs and sugar-smears, the

16 See Molly Hite, *Ideas of Order in the Novels of Thomas Pynchon* (Columbus: Ohio State University Press, 1983).

17 LeClair, *The Art of Excess*, 58.

18 On the representation of children and childhood in *Gravity's Rainbow*, see Katherine Hume, *Pynchon's Mythography: An Approach to "Gravity's Rainbow"* (Carbondale: Southern Illinois University Press, 1987), ch. 5; Strother Purdy, "*Gravity's Rainbow* and the Culture of Childhood," *Pynchon Notes* 22–23 (1988): 7–24; Monika Fludernik, "Hänsel und Gretel, and Dante: The Coordinates of Hope in Pynchon's *Gravity's Rainbow*," *Arbeiten aus Anglistik und Amerikanistik* 14, 1 (1989): 39–55.

> black indomitable Oven all that remains, and the two children, the peak of sweet energy behind them, hunger beginning again, wandering away into a green blankness of trees. . . . Where will they go, where shelter the nights? The improvidence of children . . . and the civil paradox of their Little State, whose base is the same Oven which must destroy it . . . (Ibid., 117)

Reworked in a Nazi key,[19] the fairy tale of Hansel and Gretel alludes to the condition of contemporary man who lives separated from Gaia, the Earth, understood as a living organism of which we are all a part and in which we are, or rather should be, profoundly integrated.[20] A guiding idea of the novel is that of acquiring a new awareness of being part of a whole, Gaia, to be precise; a whole with relation to which we should no longer think of ourselves separately, but in terms of interconnection. This conviction is elaborated in opposition to the Judeo-Christian myth of a future return to the Creator because it is in the here and now, according to Pynchon, that there is a need of renewed rules for a more civil cohabitation among men; rules which would also guarantee a greater respect for our planet.[21] The leitmotiv of the "child separated from home" is, then, something more than a recurring motif in the narrative. It becomes the vehicle for a utopian strain without which a large part of the novel would be, frankly, incomprehensible. It is a motif, that is to say, that becomes a structure.

A final leitmotiv can be found in *White Teeth* and is, precisely, "white teeth," understood as a metaphor for alterity. In a conversation between Irie, Magid, and Millat with Mr Hamilton on the importance of brushing one's teeth, we read how the whiteness of the teeth of the Congolese was of great assistance to the young soldier Hamilton in identifying his enemies. A physiognomic mark of alterity transformed into a sinister catalyzer of death by the British army:

> But like all things, the business has two sides. Clean white teeth are not always wise, now are they? Par exemplum: when I was in the Congo, the only way I could identify the nigger was by the whiteness of his teeth, if you

[19] See Susan Sontag, "Fascinating Fascism" [1975], in Sontag, *Under the Sign of Saturn: Essays* (New York: Picador, 2002), 73–108; Valerie Steele, *Fetish: Fashion, Sex, Power* [1976] (New York: Oxford University Press, 1997), ch. 7.

[20] The obligatory reference is to James Lovelock, *Gaia: A New Look at Life on Earth* (New York: Oxford University Press, 1979), and to Lovelock's more recent *The Revenge of Gaia: Earth's Climate Crisis & the Fate of Humanity* [2006] (New York: Basic Books, 2007).

[21] LeClair, *The Art of Excess*, 61–3.

> see what I mean. Horrid business. Dark as buggery, it was. And they died because of it, you see? Poor bastards. Or rather I survived, to look at it in another way, do you see? (*White Teeth*, 144)

In the last part of the novel, when Marcus Chalfen is at the airport to meet Magid, his favorite disciple returning at long last from Bangladesh, the crowd of passengers getting off the plane is described as follows:

> Before he had a chance to think what this meant, whether it meant anything, they were coming toward him, the passengers of BA flight 261; a talkative but exhausted brown mob who rushed toward him like a river, turning off at the last minute as if he were the edge of a waterfall. *Nomoskār . . . sālām ā lekum . . . kāmon āchō?* This is what they said to each other and their friends on the other side of the barrier; some women in full purdah, some in saris, men in strange mixtures of fabrics, leather, tweed, wool, and nylon, with little boat-hats that reminded Marcus of Nehru; children in sweaters made by the Taiwanese and rucksacks of bright reds and yellows; pushing through the doors to the concourse of gate 32; meeting aunts, meeting drivers, meeting children, meeting officials, meeting suntanned white-toothed airline representatives . . . (Ibid., 349)

The phantasmagoria of otherness that rushes toward Marcus like a swollen river is seen through eyes sensitive to the signs of alterity, on the wavelength of a stereotyped and stereotyping gaze: Arabic language, exotic clothes, waiting relatives.[22] But what is especially striking in such a climax of altery are the physical features: the tanned skin, and, once again, the white teeth of the airline representatives. Two characteristics capable of condensing, albeit in a superficial way, the fascination that the Other exerts on Marcus.

1.3.2 Myth

The ordering function of myth was famously theorized in his day by T. S. Eliot with regard to Joyce's *Ulysses*:

> In using the myth, in manipulating a continuous parallel between contemporaneity and antiquity, Mr Joyce is pursuing a method which others must pursue after him. They will not be imitators, any more than the scientist

[22] On the stereotype as a cognitive strategy, see Homi K. Bhabha, *The Location of Culture* [1994] (New York: Routledge, 2005), ch. 3.

> who uses the discoveries of an Einstein in pursuing his own, independent, further investigations. It is simply a way of controlling, of ordering, of giving a shape and a significance to the immense panorama of futility and anarchy which is contemporary history. . . . It is a method already adumbrated by Mr Yeats, and of the need for which I believe Mr Yeats to have been the first contemporary to be conscious. It is a method for which the horoscope is auspicious. Psychology (such as it is, and whether our reaction to it be comic or serious), ethnology, and *The Golden Bough* have concurred to make possible what was impossible even a few years ago. Instead of narrative method, we may now use the mythical method. It is, I seriously believe, a step toward making the modern world possible for art.[23]

A horoscope that was quite auspicious, Eliot had seen correctly. Just think of the innumerable revivals of myth in the twentieth century. And also in two of the maximalist novels examined here, *Infinite Jest* and *2005 dopo Cristo*, which take systematic recourse to the mythical method to impart order to their diegetic material, that is to say, to the same structuring function of myth at work in *Ulysses*.

The references to Greek, Christian, and Nordic mythology are everywhere in *Infinite Jest*, from Gately and Marathe, who are repeatedly and respectively likened to Heracles and Perseus, to the superhuman beauty of Joelle, capable of unleashing in men a paralyzing "Actaeon Complex,"[24] and concluding with the mysterious non-seeing tennis player Dymphna, whose name alludes to a Catholic saint who probably lived in the seventh century. These are references which, on more than one occasion, act as ordering principles and interpretive coordinates of the text.

In *David Foster Wallace's "Infinite Jest,"* Stephen Burn has traced a precise map of the mythical materials which have a structural function in Wallace's novel, with results that are surprising, to say the least.[25] For example, the night on which Marathe and Steeply meet on a rise on the outskirts of Tucson to discuss the death of the medical attaché who fell victim after viewing *Infinite*

[23] T. S. Eliot, "*Ulysses*, Order and Myth," *The Dial*, LXXV, November 1923, 480–3, cited in *James Joyce 1902-1927: The Critical Heritage*, ed. Robert H. Deming (London: Routledge & Kegan Paul, 1970), vol. I, 271.

[24] See Marshall Boswell, *Understanding David Foster Wallace* (Columbia: University of South Carolina Press, 2003), 126–7.

[25] Stephen Burn, *David Foster Wallace's "Infinite Jest,"* 56–65.

Jest, the night, that is, between 30 April and 1 May (a night whose story is strewn over the span of hundreds of pages), was, according to James Frazer, the moment of the year in which an ancient Celtic ritual took place, consisting in the lighting of sacred fires which were supposed to "measure" the morality of the community.[26] It was thought that if those lighting the fires had been guilty of murder, adultery, or theft, the fire would reveal them by behaving in an unusual way. Burn writes:

> Frazer's list of offenses noticeably summarizes the three major crimes of the novel—the murder of DuPlessis, Avril's adulteries and Gately's theft of the film—and, intriguingly, on the floor of the desert below Steeply and Marathe's outcrop, they see the flickers of a "celebratory fire" (422), but the flames are "burning in a seeming ring instead of a sphere," as Marathe expects. (423)[27]

In addition, most of the events of the YDAU, by far the most important year of the novel, are recorded from the beginning of November, the Christian month of the dead, which begins with the ancient and pagan holiday of Halloween, a festivity that most likely goes back to the Celtic calendar, according to which the celebrations of the new year took place on the first of November. The night before, between 31 October and 1 November, was known as the night of *Samhain*; a night in which the world of the dead and the world of the living entered into communication, and the dead spirits were permitted to return.[28] The ancient Celts, to protect themselves from these spirits, lit bonfires and wore masks. These masks are referred to frequently in the novel and are worn, for example, by Gately and Kite the day of the burglary, full of terrible and unforeseen consequences, in DuPlessis's home, a burglary that results in the accidental death of the latter, and in the theft of the entertainment *Infinite Jest*. In Wallace's novel, the mythical subtexts not only provide useful guidelines the reader can follow in order not to become lost in the novel's dizzying diegetic exuberance, they also function to extend retrospectively the temporal parabola of *Infinite Jest*—the narrative of which unfolds almost

[26] James Frazer, *The Golden Bough: A Study in Magic and Religion* [1890-1922] (London: Oxford University Press, 1994), 717. Frazer also notes that the twilight of "May Day," 1 May, marks the beginning of the Walpurgis Night (a belief rendered immortal in Goethe's *Faust*), when "the witches are everywhere, speeding unseen through the air on their hellish errands" (Frazer, *The Golden Bough*, 721). And Wallace refers to this directly, quoting Faust, in note 38 of *Infinite Jest* (63).

[27] Burn, *David Foster Wallace's "Infinite Jest,"* 63.

[28] Ibid., 64–5.

entirely in a near future—to a very distant past, making explicit once again the omnivorous relationship the maximalist novel has with time and which we have already observed in *Underworld* and *White Teeth*. Moreover, these mythical subtexts hint at an important interpretive thread. As Burn has written, the mythical calendar of the novel is literally *obsessed* with death.[29] This obsession drives a recurring idea in the narrative, that of a nation, the United States, on the brink of an apocalypse. It is a nation that has ended up becoming the victim of its own dreams and has demonstrated itself to be totally incapable of renewal.

2005 dopo Cristo is also constructed on the basis of a mythical paradigm, the well-known myth of the ritual murder of the king in the woods of Nemi. It is a myth that Frazer made famous in *The Golden Bough*, and which has enjoyed enormous fortune, from Conrad's *Heart of Darkness* to *The Waste Land* by T. S. Eliot, from Francis Ford Coppola's *Apocalypse Now* to the music of the Doors.[30] This mythical substratum is presented as the ideological grounds of the plot hatched to assassinate Berlusconi, in that the latter is compared several times to a king who has to be killed to regenerate Italy:

> La sua morte [di Berlusconi] deve avvenire al centro perfetto di un'intersezione di linee. È una morte generatrice, ma che ha bisogno a sua volta di essere generata. (*2005 dopo Cristo*, 154)
>
> [His [Berlusconi's] death must take place at the perfect center of an intersection of lines. It is a generative death, but which needs in its own stead to be generated.]
>
> Sa cosa succedeva nelle comunità primitive quando veniva ucciso il re? Passata la fase di partecipazione orgiastica all'evento, *qualcuno* faceva sempre in modo che le cose riprendessero il loro corso naturale. Ma quale corso? C'è bisogno che *qualcuno* riporti l'ordine, dal caos al cosmos. (Ibid., 162)
>
> [Do you know what happened in primitive communities when the king was killed? Once the phase of orgiastic participation in the event had passed, *somebody* always did something to have things reassume their normal course. But what course? It is necessary that *somebody* restore order, from chaos to cosmos.]

[29] Ibid., 65.

[30] Laurence Coupe, *Myth (The New Critical Idiom)* [1997], 2nd edn (New York: Routledge, 2009), 13–81.

This conviction not only provides an ancient and noble mythological (pseudo-) motive for the assassination attempt against Berlusconi organized by Sinisgalli and his coterie, it also acts as a glue and a mirror to the grievous reality of Berlusconi's Italy. A double function, then, a purely structural one, Eliot's, in which myth is used to impart order to the "immense panorama of futility and anarchy which is contemporary history," and another one which, in a complementary way, thrusts important thematic nuclei onto the conceptual frame of the novel, that is to say, Italy's deep need for political and moral renewal.

1.3.3 Intertextual forms

With the expression "intertextual forms," I am referring to that particular maximalist structural practice consisting in the use of rhetorical strategies, or of thematic sparks, taken from other literary texts.

One of the discursive frameworks on which the overflowing narrative material of *Gravity's Rainbow* is organized is inspired by the estrangement effect of Bertolt Brecht's epic theater. This is a macroscopic phenomenon that is manifest through the insertion of numerous "Brechtian" songs in the course of the narrative, and it is linked by LeClair to the presumed construction on Pynchon's part of a meandering maieutic journey meant to instill in the reader the awareness of belonging to Gaia.[31] Nevertheless, Pynchon should not need to resort to Brecht to attain estrangement effects in his readers. The narrative as is, with its informative hypertrophia and its exhausting digressions, would be enough for that. Reader identification is not a very concrete risk when reading *Gravity's Rainbow*, or when reading any of the maximalist novels under discussion here, with the exception of *2666*, perhaps. Rather than considering the rhetorical strategies of the epic theater as techniques capable of generating a fertile estrangement in the reader, it would perhaps be more precise to view them as mere ordering devices, able to create strong intertextual references within an otherwise chaotic narrative.

Two other intertextual forms which generate great explicative potential in *Infinite Jest* can be found in the insistent quotations from William Shakespeare's

[31] On the textual function exercised in Pynchon's novel by the formal procedures of Brechtian theater, see the second section of the chapter dedicated to *Gravity's Rainbow* in LeClair, *The Art of Excess*, 48–57.

Hamlet and from Fyodor Dostoevsky's *The Brothers Karamazov*. Marshall Boswell writes:

> Wallace makes overt this complex theme of artistic patricide through the novel's intricate allusions to two primary texts of patrimonial anxiety, Shakespeare's *Hamlet* and Dostoevsky's *The Brothers Karamazov*. The *Hamlet* references are ubiquitous, beginning with the novel's (and the film's) title, which is culled from that play's famous graveyard sequence, while the Dostoevsky references are a bit more muted and hence less important.[32]

In reality, the importance of *The Brothers Karamazov* is not secondary in the novel.[33] The members of the Incandenza family are at the center of one of the two main narrative threads in the novel, and, with the exception of Avril, appear to be perfectly superimposable on those of the Karamazov family: Orin, the oldest son, is in love with Joelle who, in her turn, has an ambiguous relationship with his father James, the moviemaker who often uses her as an actress and who is the author of *Infinite Jest*. It is clear enough: Dmitri-Grushenka-Fyodor Pavlovic (the father of Dmitri). Hal, for his part, brazenly plays the role of Ivan: cold and excessively brainy, a character who before falling asleep, perhaps with subtle parodic intent with regard to his Dostoevskian model, discusses several times with his brother Mario about the nonexistence of God. And finally, Mario, the good one, the deformed and retarded brother, perhaps the only truly positive figure in the novel, cannot be other than Alyosha. As can be seen, we are presented with something more than a simple allusion, but rather with a true structural copy, the Karamazovs merge and blur with the Incandenza family, offering a possible interpretive key to it. Almost as if Wallace has wanted to suggest, in accordance with the universalizing thrust of the maximalist novel, that certain (non-)affective family realities are no longer characteristic of America at the end of the twentieth century, just as they were not of Russia in the second half of the nineteenth century.

Finally, as Boswell reminds us, the references to *Hamlet* are barefaced, beginning with the very title of the novel. All the more barefaced given just

32 Boswell, *Understanding David Foster Wallace*, 165.

33 This is made clear by Timothy Jacobs in an article dedicated entirely to *Infinite Jest*'s debt to Dostoevsky's masterpiece. See Timothy Jacobs, "The Brothers Incandenza: Translating Ideology in Fyodor Dostoevsky's *The Brothers Karamazov* and David Foster Wallace's *Infinite Jest*," *Texas Studies in Literature and Language* 9, 3 (2007): 265–92.

how famous the episode is in Shakespeare's tragedy from which it is taken, the disinterment of the skull of Yorick, the court jester: "Alas, poor Yorick! I knew him, Horatio, a fellow of infinite jest, of most excellent fancy. He hath bore me on his back a thousand times, and now—how abhorred in my imagination it is!"[34]

Hamlet is everywhere in *Infinite Jest*. Beginning with the death of Hal's father, James—who, moreover, appears in the form of a ghost to Gately in his hospital bed—and with Avril's relationship with Hal's uncle, Charles Tavis, who, after James's death, takes his place as the head of the Enfield Tennis Academy; not to mention the multiple infidelities committed by Avril with that latter, of which Hal is perfectly aware. Hal plays the part of Hamlet, and his uncle Charles that of Claudius, the usurper. Hal also shares numerous character affinities with Hamlet, which are efficaciously synthesized in a veiled autobiographical essay written by Hal himself on the "post-postmodern" hero, described as a hero of nonaction: ". . . the catatonic hero, the one beyond calm, divorced from all stimulus, carried here and there across sets by burly extras whose blood sings with retrograde amines."[35] But, above all, the citing of Shakespeare's text is overt in the aforementioned scene of the disinterment of the head of Hal's father by his son and Gately, a scene constructed in evident parallelism to the one from Shakespeare and which supplies the title of the novel and that of the fatal entertainment created by James. Other points of contact between Wallace and Shakespeare could be pointed out—such as the name of the movie production company founded by James Incandenza, *Poor Yorick Entertainment*—but this would only go to confirm what should already be clear, that Shakespeare's text, as well as *The Brothers Karamazov*, is used by Wallace not just as an intertextual trace, but also as a semantic device, with the intent to organize and give meaning to the immense narrative material composing the diegesis.

Thus, we have seen up to now how the maximalist novel tends to erect structures to impart order to the narration. Ironclad structures which provide it with a solid framework and under whose aegis the entire representation unfolds. But let us now ask ourselves if a novel resting on such peremptory ordering principles can truly be considered to be incomplete. The idea of

[34] William Shakespeare, *Hamlet*, V, I, lines 169–72.
[35] Wallace, *Infinite Jest*, 142.

incompleteness, which permeates the theoretical hypotheses formulated by Moretti[36] and Karl,[37] should probably be reassessed. The fact that world texts are constitutionally open[38] because they are constructed on the basis of a mechanical form that is aggregational in nature, does not mean that they are incomplete.[39] This concept has been expressed in passing by Massimo Fusillo in his aforementioned "Epic, Novel" with regard to the analogy between the multiple endings of *War and Peace* and the open ending of the *Iliad*[40]: "This perspective clearly recalls the open ending of the *Iliad*—in which openness does not signify incompletion and does not preclude a satisfying feeling of wholeness."[41]

In fact, the completeness or incompleteness of a literary work is not measured in relation to the plot or to the mechanisms of its production, but rather at the level of their arrangement into a specific form which guarantees their *control*. We need to look at the structural practices of the maximalist novel in order to understand to what extent it should be considered to be a completed literary product, that is to say, *hypertrophically* completed, governed by a rigid structural logic which shapes its narration, and which, at the same time, is charged with delivering some of its fundamental contents.

[36] Moretti, *Modern Epic*, 96–8.

[37] "Yet despite all the care which goes into binding elements, the Mega-Novel is incomplete and must remain so. The form uses its great extension, paradoxically, to suggest incompleteness. . . ." Karl, *American Fictions: 1980-2000*, 160.

[38] Moretti, *Modern Epic*, 48–9.

[39] This thesis is advanced by Moretti more than once, as when he writes: "That long . . . It is the sincere surprise of the aged Goethe, who apparently never expected to finish *Faust*; the deaths of Flaubert and Musil, which cut short *Bouvard et Pécuchet* and *The Man Without Qualities*. Between the brief span of individual existence and the continuous growth of the social totality, the game has become unequal: the aggregation of the mechanical form seeks in some way to confront it; but vying in extent with the world, in the long run, makes no sense." Moretti, *Modern Epic*, 92. Speaking in material terms, maximalist novels are all concluded by their authors, so much so that at times they have written other ones, such, for example, as Pynchon did, who, after *Gravity's Rainbow*, published two other maximalist novels: *Mason & Dixon* and *Against the Day*. The only case considered here of a maximalist novel interrupted by the death of its author is *2666*. It must be said, however, that Bolaño died at just 50 years after a long illness and that his novel, despite his early death, has a clear internal structure.

[40] The problem of the ending of the *Iliad*, as with the epic in general, is notoriously complex. See *Classical Closure: Reading the End in Greek and Latin Literature*, eds. Deborah H. Roberts et al. (Princeton: Princeton University Press, 1997), especially the contributions of Dan Fowler, "Second Thoughts on Closure" (ch. 1), and Sheila Murnaghan, "Equal Honor and Future Glory: The Plan of Zeus in the *Iliad*" (ch. 2). See Fusillo, "Epic, Novel," 60.

[41] Fusillo, "Epic, Novel," 60.

6

Narratorial Omniscience

The seven novels considered in this study are all characterized by the presence of an omniscient narrator. They vary from a more overt, "traditional" omniscience, as in *Gravity's Rainbow*, *White Teeth*, and *The Corrections*, to a different, more complex type of omniscience, which we might define as *omniscience through recomposition* or *derived omniscience*, present in a radical manner in *Infinite Jest* and *Underworld* and, in a more attenuated form, in *2005 dopo Cristo* and *2666*.[1]

Taking up and refining a classification proposed by Jean Pouillon,[2] Tzvetan Todorov defines three narrative "aspects" (whereby "aspect" he means the way in which the reader perceives the narrated facts through the mediation of the narrator): the narrator knows more than the character (N > C); the narrator knows as much as the character (N = C); the narrator knows less than the character (N < C).[3] In the first case we have classical omniscience; the second situation is basically that of a story with a point of view; and the third, more difficult to find in its absolute form, is widely used in behaviorist stories such as Hammett's. The first aspect is the one of most interest to us. Todorov:

> NARRATOR > CHARACTER (VISION "FROM BEHIND"). The classical story most often uses this formula. In this case, the narrator knows more

[1] An articulate discussion of narratorial omniscience—even if it is not of direct consequence for my analysis—is that proposed by Norman Friedman in "Point of View in Fiction: The Development of a Critical Concept," in *The Theory of the Novel*, ed. Philip Stevick (New York: The Free Press, 1967), 108–36. Within the framework of a more ample examination of "narrative situations," Friedman identifies four types of omniscience: (1) with (Fielding), or (2) without (Hardy), "authorial intrusions"; "selective" omniscience with the use of (3) a single point of view (James Joyce, *A Portrait of the Artist as a Young Man*), or of (4) multiple points of view (Virginia Woolf, *To the Lighthouse*). On the limits of Friedman's proposal see Genette, *Narrative Discourse*, 187–8.

[2] In *Temps et roman* (Paris: Gallimard, 1946), Jean Pouillon proposed a taxonomy of narrative "vision" based on the different perspectives the narrator assumes with respect to the character: *vision par derrière* (identifiable with Todorov's typology N > C); *vision avec* (N = C); and *vision du dehors* (N < C).

[3] Tzvetan Todorov, "Les categories du récit littéraire," *Communications* 8, 1 (1966): 141–3.

> than his character. He does not worry about explaining to us how he has acquired this knowledge: he sees through the walls of the house just as well as through the skull of his heroes. His characters keep no secrets from him. As is obvious, this form offers different degrees. The narrator's superiority may manifest itself in the knowledge of the secret desires of someone (which this someone himself is unaware of), in the simultaneous knowledge of the thoughts of more than one character (something of which no one of them would be capable), or simply in the narration of events that are not perceived by an individual character. Thus Tolstoy, in the tale "Three Deaths," narrates, in succession, the story of the death of an aristocrat, of a peasant, and of a tree. None of the characters have perceived these three jointly; we are thus in the presence of a variant of the vision "from behind."[4]

Narratorial omniscience would consist, therefore, in knowing things before they happen and in having free access to the most hidden thoughts and desires of all the characters. However, what seems most interesting for our discussion is the specification, on Todorov's part, that this omniscience has "different degrees," that it does not manifest itself always in the same way. Todorov's proposal has been elaborated further by Genette in terms of "focalization." As is well known, for Genette, focalization represents, together with "distance," one of the two fundamental modalities for the regulation of narrative information, that is to say of "mode": to instances of $N > C$, Genette associates zero focalization; to instances of $N = C$, internal focalization (whether it is fixed, variable, or multiple); and to instances of $N < C$, external focalization.[5] As he himself points out, rarely is each of the three types of focalization present in an absolute and coherent way in a given narrative.[6] Very often, if not almost always, the three focalizations *coexist*, sharing the space of the novel and cooperating in the production of meaning. This is precisely the key for understanding the nature of maximalist omniscience.

First of all, it must be noted that in order to define the narrative regime of the maximalist novel it is necessary to take into account two distinct levels: the

4 Ibid., 141–2.

5 Genette, *Narrative Discourse*, 161–94.

6 It is what happens, for example, in a novel that does not give much space to external focalization, *Madame Bovary*, in which the famous carriage scene is told as if it were seen by an external witness. See Genette, *Narrative Discourse*, 191.

single fragment, or the *microstructural* level, and the narrative as a whole, the *macrostructural* level. From one narrative unit to another—and sometimes even within the same fragment—the focalization can change radically, as in *Infinite Jest* or *Underworld*, in which one moves freely among the three focalizations; or it can remain substantially unaltered, as is the case in *Gravity's Rainbow*, *White Teeth*, and *The Corrections*, in which a zero focalization, onto which are grafted large segments of mostly internally focalized story, is almost always discernible. However, if we take the narrative as a whole, we always have omniscience, and thus zero focalization. In a novel such as *Gravity's Rainbow*, it is understandable how zero focalization at the microstructural level should imply and then *de facto* reveal the presence of an omniscient narrator also at the macrostructural level; for a novel such as *Underworld*, on the other hand, constituted almost in its entirety by narrative units with a strictly internal focalization,[7] it is much more problematic to speak of an omniscient narratorial regime. Genette writes:

> Any single formula of focalization does not, therefore, always bear on an entire work, but rather on a definite narrative section, which can be very short. . . . Similarly, the division between variable focalization and nonfocalization is sometimes very difficult to establish, for the nonfocalized narrative can most often be analyzed as a narrative that is multifocalized *ad libitum*, in accordance with the principle "he who can do most can do least" (let us not forget that focalization is essentially, in Blin's word, a *restriction*); and yet, on this point no one could confuse Fielding's manner with Stendhal's or Flaubert's.[8]

The nonfocalized story understood as a story composed of innumerable focalizations: this is exactly what occurs in *Underworld* or *Infinite Jest*, in which narratorial omniscience is the sum of all of the narrative information advanced

[7] With an exception made for the sections dedicated to Nick Shay, all narrated by Nick himself, and thus by a necessarily omniscient extradiegetic-homodiegetic narrator, since Nick re-evokes his own story clearly after having lived it. Although for *Underworld*, as for *Infinite Jest*, it probably does not make much sense to speak of extradiegetic or intradiegetic levels (Genette, *Narrative Discourse*, 245). As we know, the individual fragments are arranged paratactically, and, in addition, the scene prevails for the most part. The differentiation between extradiegetic and intradiegetic levels would be more suitable for *2666*, in which various diegetic embeddings can be found within each fragment.

[8] Genette, *Narrative Discourse*, 191–2.

by each of the focalizations of the different units constituting the narrative. It is an omniscience attained through the *recomposition* of the single points of view adopted by the narrator at various times at the *microstructural level*, in a *derived* zero focalization that is defined, instead, at the *macrostructural level*. In DeLillo's novel, for instance, from the moment the narrative goes back in time, it can only be illuminated in its journey by an absolute narratorial omniscience. When the narrator speaks to us in "Part 2" of the novel about Klara Sax between the mid-1980s and the beginning of the 1990s, he *knows* what will happen to her in the spring-summer of 1992 because he has already told us about that in "Part 1." Moreover, when the narrative—as it occurs in *Underworld* and in *Infinite Jest*—is systematically carried on through an uninterrupted alternation of points of view, it is inevitable that sooner or later they will mutually *interfere* at the macrostructural level, thereby giving rise to changes in perspective that clearly reveal the omniscience of the narrator. In *Infinite Jest*, the A. F. R. look everywhere for Joelle, not aware that she is at the Ennet House; something that Gately instead is well aware of since he too, like Joelle, lives there. But, in his turn, Gately does not know what the A. F. R. know about Joelle, that is to say, her relations with the Incandenza family. We are confronted with a clear example of the arrangement of narrative information by an omniscient narrator. This is a particularly compelling exigency in maximalist narratives.

Beyond the means through which omniscience is produced—whether in focal correspondence or opposition between the microstructural and macrostructural levels—there is a fundamental need in the maximalist novel to construct a narratorial gaze capable of perceiving from *above*, and thus of dominating, the entire narrative flow. In the end, it is a question once again of the need to order that we have seen in operation at various levels in the preceding chapter. This of course does not mean that in every maximalist novel the narrator must necessarily be omniscient, but rather that omniscience is a narrative modality that adapts itself more efficiently than others to the control of the narrative material that is so abundant in maximalist narratives. Through a strict control of the diegesis, it is easier to effect a narrative project attempting at a totalizing representation of reality. Moreover, it is precisely through the constant play between the microstructural and the macrostructural levels, between a partial and a total vision, that the comprehensive *sense* of the narration is produced. It is a question, in other words, of reproposing on a (much) vaster scale the tension between point of view and "point of view" of which Paola Pugliatti has written in a more limited way concerning the focal point of a story, in which the first is understood, in an orientative-evaluative sense, as opinion.[9] A painterly example might help us to elucidate the question better.

In *Underworld*, in a dialogue between Klara Sax and her husband Bronzini, reference is made to an interesting painting by Bruegel, *Kinderspielen* (figure 6.1):

> "Do you know the old painting," he said, "that shows dozen of children playing games in some town square?"
>
> "Hundreds actually. Two hundred anyway. Bruegel. I find it unwholesome. Why?"
>
> "It came up in conversation."

Figure 6.1 Pieter Bruegel, *Children's Games*, oil on canvas, 118 × 161 cm, Vienna, Kunsthistorisches Museum, 1560. Reprinted with permission from the Kunsthistorisches Museum, Wien.

[9] Paola Pugliatti, *Lo sguardo nel racconto: Teorie e prassi del punto di vista* (Bologna: Zanichelli, 1985), 2.

> "I don't know what art history says about this painting. But I say it's not that different from the other famous Bruegel, armies of death marching across the landscape. The children are fat, backward, a little sinister to me. It's some kind of menace, some folly. *Kinderspielen*. They look like dwarves doing something awful." (*Underworld*, 682)

In juxtaposing *Kinderspeilen* to the celebrated *Triumph of Death*—an important visual intertext for the novel we will discuss in the chapter on visuality—Klara expresses her unease regarding the painting: a painting that is an eloquent *mise en abyme* of the perspectival strategies used by DeLillo in the novel.

Bruegel depicts more than two hundred disturbing children with adult faces playing the most disparate games: a choice with an allegorical meaning, consisting of a warning to adults not to "fritter their life away as if it were a childlike game."[10] The most interesting aspect of the painting lies, however, not in its allegorico-moralistic intentions, but rather in its use of perspective. Placing oneself in front of the painting and looking at its center, one has an immediate impression of chaos: scores of people engaging in very different, and for the most part, incomprehensible activities. Only by drawing our gaze very near to each figure can we clearly distinguish the type of game being depicted, but, in so doing, we completely lose the impression of the whole, which, albeit chaotic, we had by looking at the painting from a frontal perspective. This sensation of chaos is suddenly lost, however, if one looks at the represented space from the observation point set on the high right by Bruegel, following strict rules of perspective.[11] By so doing, we see how what in a first moment seemed chaotic, in reality, is not so at all: children playing in a square. This is the "literal" meaning of the painting, which emerges by orienting our vision perspectively along the painting's vanishing point. The deepest meaning of the work only becomes manifest if we take into consideration the individual figures as well. By doing so, we realize that the children have adult faces and that, although they are playing, they do not have happy expressions; and we

[10] See Rose-Marie Hagen and Rainer Hagen, *Pieter Bruegel the Elder, c. 1525-1569: Peasants, Fools, and Demons* (Cologne: Benedikt Taschen, 1994), 33.

[11] See *Brueghel*, ed. Pietro Allegretti (Milan: Rizzoli/Skira, 2003), 96.

also see that some of them are engaged in solitary games, while others, the majority, are playing in groups. And it is only at this point that we begin to intuit the allegorical meaning of the representation.[12] Without the double movement between the individual and collectivity, the detail and the vision of the whole, the partial point of view and the general perspective, we would never fully comprehend the sense of what we are watching. We would lose sight of the fact that, first, it is the representation of many children at play at the same time in a square, then, the representation of the type of game they are playing; and we would never imagine that hidden within the painting is an allegory. It is, indeed, the *tension* between the particular and the general that generates the profound meaning of the work. Exactly what takes place in *Underworld*, in *Infinite Jest*, in *2005 dopo Cristo*, and in *2666*, in which only by taking into account the conflict in focus occasioned by the divarication between the microstructural and macrostructural levels of the story can we grasp the overall sense of the representation. And this conflict is precisely the main determinant of the production of meaning; the virtual place in which to seek out, to put it in Pugliatti's words, the "point of view" which, understood in orientative-evaluative terms, is expressed by the narrator with regard to the work as a whole.

Lastly, maximalist omniscience, or "super-omniscience" as DeLillo has well defined it,[13] is not only a particularly effective narratorial tactic for managing a series of expressive exigencies dictated by the need to control an overabundance of narrative information. It can also be seen as part of that galaxy of discursive strategies which have flourished in recent years in the attempt to restore the role of the author within the sphere of literary communication,[14] following

[12] This, according to a procedure that could be defined as "iconological," following Panofsky's well-known methodological tripartition concerning the interpretation of the work of art, which consists in a "pre-iconographic" level, an "iconographic" level in a strict sense, and an "iconological" level. See Erwin Panofsky, "Iconography and Iconology: An Introduction to the Study of Renaissance Art," in Panofsky, *Meaning in the Visual Arts* (Garden City: Doubleday, 1955), 26–54. See also Erwin Panofsky, *Studies in Iconology* (Oxford: Oxford University Press, 1939).

[13] DeLillo uses this expression in relation to the technique that he himself employs in the construction of the multi-perspective framework of the "Prologue" to *Underworld*. See David Remnick, "Exile on Main Street: Don DeLillo's Undisclosed Underworld" [1997], in *Conversations with Don DeLillo*, ed. Thomas DePietro (Jackson: University Press of Mississippi, 2005), 136.

[14] See Carla Benedetti, *The Empty Cage: Inquiry into the Mysterious Disappearance of the Author* [1999] (Ithaca-London: Cornell University Press, 2005).

upon Roland Barthes's vociferous proclamation of his death.[15] Omniscience is, in fact, the distinctive sign of a *strong* idea of authorship that seems to affirm itself in the maximalist novel, and which can be interpreted as a specific form of the complex and manifold phenomenon of the "return of the author" occurring in contemporary fiction.[16]

[15] Roland Barthes, "The Death of the Author" [1968], in *The Rustle of Language*, trans. Richard Howard (New York: Hill and Wang, 1986), 49–55.

[16] On the function and importance of the figure of the author in contemporary narrative, see *Rückkehr des Autors: Zur Erneuerung eines umstrittenen Begriffs*, eds. Fotis Jannidis et al. (Tübingen: Niemeyer, 1999); Fusillo, *Estetica della letteratura*, 111–20; Stefano Ercolino, "Il difficile ritorno dell'autore," in *Lezioni di dottorato 2009*, ed. Francesco Pontuale (Rome: Palombi Editori, 2011), 253–72.

7

Paranoid Imagination

It is generally recognized that paranoia is one of the most characteristic elements of the postmodern narrative universe.[1] Manifold and suggestive hypotheses have been advanced as to its origins, but even if it has been pervasively present in a consistent portion of Western narrative of the past 50 years, it has almost always been considered to be a North American phenomenon.[2] Not that this is inaccurate; quite the contrary. American postmodern narrative has been so profoundly obsessed with conspiracies and intrigues of every kind for such a long time that it has certainly earned the uncontested (and dubiously flattering) prize for the most paranoid fiction in Western literature. Nevertheless, I will attempt in this chapter to demonstrate how paranoia, more than being tied to a single national literary context, is a transversal cultural phenomenon characteristic of the maximalist novel as a genre of the contemporary novel. The deep-seated reasons for this phenomenon are to be located in a few *constants* present within different national literatures. But first let us try to understand what we mean by "paranoid imagination."

On the basis of the distinction underscored by Derrida between the French words "conjuration" and "conjurement," with the first referring properly to

[1] So much so that it has been included in the Routledge guide to postmodernism among the most typical features of postmodern fiction. See Barry Lewis, "Postmodernism and Fiction," in *The Routledge Companion to Postmodernism* [2001], ed. Stuart Sim (London-New York: Routledge, 2005), 111–21.

[2] See Richard Hofstadter, *The Paranoid Style in American Politics* (New York: Knopf, 1946); *Conspiracy: The Fear of Subversion in American History*, eds. Richard O. Curry and Thomas M. Brown (New York: Holt, 1972); Mark Fenster, *Conspiracy Theories: Secrecy and Power in American Culture* (Minneapolis: University of Minnesota Press, 1999); Timothy Melley, *Empire of Conspiracy: The Culture of Paranoia in Postwar America* (Ithaca: Cornell University Press, 2000); Patrick O'Donnell, *Latent Destinies: Cultural Paranoia and Contemporary United States Narrative* (Durham: Duke University Press, 2000); Robert Alan Goldberg, *Enemies Within: The Culture of Conspiracy in Modern America* (New Haven: Yale University Press, 2001); *Conspiracy Nation: The Politics of Paranoia in Postwar America*, ed. Peter Knight (New York: New York University Press, 2002); Samuel Chase Coale, *Paradigms of Paranoia: The Culture of Conspiracy in Contemporary American Fiction* (Tuscaloosa: University of Alabama Press, 2005).

conspiracy and the second, to the act of evoking a spirit,[3] Remo Cesarani has proposed an interpretation of the works of Philip K. Dick that might help us to better grasp the object of our discussion:

> [T]he obsessive theme of Dick's novels is not the one so often highlighted by critics concerning the "ontological" uncertainty of the nature and location of our existence in the world, or worlds, but rather the "hauntological" presence in our world of some sort of phantasmatic or spectral essence, whether consisting of the occult powers governing the world from behind the scenes of our democratic institutions, or of the egoistic interests and instincts governing the financial markets, or the ideological interpretations of reality which defy the conviction, it too ideological, that all ideologies are now dead.[4]

Paranoid imagination enshrouds, literally infests, the maximalist narrative universe. Its presence shapes and gives substance to the plot, which from novel to novel assumes the most diverse forms: indecipherable and extended conspiracies by unscrupulous multinationals (*Gravity's Rainbow*)[5]; political terrorism and Islamic fundamentalism (*Infinite Jest* and *2005 dopo Cristo* on the one hand, *White Teeth* on the other)[6]; nuclear psychosis (*Underworld*)[7]; corrupt state apparati (*2666*); psychotic disturbances (*The Corrections*, and, once again, *Infinite Jest*). These are often hypothetical threats, at times absolutely implausible or ridiculous but, nevertheless, always mortally feared; all the more obsessively present and paranoidly concrete, the more ephemeral they are. Paranoia is the *motor* of the maximalist literary imagination, and in each of the seven novels analyzed it plays a fundamental role both in the *poïesis* of fiction, and in the weaving of the plot. Let us articulate the question a bit better.

3 Jacques Derrida, *Specters of Marx: The State of the Debt, the Work of Mourning, and the New International* [1993], trans. Peggy Kamuf (New York: Routledge, 1994), 62.

4 Remo Ceserani, "Immaginazione cospiratoria," in *Cospirazioni, trame: Quaderni di Synapsis II*, ed. Simona Micali (Florence: Le Monnier, 2003), 16.

5 See Mark Richard Siegel, *Pynchon: Creative Paranoia in "Gravity's Rainbow"* (Port Washington: Kennikat Press, 1978).

6 See Margaret Scanlan, *Plotting Terror: Novelists and Terrorists in Contemporary Fiction* (Charlottesville: University Press of Virginia, 2001).

7 See Peter Knight, "Everything is Connected: *Underworld*'s Secret History of Paranoia," *Modern Fiction Studies* XLV, 3 (1999): 811–36.

Samuel Coale argues that the conspiratory imagination from which a consistent number of American narrative works have originated in the last 50 years is an antidote against the radical skepticism of certain postmodern theoretical positions:

> Thus the contemporary human dilemma: the postmodern celebration of radical skepticism clashes with a deeper yearning for unity and wholeness, however it is defined. . . .
>
> Conspiracy, whether actual or theoretical, provides an antidote to postmodernism: everything becomes a sign, a clue, a piece of a larger puzzle.[8]

A sort of new and potent metanarrative produced, paradoxically, precisely in an era in which there should no longer be any place, at least in accordance with Lyotard, for strong and univocal interpretations of the world. Not only; it is also, for Coale, a modality of the cultural imagery strictly linked to the shape that the sublime has assumed in the postmodern. Taking his distance from two of the most noteworthy theoretical treatments of the matter, Jameson's and Joseph Tabbi's—the first defining the postmodern sublime as a "hysterical sublime," an exhilarating and playful experience deriving from an oxymoronic mix of camp aesthetics and the Kantian sublime[9]; the second describing it instead as an ambivalent attitude between fascination and fear in the face of technology[10]—and referring to the Burkean-Kantian tradition in which the sublime is defined as the feeling produced by the experience of a limit,[11] Coale accentuates those aspects of the sublime linked to mystery and ambiguity, inflecting it in a postmodern key in association with the conspiratory imagination. The entirely postmodern passion and obsession for extremely intricate, fleeting, and unfathomable conspiracies can be suggestively interpreted, in fact, as an attempt to represent the unrepresentable; an attempt to recount an extreme experience that threatens us, and in the face of which, we are completely powerless; a postmodern attempt, in the end, to speak the

[8] Coale, *Paradigms of Paranoia*, 4.
[9] Jameson, *Postmodernism*, 34–5.
[10] Joseph Tabbi, *Postmodern Sublime: Technology and American Writing from Mailer to Cyberpunk* (Ithaca: Cornell University Press, 1995).
[11] Baldine Saint Girons, *Le sublime de l'Antiquité à nos jours* (Paris: Desjonquères, 2005), ch. 6.

sublime.[12] In this sense, the conspiratory fantasy would be at one and the same time the principal source of the sublime, and one of the most characteristic aspects it assumes within the postmodern cultural horizon: the controversial fruit of and paradoxical antidote against the relativistic drifts of meaning produced by deconstructionism.

Now let us confront the problem we had formulated at the beginning of this chapter: how to define paranoid imagination as a transversal cultural phenomenon. One determinant probably responsible for the specificity of the paranoid fantasy running throughout North American fiction is its strong tie with the apocalyptic tradition.[13] It is an extremely sturdy tie due to the Puritan roots of American society, which finds the template for every possible intrigue and machination in the original, anguished Calvinist opposition between the elected and the damned, there being in every conspiracy worthy of the name evildoers who plot against the good.[14] An ancient tale aestheticized and given new meanings in the postmodern, the apocalypse has been transformed into an efficacious textual strategy used to contest power, taking advantage of the palingenetic potential unleashed by its mindset.[15] And it was probably the utopian tension implicit in the idea of the apocalypse that led authors such as Pynchon and Wallace to the elaboration of the extended and tentacular conspiracies we find in *Gravity's Rainbow* and *Infinite Jest*. These conspiracies

[12] See George Hartley, *The Abyss of Representation: Marxism and the Postmodern Sublime* (Durham: Duke University Press, 2003); Massimo Carboni, *Il sublime è ora: Saggio sulle estetiche contemporanee* (Rome: Castelvecchi, 2003).

[13] See Douglas Robinson, *American Apocalypses: The Image of the End of the World in American Literature* (Baltimore-London: The Johns Hopkins University Press, 1985); Norman Cohn, *Cosmos, Chaos, and the World to Come: The Ancient Roots of Apocalyptic Faith* (New Haven: Yale University Press, 1993); Daniel Wójcik, *The End of the World as We Know It: Faith, Fatalism, and Apocalypse in America* (New York: New York University Press, 1997); Eugen Weber, *Apocalypses: Prophecies, Cults, and Millennial Beliefs through the Ages* (Cambridge, MA: Harvard University Press, 1999).

[14] In Jane Kramer's telling of the mad exploits of John Pitner, the founder and head of the Washington State Militia, we read: ". . . John understood that in millennial America the idea of making good had become so fatally confused with the idea of getting saved that the choice for the failed and the poor was either to believe that they were damned themselves or else, like John, to believe that they were victims of a great conspiracy of the damned against them." Jane Kramer, *Lone Patriot* (New York: Pantheon, 2002), 35. See Coale, *Paradigms of Paranoia*, 218–19.

[15] See Richard Dellamora, *Postmodern Apocalypse: Theory and Cultural Practice at the End* (Philadelphia: University of Pennsylvania Press, 1995); Michele Cometa, *Visioni della fine: Apocalissi, catastrofi, estinzioni* (Palermo: :duepunti Edizioni, 2004); Timothy Parrish, *From the Civil War to the Apocalypse: Postmodern History and American Fiction* (Amherst: University of Massachusetts Press, 2008); Elizabeth K. Rosen, *Apocalyptic Transformation: Apocalypse and the Postmodern Imagination* (Lanham: Lexington Books, 2008); Mirko Lino, *L'apocalisse postmoderna tra letteratura e cinema: Catastrofi, oggetti, metropoli, corpi.* (Florence: Le Lettere, 2014, forthcoming).

always start with the palingenetic urge to instate a new world order, and they draw substance from the attempt to impose a system of power often with a more sinister face than the one they wish to bring down. But the multiple inflections paranoia assumes in the maximalist novel are not always explicable in these terms. For novels such as Bolaño's or the one by Babette Factory, which cannot of course be tied to a puritan culture pervaded with apocalyptic overtones, it is necessary to seek out a different explanation; an explanation by means of which we can attempt to identify the common ground of the maximalist paranoid imagery.

According to John McClure, the conspiratory imgination

> replaces religion as a means of mapping the world without disenchanting it, robbing it of its mystery. For conspiracy theory explains the world, as religion does, without elucidating it, by positing the existence of hidden forces which permeate and transcend the realm of ordinary life. It offers us satisfactions similar to those offered by religions and religiously inflected romance: both the satisfaction of living among secrets, in a mysterious world, and the satisfaction of gaining access to secrets, being "in the know."[16]

Mapping the world *without disenchanting it:* this is the first fundamental element for understanding the maximalist paranoid imagination. To imagine that everything is connected and that hidden forces are constantly plotting to overthrow the constituted power is the paradoxical strategy employed by postmodern narrative to defend itself from the logic of suspicion which permeates the postmodern. To defend itself from suspicion with suspicion is not so surprising in a literature, postmodern literature, in which the confines between theory and literary practice often are uncertain. This reaction undoubtedly qualifies the maximalist novel as a product of the postmodern cultural temperament, but at the same time, it constitutes an attempt to rethink and restrain the theoretical extremism of post-structuralism, in the name of an overwhelming desire to preserve a scrap of enchantment

[16] John A. McClure, "Postmodern Romance: Don DeLillo and the Age of Conspiracy," in *Introducing Don DeLillo* [1991], ed. Frank Lentricchia (Durham: Duke University Press, 1999), 99–115. Quotation from p. 103.

in the world; an enchantment crushed by the epistemological opacities of the postmodern, denounced and legitimized at the same time by theory. Even if it is fairly grotesque to observe that it is paranoid fantasy itself which threatens to disenchant the world,[17] to see conspiracies and lethal dangers everywhere, orchestrated in the name of hidden and worrisome interests, is, in the end, a way to *explain* reality. And once explained, albeit on the basis of improbable fantasies, it will inevitably lose the halo of mystery that surrounded it, and its enchantment will suddenly disappear. Nevertheless, it is precisely in this ambiguous and partially failed attempt to resuscitate enchantment in a world dominated by doubt and diffidence that we can identify a common ground for the maximalist conspiratory imagination. A ground certainly shared with a lot of other postmodern fiction, but which, precisely for this reason, allows us to view the maximalist novel as a literary product deeply rooted in the historical and cultural context in which it was conceived and not as a non-identified object that at a certain point toppled into the postmodern literary system, in complete isolation with respect to the aesthetic context.

One final question concerns the role of the paranoid imagination in the plot of the maximalist novel. As we know, multiple stories isolated from one another, are narrated in maximalist novels; stories which continually intertwine, and thereby contribute to making tangible at the level of the management of narrative information the narratorial "super-omniscience" we spoke of in the preceding chapter. But in the light of what we have just said, the osmotic nature of the various narrative threads that constitute the maximalist diegesis could easily be interpreted as an *objective correlative* of the paranoid imagination. Pynchon:

> About the paranoia often noted under the drug, there is nothing remarkable. Like other sorts of paranoia, there is nothing less than the onset, the leading edge, of the discovery that *everything is connected*, everything in the Creation, a secondary illumination—not yet blindingly One, but at least connected, and perhaps a route In for those like Tchitcherine who are held at the edge . . . (*Gravity's Rainbow*, 834)

[17] See Coale, *Paradigms of Paranoia*, 15.

Everything is linked: this is the unshakeable conviction of the paranoid,[18] a conviction that finds its structural equivalent in the direct or indirect interconnection of all the stories, of all the characters, and of all the events that proliferate in maximalist novels.[19] Such a situation could not be underpinned by a more efficient narratorial procedure than omniscience, in which the hyper-vigilant gaze of the narrator dominates the narrative material in its entirety. Moreover, the paranoid production of the plot would also seem to imply a certain *holistic* concept of mimesis on the part of maximalist novelists.

Reflections on holism developed in the philosophy of language beginning with Frege's formulation of the "context principle," in accordance with which, the significance of words is not considered in isolation but within the context of a statement.[20] In the wake of an extension of that principle, first with Ludwig Wittgenstein,[21] then with Willard Van Orman Quine[22] and Donald Davidson,[23] the idea has been asserted that the meaning of a word, or of a statement, does not depend simply on their context, but rather on language in its entirety. That is, this is the assertion of a holistic conception of meaning: a fascinating idea, destined to raise many problems in the philosophical debate.[24]

What is more important to underscore for our analysis is that, at the core of the maximalist paranoid imagination, a veritable *holistic ontology* seems to take shape because of which no event can be either conceived or fully comprehended if not within a much more far-reaching design. This is what happens in *Infinite Jest* and in *2666*, in which only at the end of the narration

18 See Thomas Moore, *The Style of Connectedness: "Gravity's Rainbow" and Thomas Pynchon* (Columbia: University of Missouri Press, 1987).

19 On the obsession with links in a certain type of the contemporary novel see James Wood, *The Irresponsible Self: On Laughter and the Novel* (New York: Picador, 2004), 181–3. We will return to Wood in the final chapter with regard to "hysterical realism."

20 Gottlob Frege, *The Foundations of Arithmetic: A Logico-Mathematical Enquiry into the Concept of Number* [1884], trans. J. L. Austin (Oxford: Basil Blackwell, 1959).

21 Ludwig Wittgenstein, *Philosophical Investigations* [1953] (Oxford: Blackwell Basil, 1968).

22 A notion developed beginning with his celebrated essay on the two dogmas of empiricism. See Willard Van Orman Quine, "Two Dogmas of Empiricism" [1951], in Quine, *From a Logical Point of View: 9 Logico-Philosophical Essays* (Cambridge, MA: Harvard University Press, 1953), 20–46.

23 Donald Davidson, "Truth and Meaning" [1967], in Davidson, *Inquiries into Truth and Interpretation* (Oxford: Clarendon Press, 1984), 17–36.

24 In particular as concerns (1) the constitution of the meaning of an expression, (2) the communication and sharing of meanings, (3) the compositionality of meaning. See Nicla Vassallo, *La naturalizzazione dell'epistemologia: Contro la soluzione quineana* (Milan: Franco Angeli, 1997); Carlo Penco, *Introduzione alla filosofia del linguaggio* (Rome-Bari: Laterza, 2004), 148–71.

do we understand the facts related to us in the opening pages; or in *2005 dopo Cristo*, with the progressive and inescapable involvement of all of the novel's characters in the failed plot against Berlusconi. Connect everything, include the particular in the general, the individual in a collective destiny, render the plot *pansemantic*[25]—this is the aesthetic imperative that guides the production of the maximalist plot. Every narrative cell becomes part of a whole, a whole that acquires consistency and coherence only within the perspective of the *interconnection* of each individual story and existence. And if the paranoid obsession for connections seems evident at the level of the organization of the contents into a plot, it also exercises a strong influence for determining the overall effects of meaning within the novel: we know well that it is precisely the perspective positioning of each fragment that ends up constituting itself, as in a game of mirrors, into a sort of narratorial macro-perspective with regard to the mimesis. The paranoid imagination involves much more, in fact, than merely contriving conspiracies, or giving life to psychotic characters. In the maximalist novel, it acts as a compositional principle, as both an *ontological and an epistemological grounding*.

The desire for re-enchantment and holistic ontology, then; these seem to be the constants of the maximalist paranoid imagination. A paranoid imagination that serves as a privileged access key for understanding our cultural imagery, as much so as certain formal choices in contemporary fiction, and whose obstinate deep-rootedness in the maximalist novel is summed up grotesquely by Pynchon in the buffoonish song of paranoia:

> Pa—ra—nooooiiiia, Pa-ra-noia!
> Ain't it grand ta see, that good-time face, again!
> Pa-ra-*noi*-ya, boy oh boy, yer
> Just a bit of you-know-what
> From way back when!
> Even Goya, couldn't draw ya,
> Not the way you looked, just kickin' in that door—
> Call a lawyer, Paranoia,

[25] In a different sense than what is commonly understood for paraliterature. See Daniel Couégnas, *Introduction à la paralittérature* (Paris: Seuil, 1992).

Lemme will my ass to you, for-ever-more!
Pa- ra- noi—(clippety-clippety-clippety cl[ya,]op!)
Pa- ra- noi—(shuffle*stomp!* shuffle*stomp!* shuffle*stomp!*
    [and] cl[ya,]op! clickety cl[Ain't]ick) it grand (clop)
    ta (clop) see (clippy*clop*) yer good-time face again! etc. (*Gravity's Rainbow*, 778–9)

Internal Dialectic: Chaos-Function/Cosmos-Function

It would be erroneous to think of the maximalist novel as a literary object defined by a series of features all having the same weight or function. If, up until this point, we have considered each characteristic in itself or in reference to particular literary and cultural systems, this does not mean that internal genre dynamics do not exist among them.

A literary genre is not a metadiscursive formation composed merely of juxtaposed elements. To varying degrees, a *hierarchy* of the materials is always presupposed which guarantees the genre's morphological and symbolic *hold*. In this sense, we could think of a literary genre as a *system* the formal components of which contribute to a common goal, to the satisfaction of very precise symbolic needs. And just as it happens in a system, the individual elements that identify a genre carry out specific functions and relate to one another. This being said, every genre-system organizes itself in different ways. Let us analyze our case.

Length, encyclopedic mode, dissonant chorality, and diegetic exuberance on the one hand; completeness, narratorial omniscience, and paranoid imagination on the other: seven characteristics of the maximalist novel we have come to know. Seven characteristics which play different roles in the *internal dialectic* of the genre. In particular, the first four are responsible for an increase in the narrative entropy, expressing what we could define as a *chaos-function*, while the remaining three work in the opposite direction, toward a containment of the complexity of the diegesis, executing a *cosmos-function*. Length, encyclopedic mode, dissonant chorality, and diegetic exuberance are all attributes which would take the maximalist form toward complete dispersion and ungovernability if there were not others to oppose them. In other words, the paroxysmal accumulation of narrative materials enabled by the length of the novels in question, the anomalous cognitive openings made possible by the encyclopedic mode, the amalgam of chorality and polyphony, and the systematic use of fragments and digressions would generate a guaranteed deflagration of the maximalist novel if a series of countermeasures were not provided for: rigid structural practices, a capillary control of the narrative material through a super-omniscient narrator, and a holistic construction of the plot. Even though each of these categories is provided with a strong specificity and autonomy, within the structural dialectic of the genre, they split into two monolithic and opposing camps: anarchy versus order, centrifugal forces versus centripetal forces, chaos versus cosmos. Two camps exercising antithetic functions to ensure the delicate *equilibrium* of the maximalist novel as a genre-system. An internal equilibrium as necessary as it is indispensable to enable the maximalist novel to fulfill its fundamental symbolic need: to relate the complexity of the world we live in, by providing a totalizing representation of it. The internal dialectic of the maximalist novel would appear then to work toward the *synthesis* of two opposing functions exercised by some of its elements, a chaos-function and a cosmos-function. But let us take one step further toward formal abstraction and attempt to reason in terms of single procedures.

There certainly exist narrative devices which intrinsically hold a chaos-function or a cosmos-function. In this sense, it is necessary to establish an important distinction between *function* and *effect*. It is not the procedure in itself which directly determines a *chaos effect* or a *cosmos effect* in the narrative taken as a whole, but rather its *combined* use with other factors which have the same function. Take the example of fragments and digressions. In the maximalist novel, the structural use of fragments and digressions in the diegesis has the consequence of drastically increasing the polyphony of representation. In fact, to reject a compact narrative *continuum* and to systematically substitute it with autonomous and juxtaposed diegetic units—fragments— and, at the same time, to multiply the materials inserted into the narrative through countless digressions, results in a notable upsurge of narrative entropy. But this does not automatically take place in all literary texts which make use of the same procedures.

In *Flesh and Blood*,[1] Michael Cunningham constructs the diegesis on a markedly choral foundation: from 1935 to 2035, the story of the Stassos family is narrated from the point of view of each of its members. Following a chronologically linear progression, each chapter of the novel is typically subdivided into fragments of varying lengths, each usually concerned for the most part with a particular character. Through these fragments, the utilization of scenes is asserted in the narrative, and less often, changes in the point of view are also determined. Cunningham's use of the fragment is pervasive, just as in the maximalist novel, and yet, here, the fragments do not generate any chaos effect. Polyphony remains relatively contained, and we never have the sensation of even the slightest dispersion in the plot. This is because in *Flesh and Blood* Cunningham *does not* intend whatsoever to devise a totalizing narrative of the world. In accordance with the dictates of the family novel, the affairs of the Stassos family do indeed hypostatize a particular historico-economic juncture, as in Roth's *American Pastoral*, but always from a very circumscribed perspective, that of a rich New England family, even if the views of Constantine, Mary, Susan, Billy, and Zoe may be resistant to assimilation. In Cunningham's novel, fragments and a variable internal focalization do confer a choral aspect to the diegesis, but it is a chorality which is qualitatively different from that of the maximalist novel. Let us consider the case of Franzen's *The Corrections*.

In Franzen's novel, as in Cunningham's, the narrative is concentrated on one family in particular and the perspective on the world offered to the reader results from the interaction of the various points of view of the family members. But in *The Corrections*, Franzen goes far beyond the standard formulas of the family novel, within which it seems possible instead to circumscribe *Flesh and Blood*. Encyclopedic opening ushers into Franzen's novel a dialogical richness absent in Cunningham's. Reading *The Corrections*, one quickly has the certitude of listening not only to the voices of the members of a family, particularly representative of American middle-class at the beginning of the twenty-first century, but of witnessing the representation of a whole, that is to say, of America today viewed as a plural cosmos, whose manifold aspects need

[1] Michael Cunningham, *Flesh and Blood* (New York: Farrar, 1995).

to be told: from high finance to depression, from pharmaceutical research to drug addiction. In this sense, we could say that in the family novel, the relationship between the representation and the social totality is metonymic in nature, while, in the maximalist novel, it is synecdochal.

As we have said, the procedure in and of itself is not sufficient to ensure a comprehensive chaos or cosmos effect, since the outcome will be determined by the procedure's interaction with other elements kindred to it. The fragment may well indeed be a device evincing a chaos-function, but the chaos effect is something different, resulting from a *summation* of the individual centrifugal factors of the diegesis: in the case of *The Corrections*, the use of fragments joins, indeed, with the encyclopedic mode. Moreover, in the maximalist novel, the chaos effect is never predominant. It is always balanced by a cosmos effect, determined in its turn by the convergence of a multiplicity of centripetal elements: structural practices, narratorial omniscience, and a holistic set up of the plot. But, before concluding, a small parenthesis on *The Corrections* is needed.

It goes without saying that maximalist novels are not all the same. The presence of a series of shared features certainly does not imply that they can be grasped in their entirety solely in accordance with the formula of genre membership. As a matter of fact, there is a vast diversity in authorial choices especially with regard to the degree of narrative experimentalism. Franzen's novel is emblematic in this way. If, on the one hand, *The Corrections* is undoubtedly definable as a maximalist novel, on the other, it demonstrates a strong continuity with classical narrative forms such as the realist novel.[2] It would be misleading to impoverish *The Corrections* under the sign of the recently coined slogan of the "return of the real"[3]: a somewhat problematic formula, in truth, pointing to a supposed overcoming, registered in some works of literature over the last 20 years, of a literary season-well represented by a specific kind of postmodernist fiction-characterized by a distinct loss in the referentiality of the word. Nonetheless, there is a certain "similarity" between Franzen's masterpiece and a novel such as *Flesh and Blood*—a similarity

[2] See Wood, *The Irresponsible Self*, 195–209.

[3] See Romano Luperini, *L'incontro e il caso: Narrazioni moderne e destino dell'uomo occidentale* (Rome-Bari: Latereza, 2007), 311–12; VV.AA., *Allegoria* XX, 57 (2008).

the reason for which is easy to point out: *The Corrections* is simply less experimental than other maximalist novels. This fact is evident, for instance, in its use of digressions. In Franzen's novel, the number of digressions is not even remotely comparable to their number in *Infinite Jest*, but each time one is inserted in the novel, it contributes nevertheless to the overall chaos effect, in concourse with length, encyclopedic openness, and the use of fragments. Such is the case, for instance, for the long tale of Sylvia Roth, incorporated into the section dedicated to the narration of Alfred and Enid's cruise. The insertion of *The Corrections* into our textual corpus was in keeping, in fact, with a very precise intention: to provide a composite and multifaceted image of the maximalist novel, one that permits us, at the same time, to effectively mark out the confines between what can and cannot be defined as maximalist. The intent was to convey an idea of the maximalist novel as a literary form in which can be identified, to the extent possible, continuities with respect to other tendencies in contemporary narrative; a literary genre in which one can trace continuities within discontinuity. And whereas a discussion of this sort would be difficult, if not impossible, to have through the comparison of a text such as Pynchon's *Gravity's Rainbow* with one like Cunningham's *Flesh and Blood*, Franzen's novel, on the contrary, thanks to its proximity to more traditional types of writing, lends itself very well to this operation.

Part Two

8

Intersemioticity

When Gotthold Ephraim Lessing theorized painting in *Laocoön* as a spatial and synchronic art form and poetry as a temporal and diachronic art form, he laid the groundwork for a codification which would have an immense critical fortune, underpinning for a long time purist conceptions of artistic languages.[1] We now know well, however, that space and time cannot be kept distinct, either in the enjoyment or in the creation of a work of art, since, as Georges Didi-Huberman has shown,[2] even the image possesses a complex temporality, "made up of unconscious unforeseen events and sudden returns."[3] Moreover, Lessing's opposition did not take long to disclose its ideological component.[4] Massimo Fusillo writes:

> In *Laocoön*, we find a tendency very rooted in all of Western culture which considers the image to be a natural product, putting it on the same plane as beauty and femininity, and setting it in opposition instead to the sublime and masculine eloquence of the word. . . .[5]

1 A success testified to by the composition of other Laocoöns in the twentieth century: Irving Babbitt, *The New Laokoon: An Essay on the Confusion of the Arts* (Boston: Houghton Mifflin, 1910); Rudolf Arnheim, "A New Laocoön: Artistic Composites and the Talking Film" [1938], in Arnheim, *Film As Art* (Berkeley-Los Angeles: University of California Press, 1969), 199–230; Clement Greenberg, "Toward a Newer Laocoon," *Partisan Review* 7, 4 (1940): 296–310; Galvano Della Volpe, "Laocoonte 1960," in Della Volpe, *Critica del gusto* [1960] (Milan: Feltrinelli, 1996), ch. 3. Not to mention a recent anti-Laocoön conceived on the background of multimedial semiotics: *Electric Laokoon: Zeiche und Mieden, von der Lochkarte zur Grammatologie*, eds. Michael Franz et al. (Berlin: Akademie, 2007).

2 Georges Didi-Huberman, *Devant le Temps: Histoire de l'art et anachronism des images* (Paris: Éditions de Minuit, 2000); Georges Didi-Huberman, *L'Image survivante: Histoire de l'art et temps des fantômes selon Aby Warburg* (Paris: Éditions de Minuit, 2004).

3 Fusillo, *Estetica della letteratura*, 176.

4 An opposition between poetry and painting conceived politically by Lessing in an anti-French key. See W. J. T. Mitchell, *Iconology: Image, Text, Ideology* (Chicago-London: The University of Chicago Press, 1986), 110.

5 Fusillo, *Estetica della letteratura*, 176.

In the postmodern era, the separation of the languages of the arts has revealed itself to be an obsolete aesthetic myth, glaringly contradicted by numerous artistic practices.[6] And if the influence of the arts, especially cinema, was already crucial in literary modernism in dictating compositional procedures and suggesting subjects matter—such as the use of the cinematographic technique of montage as a reference for the construction of the narrative structure of *Manhattan Transfer* by Dos Passos, for instance,[7]—on various levels the contemporary literary imagery seems to lean firmly on a semiotic exchange: a polymorphic imagery, oriented toward the overcoming of centuries-old aesthetic taboos.

The ever closer conversation going on between the different media enriches and regenerates the individual artistic languages in their *hybridization*.[8] This is an invaluable wealth, and one too often scorned, for in it probably lies one of the keys to the successful adaptation of literature to the contemporary cultural system. An adaptation all the more necessary, the higher the stakes: survival. In the shadow of cinema, the uncontested artistic power of our time, literature has undergone an increasing marginalization, often the victim of a paralyzing incapacity to rethink itself in truly radical ways and to propose alternative visions of the world. But this process is by no means irreversible; quite the contrary. The sclerosis of literary language, contributed to by aesthetic dogmas such as the one established by Lessing,[9] or by iconophobic attitudes in line with Baudrillard's,[10] could be cured by

[6] As is the case, for example, in W. G. Sebald's *Austerlitz*—an "iconotext" (see *Icons—Texts—Iconotexts: Essays on Ekphrasis and Intermediality*, ed. Peter Wagner [Berlin-New York: Walter de Gruyter, 1996], 15)—in which the narrative is alternated with evocative black and white photographs. W. G. Sebald, *Austerlitz* [2001], trans. Anthea Bell (New York: Random House, 2001). See Stefano Ercolino, "Per un'estetica dell'irrappresentabile: Le immagini della Shoah in *Austerlitz* di W. G. Sebald," *Contemporanea* 9 (2011): 93–107.

[7] See Antonio Bibbò, "'There can't be two Jameses can there?': Il montaggio di *Manhattan Transfer* e l'indeterminatezza," in *Il personaggio: Figure della dissolvenza e della permanenza*, ed. Chiara Lombardi (Turin: Edizioni dell'orso, 2008), 323–35. For a general approach to the question, see P. Adams Sitney, *Modernist Montage: The Obscurity of Vision in Cinema and Literature* (New York: Columbia University Press, 1990).

[8] Fusillo, *Estetica della letteratura*, 177.

[9] The groundlessness and "posteriority" of which are demonstrated, among other things, by the long tradition of *ekphrasis*, going all the way back to Homer's *Iliad*. See Murray Krieger, *EKPHRASIS: The Illusion of the Natural Sign* (Baltimore-London: The Johns Hopkins University Press, 1992), and James A. W. Heffernan, *Museum of Words: The Poetics of Ekphrasis from Homer to Ashbery* (Chicago-London: The University of Chicago Press, 1993).

[10] The reference is to his well-known critique of the simulacrum: Jean Baudrillard, *Simulacra and Simulation* [1980], trans. Sheila Faria Glaser (Ann Arbor: University of Michigan Press, 1995). See Martin Jay, *Downcasts Eyes: The Denigration of Vision in Twentieth-Century French Thought* (Berkeley-Los Angeles: University of California Press, 1994).

taking up the challenges proposed by the "visual turn" we have witnessed in the last few decades.[11] These challenges, if accepted, might inject new and precious blood into the aged veins of literature, conferring on it a renewed heuristic vitality. Nowadays, it is only by surrendering to multiplicity that one can hope to voice contemporaneity, and this is precisely what happens in the maximalist novel.

The maximalist novel is literally overrun with images. Cinema, television, video, painting, comics, pop icons: the visual dimension cloaks and molds the maximalist imagery; a *hybrid* imagery which, at its intersection with other artistic media, acquires powerful expressive tools and obsessive themes. A first and important intersemiotic hybridization for the maximalist novel is with cinema. As Fusillo writes, in contemporary narrative cinema is not only a privileged theme of literary discourse, but

> . . . becomes the object of continual allusions and quotations, which confide in the filmic memory of the reader; it influences techniques and narrative time, prompting frenetic montages; it evokes fragmentary and obsessive modes of reception, through the new props of dvds and computers. . . .[12]

An influence which is articulated on two levels: one *thematic* and the other *formal*. Let us see in what sense.

Antonio Costa identifies four fundamental types of cinematic citation in literary texts: cinema is referred to as (1) an institution, (2) a visual device, (3) a language, and (4) an individual film or genre.[13] From a thematic point of view, cinema is present in the maximalist novel both as citation and as subtle

[11] A guiding idea which runs throughout the above-cited pages of Massimo Fusillo's *Estetica della letteratura*, an idea which advocates a revival of aesthetics and of literature under the aegis of pluralism. See Fusillo, *Estetica della letteratura*, 9–10. On the visual turn which seems to have influenced a large part of contemporary artistic production, see *The Visual Turn: Classical Film Theory and Art History*, ed. Angela Dalle Vacche (Piscataway: Rutgers University Press, 2003). See also W. J. T. Mitchell, *Picture Theory: Essays on Verbal and Visual Representation* (Chicago: The University of Chicago Press, 1994).

[12] Fusillo, *Estetica della letteratura*, 177–8. See Vincenzo Maggitti, *Lo schermo fra le righe: Cinema e letteratura del Novecento* (Naples: Liguori, 2007).

[13] Antonio Costa, "Nel corpo della parola, l'immagine: quando la letteratura cita il cinema," in *La letteratura e le altre arti: Atti del convegno annuale dell' Associazione di teoria e studi di Letteratura comparata—L'Aquila, Febbraio 2004*, eds. Massimo Fusillo and Marina Polacco, *Contemporanea* 3 (2005): 66.

allusion—as it occurs frequently in *Gravity's Rainbow*, from Merian Cooper and Ernest Schoedsack's *King Kong* to Clark Gable—and as an obsessive presence, the object of a fetishistic adoration, as in the case of *White Teeth*, with Millat's fixation on gangster movies—especially *The Godfather*—and on Robert De Niro's famous dialogue/monologue with his reflected image in a mirror in *Taxi Driver*.

Cinema influences the discursive strategies of the maximalist novel at the formal level as well. In this sense, the use of fragments can be easily interpreted as a significant rhetorical debt to cinematic language.[14] Eisenstein's conception of montage as the juxtaposition of the heterogeneous seems in fact to be presumed in the segmentation of the plot into fragments, part of a strong continuity with the most experimental and semiotically hybrid outcomes of literary modernism, first among which are the novels of Dos Passos. In particular, the search for overall sense effects through the summation of individual signifying units, a strategy on which the construction of maximalist perspective depends, appears to present some analogies with the "montage of attractions," defined by Eisenstein as the "free montage of arbitrarily chosen independent (of both the PARTICULAR composition and any thematic connection with the actors) effects (attractions)—but with the precise aim of a specific final effect."[15]

Another eloquent example of the intersection between literary and cinematographic rhetorics can be found in the widespread use in the maximalist novel of narrative syntagms typical in the organization of filmic information. In *2666*, at the end of the "Part of the Critics," the narrator alternates snippets of Liz Norton's e-mail to Pelletier and Espinoza—an e-mail in which she reveals the reason for her sudden departure from Mexico and for her abandonment of the two lovers with whom she had gone in search of Arcimboldi—with the reactions of the latter two after having read it. The reader is not immediately informed as to the contents of Norton's e-mail, rather only at the end of the

[14] See Keith Cohen, *Film and Fiction: The Dynamics of Exchange* (New Haven: Yale University Press, 1979).

[15] Sergei M. Eisentein, "The Montage of Attractions" [1923], in *The Eisenstein Reader*, ed. Bruce Taylor, trans. Richard Taylor and William Powell (London: British Film Institute, 1998), 31.

section, throughout which the actions of the three characters seem, therefore, to be unmotivated, although the rhythmical insertion of passages from the e-mail continually offers glimpses of a denouement. On the one hand, the alternation of scenes placed in chronological succession but belonging to two distinct planes of events, reminds us of the cinematic narrative technique of "alternate syntagmas"—excepting of course the relationship of posteriority between the two—as theorized by Christian Metz[16]; on the other, the effect of reticence attained through a rigorous use of external focalization creates a powerful sense of suspense, traceable to a characteristic rhetoric of film noir.

Sometimes, it is the gaze itself of the narrator which seems to reproduce the movements of a movie camera. As in *Infinite Jest*, when the purse-snatching episode perpetrated by Poor Tony Krause on Kate Gompert and Ruth Van Cleve is abruptly interrupted by a defamiliarizing horizontal panning shot of the Ennet House[17]:

> The vaporizer chugs and seethes and makes the room's windows weep as Jim Troeltsch inserts a pro-wrestling cartridge in the little TP's viewer and dons his tackiest sportcoat and wet-combs his hair down smooth so it looks toupeeish and settles back on his bunk, surrounded by Seldane-bottles and two-ply facial tissue, preparing to call the action. His roommates have long since seen what was coming, and screwed.
>
> Standing on tiptoe in Subdorm B's curved hallway, using the handle of an inverted tennis racquet whose vinyl cover he can absently zip and unzip as he moves the handle around, Michael Pemulis is gently raising one of the panels in the drop-ceiling and shifting it on its aluminum strut, the panel, changing its lie on the strut from square-shaped to diamond-shaped, being careful not to let it fall.

16 It is one of the most typical techniques of cinematic montage: "The montage presents alternately two or more series of events in such a way that within each series the temporal relationships are consecutive, but that, between the series taken as wholes, the temporal relationship is one of simultaneity." Christian Metz, *Film Language: A Semiotics of Cinema*, trans. Michael Taylor (New York: Oxford University Press, 1974), 128–9.

17 "It is a rotating movement of the camera which can be *horizontal* (a horizontal panning shot to the right or to the left; if the rotation is complete, a 360° panning shot); or *vertical* (from high to low or vice versa); or *oblique*." Antonio Costa, *Saper vedere il cinema* [1985] (Milan: Bompiani, 2004), 181.

> Lyle hovers cross-legged just a couple mm. above the top of the towel dispenser in the unlit weight room, eyes rolled up white, lips barely moving and making no sound.
>
> Coach Schtitt and Mario tear-ass downhill on W. Commonwealth on Schtitt's old BMW, bound for Evangeline's Low-Temperature Confections in Newton Center, right at the bottom of what usually gets called Heartbreak Hill, Schtitt intense-faced and leaning forward like a skier, his white scarf whipping around and whipping Mario's face, in the sidecar, as Mario too leans way forward into their downhill flight, preparing to whoop when they bottom out.
>
> Ms. Avril Incandenza, seeming somehow to have three or four cigarettes all going at once, secures from Information the phone and e-mail #s of a journalistic business address on East Tucson AZ's Blasted Expanse Blvd., then begins to dial, using the stern of a blue felt pen to stab at the console's keys. (*Infinite Jest*, 700–1)

However, the maximalist novel's relationship with cinema also follows more twisting paths. Paths which lead away from the beaten track of classical citation, of pop aestheticization, or of the use of formal procedures typical of cinema, to penetrate into the dimension of the fictitious.[18] This relationship can be in the guise of an *amalgam* between the real and the fictitious, and/or of a *pure fiction*. We find the first type in *Underworld* and *2666*, in which there is much talk of lost or extremely rare masterworks of great directors of the past, or of directors still living, who become the object of passionate cults: the dark and apocalyptic *Unterwelt* of Sergei M. Eisenstein[19] and an unidentified first work by Robert Rodriguez, made 2 years before *El Mariachi* (1992), his debut film, respectively.[20] We find the second type instead in *Gravity's Rainbow*, *Infinite Jest*, and *2005 dopo Cristo*, in which we encounter talented and mad directors who hold a primary place in the narrative—in Pynchon's novel, Gerhardt von Göll, in Wallace's, James Incandenza, and in the novel by

[18] See *Fictional Cinema: How Literature Describes Imaginary Films*, eds. Stefano Ercolino et al. (Göttingen: Vandenhoeck and Ruprecht Unipress, 2014, forthcoming).

[19] See Timothy L. Parrish, "From Hoover's FBI to Eisenstein's *Unterwelt*: DeLillo Directs the Postmodern Novel," *Modern Fiction Studies* XLV, 3 (1999): 696–723.

[20] If we exclude the short film *Bedhead*.

Babette Factory the Underscore Sisters—all with their memorable works and detailed filmography.[21]

Leaving aside the specific forms cinematic citations assume in the maximalist novel, cinema most certainly constitutes something more than a mere reference for it; it is a powerful semantic device, able to both contribute in a decisive way to the production of the plot and to influence its compositional techniques. But cinema is not the only extra-literary medium capable of powerfully affecting the thematic and formal universe of the maximalist novel. There is, in fact, another medium, no less important which, in some cases, can assume a notable significance: painting.

A visual intertext present in an obsessive way in *Underworld* is *The Triumph of Death* by Pieter Bruegel (figure 8.1). It is a painting which haunts the thoughts

Figure 8.1 Pieter Bruegel, *The Triumph of Death*, oil on canvas, 117 × 162 cm, Madrid, Museo Nacional del Prado, 1562 c. Photo Copyright The Bridgeman Art Library. Reprinted with permission.

21 There is something similar in *The Book of Illusions* by Paul Auster (New York: Holt, 2000), in which the narrative's protagonist, Hector Mann, is an imaginary actor of the silent cinema, and whose filmography is provided. See Costa, "Nel corpo della parola," 64.

of J. Edgar Hoover—the legendary director of the FBI from 1924 to 1972—from the very first pages of the "Prologue" and is directly associated to an event of capital importance in the balance of power between the United States and the Union of the Soviet Socialist Republics, the explosion of the first Soviet atomic bomb, news of which came on 3 October 1951, the same day as the famous game between the Giants and the Dodgers:

> Edgar loves this stuff. Edgar, Jedgar. Admit it—you love it. It causes a bristling of his body hair. Skeletons with wispy dicks. The dead beating kettledrums. The sackcloth dead slitting a pilgrim's throat.
>
> The meatblood colors and massed bodies, this is a census-taking of awful ways to die. He looks at the flaring sky in the deep distance out beyond the headlands on the left-hand page—Death elsewhere, Conflagration in many places, Terror universal, the crows, the ravens in silent glide, the raven perched on the white nag's rump, black and white forever, and he thinks of a lonely tower standing on the Kazakh Test Site, the tower armed with the bomb, and he can almost hear the wind blowing across the Central Asian steppes, out where the enemy lives in long coats and fur caps, speaking that old weighted language of theirs, liturgical and grave. (*Underworld*, 50)

Bruegel's masterpiece acquires an apocalyptical meaning in the paranoid mind of Hoover, incarnating the prospect of a future dominated by death and devastation in the event of an ultimate communist victory. But beyond the catastrophizing fantasies of Hoover, the Flemish master's canvas becomes a leitmotiv in the novel—as in the conversation between Klara Sax and her husband Bronzini on *Kinderspielen* mentioned earlier—acting as an iconographic depository of the apocalyptical visions enveloping *Underworld*. From nuclear catastrophe to waste, from urban decay to crime, from drugs to AIDS, from psychological discomfort to relativism, DeLillo chronicles all the afflictions of the United States and the West. And like Bruegel's, DeLillo's apocalypse is likewise secular: God is absent from the scene, and death triumphs uncontested, so much so, that more than an apocalypse, we seem to bear witness to a cruel slaughter. But different from what happens in the anguished and dark universe of Bruegel, hope is not completely banished from the pages of DeLillo's novel. An example is the "postmodern miracle" of the final pages of *Underworld*, in which throngs of believers gather in front of a Minute Maid billboard to witness, subsequent to her tragic demise, the apparition of little Esmeralda's face: a controversial emblem of the sacred in the postmodern era. Or the ambiguous closing of the novel on the word "Peace," which appears on the computer screen after a virtual nuclear holocaust:

> . . . a word that carries the sunlit ardor of an object deep in drenching noon, the argument of binding touch, but it's only a sequence of pulses on a dullish screen and all it can do is make you pensive—a word that spreads a longing through the raw sprawl of the city and out across the dreaming bourns and orchards to the solitary hills.
>
> Peace. (*Underworld*, 827)

The virtual nuclear apocalypse becomes then a way to close the book on the cold war, and perhaps open the door to a better future, in the name of new technologies and the internet. The doubt remains, however, that, in a postatomic era, there may not be much room for yet another technological utopia, which would be inevitably encircled by a sinister halo. *Underworld* closes, then, under the sign of a deep-seated ambivalence and of the apocalypse; an apocalypse in relation to which *The Triumph of Death* acts as a sublimating device, enabling forms, even if ambiguous ones, of transcendence.

More complex and mediated, instead, is the relationship of *2666* with the paintings of Giuseppe Arcimboldo, beginning with the implausible pseudonym Benno von Arcimboldi adopted by Hans Reiter, a pseudonym referring directly to the Milanese maestro (the spelling of the last name of the latter oscillates in documents of the times between Arcimboldo and Arcimboldi, although he usually signed his paintings as "Giuseppe Arcimboldo"). But the liaison between Arcimboldo the painter and von Arcimboldi the imaginary writer goes far beyond a simple association of names. In his reading of Ansky's manuscript, the young Hans encounters the figure of Arcimboldo for the first time, and from that moment on will be obsessed with it:

> La técnica del milanés le parecía la alegría personificada. El fin de las apariencias. Arcadia antes del hombre. No todas, ciertamente, pues por ejemplo *El asado*, un cuadro invertido. . . . Pero los cuadros de las cuatro estaciones eran alegría pura. Todo dentro de todo, escribe Ansky. Como si

> Arcimboldo hubiera aprendido una sola lección, pero ésta hubiera sido de la mayor importancia. (*2666*, 917–18)
>
> [The Milanese painter's technique struck him as happiness personified. The end of semblance. Arcadia before the coming of man. Not all of the paintings, of course, because *The Roast*, for example, . . . a reversible canvas. . . . But the paintings of the four seasons were pure bliss. Everything in everything, writes Ansky. As if Arcimboldo had learned a single lesson, but one of vital importance. (*2666*, 734)]

Everything in everything: the ultimate lesson learned not only by Arcimboldo but also by Hans, in whose novels will triumph a short while later the heterogeneous and encyclopedic chaos, in a delirium of the carnivalesque and the Dionysian combined.[22] An aesthetics which, in establishing a parallel between the work of Arcimboldo and that of the key character of *2666*, Benno von Arcimboldi, indirectly reveals not only the compositional procedures of Bolaño's novel, but those of the maximalist novel itself.

Roland Barthes is the author of a compelling rhetorical analysis of Arcimboldo's paintings, and of his "Composed Heads" in particular (figure 8.2). According to Barthes, the Milanese maestro works in essence as a Baroque poet would, exacerbating the metaphorical and metonymic links between the represented objects, articulating his paintings on a *double* signifying level, and generating in this way a tension between autonomous content units and the meaning of the whole. More or less what happens in language between phonemes and words, except that in the Composed Heads, different than with phonemes, the individual elements of which they are composed also have an autonomous meaning: a shell, a bird, a flower, etc.[23] And it is precisely this double level which is of interest to us. Barthes writes:

[22] This interpretation of Arcimboldi's work is given by Pellettier and Espinoza themselves: "El público, gran parte del cual eran universitarios que habían viajado en tren o en furgonetas desde Göttingen, también optó por las encendidas y lapidarias interpretationes de Pelletier, sin ningún tipo de reserva, entregado con entusiasmo a la visión dionisíaca, festiva, de exégesis de último carnaval (o penúltimo carnaval) defendida por Pelletier y Espinoza." ["The audience, consisting mostly of university students who had traveled from Göttingen by train or in vans, was also won over by Pelletier's fiery and uncompromising interpretations, throwing caution to the winds and enthusiastically yielding to the festive, Dionysian vision of ultimate carnival (or penultimate carnival) exegesis upheld by Pelletier and Espinoza."] Bolaño, *2666*, 26; English trans., 12.

[23] Roland Barthes, *Arcimboldo* [1978], intro. Achille Bonito Oliva (Milan: F. M. Ricci, 1980), 15–32.

Figure 8.2 Giuseppe Arcimboldo, *Summer*, oil on canvas, 67 × 50.8 cm, Vienna, Kunsthistorisches Museum, 1563. Reprinted with permission from the Kunsthistorisches Museum, Wien.

> Say there is a message to be conveyed: Arcimboldo wants to signify the head of a cook, of a peasant, of a reformer, or even summer, water, fire; he encodes this message; to encode means both to conceal and not to conceal; the message is concealed insofar as the eye is diverted from the overall meaning by the meaning of details; at first I see nothing but the fruits or animals amassed in front of me; and it is only by distancing myself, changing the level of perception, that I receive another message, that of a human head: over the first message I place a hypermetropic device that like a cryptograph all at once allows me to perceive the total sense, the "true" sense.[24]

And further on:

> I imagine that an ingenious artist could take all of Archimboldo's Composed Heads, arrange them, combine them with a view to achieving a new effect

[24] Ibid., 32–4.

> of meaning, and by their disposition make, for example, a landscape, a city, a forest suddenly appear: to stand back and perceive is to engender a new meaning: perhaps no other principle governs the historical parade of forms . . . and that of the social sciences. . . .[25]

This is exactly what takes place in the maximalist novel with its tension in perspective, which, as we have seen, is generated between the microstructural and macrostructural levels of the narration, responsible indeed for a double movement of sense, but always directed toward an overall meaning, obtained by the summation of the single signifying units. And this is what happens in *2666* as well: a novel in which we witness an exceptional proliferation of narrative materials and genres, reined in and organized, however, in a marked circular structure, as well as the presentation of a large number of stories that are continually recomposed and joined by the omniscient gaze of the narrator.

Barthes probably would not have liked the maximalist novel, if it is true that the unease and sense of repulsion which, according to him, the viewer feels before a painting by Arcimboldo, derives from the fact that it is precisely a "composed" work, grounded in a brazen spectacularization of the artifice.[26] But Barthes's interpretation of Arcimboldo's paintings is not merely a valuable interpretive vantage point from which to approach *2666* and the maximalist novel in general. It helps to advocate the fundamentally *hybrid* and transmedial nature of all artistic language. In this regard, W. J. T. Mitchell writes in *Picture Theory*:

> One polemical claim of *Picture Theory* is that the interaction of pictures and texts is constitutive of representation as such: all media are mixed media, and all representations are heterogeneous; there are no "purely" visual or verbal arts, though the impulse to purify media is one of the central utopian gestures of modernism.[27]
>
> . . .

[25] Ibid., 50.

[26] Ibid., 60–8.

[27] Mitchell, *Picture Theory*, 5. See Michele Cometa, "Letteratura e arti figurative: Un catalogo," in *La letteratura e le altre arti*, eds. Fusillo and Polacco, 15–29.

> The image/text problem is not just something constructed "between" the arts, the media, or different forms of representation, but an unavoidable issue *within* the individual arts and media. In short, all arts are "composite arts" (both text and image); all media are mixed media, combining different codes, discursive conventions, channels, sensory and cognitive models.[28]

The maximalist novel seems to be aware of this and, in its peculiar practice of intersemiotic hybridization of the textual and visual spheres, it moves resolutely toward a productive, "impure view" of literature.[29]

[28] Mitchell, *Picture Theory*, 94–5.

[29] Massimo Fusillo, "Comparare la letteratura con le altre arti oggi: Per una visione 'impura,'" in *La letteratura e le altre arti*, eds. Fusillo and Polacco, 10.

9

Ethical Commitment

One of the battle cries of the adversaries of the postmodern is its presumed self-validating frivolousness. In some cases this position seems to be easily maintainable, but it cannot be generalized. In his mapping of the postmodern, Andreas Huyssen has accurately shown how it has assumed different forms in accordance with the historical moment taken into consideration.[1] From the strong utopian and avant-garde tensions of the 1960s, to the emergence of minorities and the decentering of the canon in the 1970s, to the appearance of a self-legitimizing and superficial postmodernism, Huyssen has defined the confines and distinct outcomes of the postmodern, restoring its image as a polycentric and manifold cultural phenomenon. And if Huyssen's misinterpretation probably has been to consider the postmodern almost exclusively as a critical response to modernism, and to pin the latter to univocal aesthetic principles there remains, nevertheless, a fundamental and generally unacknowledged merit to his study: to have underscored how the postmodern has been, throughout, much more than a sterile virtuosic game, the consequence and expression of a deep-seated ethical and aesthetic void.

Prejudice toward the postmodern continues still, in actual fact, to remain firmly rooted. In the wake of Wayne C. Booth's early studies,[2] and at times against the backdrop of the thought of Emmanuel Lévinas,[3] New

1 Huyssen, *After the Great Divide*, 178–221.

2 Wayne C. Booth, *The Rhetoric of Fiction* [1961] (Chicago-London: The University of Chicago Press, 1983), and *The Company We Keep: An Ethics of Fiction* (Berkeley-Los Angeles: University of California Press, 1988).

3 In particular, see Emmanuel Lévinas, *Otherwise than Being or Beyond Essence* [1978] (Pittsburgh: Duquesne University Press, 1998). For a critical evaluation see Robert Eaglestone, *Ethical Criticism: Reading After Lévinas* (Edinburgh: Edinburgh University Press, 1997); Andrew Gibson, *Postmodernity, Ethics and the Novel: From Leavis to Lévinas* (London-New York: Routledge, 1999); Battista Borsato, *L'alterità come etica: Una lettura di Emmanuel Lévinas* (Milan: EDB, 1996); Luciano Sesta, *La legge dell'altro: La fondazione dell'etica in Lévinas e Kant* (Pisa: ETS, 2005); Augusto Ponzio, *Tra Bachtin e Lévinas: Scritture, dialogo, alterità* (Bari: Palomar, 2008).

Ethics proposes a radical rethinking of what is generally considered to be the philosophical background of the postmodern, post-structuralism, in the name of a renewed ethical commitment of both criticism and literature.[4] In the last twenty years, important voices such as those of Gayatri Spivak,[5] Judith Butler,[6] Martha Nussbaum,[7] and J. Hillis Miller,[8] almost as if by tacit agreement, seem to have converged in this critical approach, with often notable results. But the rise of New Ethics—a rise which certainly responds to a legitimate need justified in particular in reference to certain extremist practices of deconstructionism, elaborated primarily in the Yale School environment—risks fueling the misunderstanding of the postmodern as a superficial and vacuous cultural phenomenon, devoid of any profound ethical impulses.

New Ethics is generally partial to the maximalist novel, and authors such as Zadie Smith[9] are often pointed to as significant examples of a new ethical commitment of fiction after postmodernism. Not that this is entirely untrue, to be sure. But the fact remains, as we shall see in a moment, that even in an author such as Pynchon, considered to be one of the champions of postmodernism, together with a playful, if not "frivolous," attitude in relation to the contents and form of the narrative, strong ethical tensions are present. Thus, more than considering the maximalist novel as the product of a literary season dominated by a new ethical strain, we will locate it in the *critical* tradition of the postmodern; a tradition which has its roots in the avant-gardism of the 1960s and, even earlier, in modernism. That is, the

4 For an introduction see *Mapping the Ethical Turn: A Reader in Ethics, Culture and Literary Theory*, eds. Todd F. Davis and Kenneth Womack (Charlottesville: University of Virginia Press, 2001). See also David Parker, *Ethics, Theory and the Novel* (Cambridge: Cambridge University Press, 1994); Dorothy J. Hale, "Fiction as Restriction: Self-Binding in New Ethical Theories of the Novel," *Narrative* 15, 2 (2007): 187–206, "Aesthetics and the New Ethics: Theorizing the Novel in the Twenty-First Century," *PMLA* 124 (2009): 896–905, "An Aesthetics of Alterity: The Art of English Fiction in the 20th Century," in *The Cambridge Companion to the 20th Century English Novel*, ed. Robert L. Caserio (New York: Cambridge University Press, 2009), 10–22.

5 Gayatri C. Spivak, "Ethics and Politics in Tagore, Coetzee, and Certain Scenes of Teaching," *Diacritics* 32, 3–4 (2002): 17–31.

6 Judith Butler, "Values of Difficulty," in *Just Being Difficult? Academic Writing in the Public Arena*, eds. Jonathan Culler and Kevin Lamb (Stanford: Stanford University Press, 2003), 199–215.

7 Martha C. Nussbaum, *Love's Knowledge: Essays on Philosophy and Literature* (New York: Oxford University Press, 1990).

8 J. Hillis Miller, *The Ethics of Reading: Kant, de Man, Eliot, Trollope, James, and Benjamin* (New York: Columbia University Press, 1987).

9 See Dorothy J. Hale, "*On Beauty* as Beautiful? The Problem of Novelistic Aesthetics by Way of Zadie Smith," *Contemporary Literature* 53, 4 (2012): 814–44.

ethical commitment of the maximalist novel should be situated within a seam of continuity with the best *engagée* literary tradition of the twentieth century, and not under the banner of a rupture with the postmodern literary system. For, as should be well apparent by now, the maximalist novel demonstrates not only its natural and full belonging to the postmodern cultural horizon, within which it reproduces itself, but also its strong consonance with certain aspects of modernism. So much so that, in a certain sense, it can been seen as a postmodern *recuperation* of modernist elements or, better still, as a genre of the contemporary novel generated by an *interference* between modernist and postmodern aesthetic codes. And if, on the one hand, it is impossible to locate it outside the postmodern literary sphere, it is also true, however, that it is far removed from works by some of the most acclaimed and canonical authors of postmodernist fiction, such as Barth,[10] (Donald) Barthelme, Nabokov, Calvino, and Eco. To better elucidate the question, the entire postmodern cultural system should probably be examined, a cultural system that is much more complex and multifaceted than one might think; but we are still, at present, far away from this undertaking. For the moment, we will conceive of the maximalist novel as the product of a mingling of different aesthetic codes, or rather as an *aesthetically hybrid* genre of the contemporary novel.

The thematic field of the maximalist novel is monopolized by themes of great historical, political, and social relevance. Maximal themes, but, above all, recurrent themes. Their presence is pervasive in each of the seven novels under analysis here, and their importance is considerable in the delineation of a precise albeit desolate thematic geography of contemporary times. A few examples:

1. *Gravity's Rainbow*: war, minorities, ecology, capitalism, the sacred, information, technology, drugs
2. *Infinite Jest*: terrorism, drugs, depression, the virtual, the sacred, information, technology

[10] With the exception of *LETTERS* (Urbana-Champaign: Dalkey Archive Press, 1994), a work which has many points of contact with the maximalist novel.

3. *Underworld*: history, the nuclear, capitalism, urban decay, drugs, the sacred, technology
4. *White Teeth*: history, minorities, drugs, fundamentalism, bioethics, the sacred, technology
5. *The Corrections*: capitalism, bioethics, sexuality, drugs, depression, technology
6. *2666*: war, the holocaust, public ethics, drugs, the sacred, madness, the condition of women, capitalism
7. *2005 dopo Cristo*: terrorism, history, information, technology, drugs, charisma

These are themes which we obviously will not be able to examine one by one in this study. I will limit myself then to the discussion of one of them in particular which exemplifies very well the *ethical commitment* of the maximalist novel. It is a relevant social question present in a transversal way in our texts, and with regard to which the maximalist imagery is highly sensitive: *drugs*.

1 "Chemically Troubled Times": Representing addiction

From the heroin and crime infested Bronx described by DeLillo in *Underworld*, to the recreational consumption of cannabis in *White Teeth*, from the sex and cocaine parties organized by splintered fragments of the Mexican police run wild in *2666*, to the narcotic-induced trips after a Forza Italia convention in *2005 dopo Cristo*, drugs extend their spectral shadow over the thematic field of the maximalist novel.

It is not easy to say what is a drug and what is not, since there is no pharmacological characteristic common to all those substances classified as narcotics missing in legal psychotropic pharmaceuticals.[11] Thus, the attempt has been made to stress the cultural component of the phenomenon, defining it on an attributive basis. For Derrida there are no drugs "in nature"; they are

[11] See Giancarlo Arnao, *Proibizionismo, antiproibizionismo e droghe* (Rome: Stampa alternativa, 1992), 5.

a category created a posteriori by language, in which have been grouped a series of substances very different in composition, effects, history, origins, and administration.[12] Thomas Szasz writes:

> . . . we had no problem with drugs until we quite literally talked ourselves into having one: we declared first this and then that drug "bad" and "dangerous"; gave them nasty names like "dope" and "narcotic"; and passed laws prohibiting their use. The result: our present "problems of drug abuse and drug addiction."[13]

Legal persecution would seem, in fact, to be the heart of the question,[14] but it would perhaps be an excess of relativism to think of drugs as a mere linguistic and cultural formation. In *Viaggi nel regno dell'illogico*, Francesco Ghelli identifies three fundamental requirements to speak of a substance as drugs: (1) psychopharmacological; (2) historico-cultural; and (3) juridico-political.[15] Any narcotic drug has a psychoactive component which on its own would not be enough to define it as such (otherwise, any commercial antidepressant would be a narcotic). Something else is needed indeed. A narcotic drug must be an "other" substance, with its origins in foreign countries and traditions, or else a chemical product, whose use has not been codified by particular social rituals or customs.[16] Whence the collective hostility and stigma, culminating in repressive legislations meant to prevent the distributions and consumption of a substance considered to be inadmissible by the cultural system.

From Thomas De Quincey until the present, drugs are a theme that has always fascinated literature; a theme capable of reflecting like few others the

12 Jacques Derrida, "The Rhetoric of Drugs" [1988], trans. Michael Israel, in Derrida, *Points . . . : Interviews, 1974-1994*, ed. Elisabeth Weber, trans. Peggy Kamuf et al. (Stanford: Stanford University Press, 1995), 229.

13 Thomas Szasz, *Ceremonial Chemistry: The Ritual Persecution of Drugs, Addicts, and Pushers* (Garden City: Anchor Press/Doubleday, 1974), 11.

14 It was only from the first decades in the twentieth century that in Europe and the United States international policies were put in place to curb the commerce and use of opiates. See Antonio Escohotado, *A Brief History of Drugs: From the Stone Age to the Stoned Age* [1996] (Rochester, VT: Park Street Press, 1999); Henri Margaron, *Le stagioni degli dei: Storia medica e sociale delle dorghe* (Milan: Raffaello Cortina, 2001), 265–77.

15 Francesco Ghelli, *Viaggi nel regno dell'illogico: Letteratura e droga da De Quincey ai giorni nostri* (Naples: Liguori, 2003), 8–11.

16 Ibid., 8. See Simonetta Piccone Stella, *Droghe e tossicodipendenza* (Bologna: Il Mulino, 1999), 13–19.

changes in perception that have occurred in the different cultural seasons traversed by literary modernity, and which has found ample attention in the maximalist novel as well. In particular, it occupies a notable place in the symbolic and conceptual configuration of the maximalist novels of Pynchon, Wallace, and Franzen with relation to one of its specific aspects: *addiction.*

In an attempt to reconsider a possible positive role for addiction as a social mechanism on which is based almost all of our interactions with the world, Albert Memmi, in *Le Buveur et l'amoureux*, defines addiction as "a constrictive, more or less accepted, relationship with a being, a thing, a group or an institution, real or ideal, and which involves the satisfaction of a need or of a desire."[17] It is a relationship based on a need and directed toward the attainment of pleasure: "It must be remembered that pleasure is the rule, that it is avidly and directly sought out in most *pourvoyances.* The satisfaction is not external, or added onto the *pourvoyance*, it is part of it."[18] This definition, however, would seem to describe only forms of addiction that do not imply a self-destructive tendency in the addicted subject; a description which comes undone when we enter the realm of excess, of the abuse of an object of *pourvoyance*; when one crosses, that is, the murky threshold of drug addiction.

As Ghelli has shown, literary tales of addiction to narcotic substances have a very specific rhetorical structure, variable in accordance with the historical moment under consideration, which reconfigures significantly the role of pleasure. In an era in which many aspects linked to the consumption of drugs were still not very clear, De Quincey declared that he turned to opium as a remedy for a neuralgic pain which afflicted him. The positive effects obtained were immediate, but when he began to make daily use of it, no longer to procure pleasure, but to find relief from the burning pangs of abstinence, these positive effects soon diminished: "It was not for the purpose of creating pleasure, but of mitigating pain in the severest degree, that I first began to use opium as an article of daily diet."[19] Already with De Quincey, two phases

[17] Albert Memmi, *Le Buveur et l'amoureux: Le Prix de la dependence* (Paris: Arléa, 1998), 29.
[18] Ibid., 25.
[19] Thomas De Quincey, *Confessions of an English Opium-eater* [1822] (Otley-Washington, DC: Woodstock Books, 2002), 14.

are distinguished in the experience of drug addiction: an *ascendant* phase, in which the subject uses the drug to obtain pleasure; and a *descendant* phase, in which the consumption of the drug no longer has anything to do with pleasure but corresponds solely to the dramatic necessities of a drug addiction that has become established in the meantime. Two different moments respectively portrayed very effectively by *Gravity's Rainbow* and *The Corrections* on the one hand, and by *Infinite Jest* on the other.

In Pynchon's novel, the consumption of narcotics is always accompanied by an ambiguous euphoria. The devastating effects of addiction are never taken into consideration. What is represented exclusively, instead, is its ascendant phase, so much so that both the Zone and the remote Kyrgyz steppes are depicted as the parturition of a mind deranged by LSD, incarnating the most forbidden dreams of the drug addict. In the description of the Chicago Bar in Berlin, for instance, almost in a parody of Émile Zola's *magasins de nouveautés*, we are witness to an aestheticizing phantasmagoria of drugs:

> What the notorious Femina is to cigarette-jobbing circles in Berlin, the Chicago is to dopers. . . . Slothrop, Säure, Trudi and Magda come in a back entrance, out of a great massif of ruins and darkness lit only here and there, like the open country. Inside, M. O.s and corpsmen run hither and thither clutching bottles of fluffy white crystalline substances, small pink pills, clear ampoules the size of pureys. Occupation and Reichsmarks ruffle and flap across the room. Some dealers are all chemical enthusiasm, others all business. (*Gravity's Rainbow*, 438)

All of this while the sailor Bodine sings *The Doper's Dream*, a revisiting of the *topos* of the land of plenty in a drug-addicted key:

> Last night I dreamed I was plugged right in
> To a bubblin' hookah so high,
> When all of a sudden some Arab jinni
> Jump up just a-winkin' his eye.
> "I'm here to obey all your wishes," he told me
> As for words I was trying to grope.
> "Good buddy," I cried, "you could surely oblige me

> By turnin' me on to some *dope*!"
> With a bigfat smile he took ahold of my hand,
> And we flew down the sky in a flash,
> And the first thing I saw in the land where he took me
> Was a whole solid mountain of hash!
> All the trees was a-bloomin' with pink 'n' purple pills,
> Whur the Romilar River flowed by,
> To the magic mushrooms as wild as a rainbow,
> So pretty that I wanted to cry. . . . (*Gravity's Rainbow*, 439)

But, in the novel, drugs are not just a substance able to generate fantasies of triumph like Bodine's. Written, if not during, in direct continuity with the psychedelic season experienced in the United States in the 1960s, *Gravity's Rainbow* seems to embrace some of the mysticizing elements traditionally associated with the consumption of hallucinatory drugs,[20] instilling them at times with a political content. On several occasions, drugs are described both as substances able to release us from pain and as substances with a revelatory power. In one of the conversations between Tchitcherine and Wimpe, the latter describes the improbable pharmaceutical research being done by Laszlo Jamf to synthesize, on the basis of morphine, molecules capable of eliminating pain without producing addiction, Oneirine and Methoneirine:

> Results have not been encouraging. We seem up against a dilemma built into Nature, much like the Heisenberg situation. There is nearly complete parallelism between analgesia and addiction. The more pain it takes away, the more we desire it. It appears we can't have one property without the other. . . . Think of what it would mean to find such a drug—to abolish pain rationally, without the extra cost of addiction. . . . We know how to produce real pain. Wars, obviously . . . machines in the factories, industrial accidents, automobiles built to be unsafe, poisons in food, water, and even air—these are quantities tied directly to the economy. We know them, and we can control them. But "addiction"? What do we know of that? Fog and

[20] See Ghelli, *Viaggi nel regno dell'illogico*, 67–85.

> phantoms. . . . we salesmen believe in real pain, real deliverance—we are knights in the service of that Ideal. It must all be real, for the purposes of our market. . . . (Ibid., 415)

By envisioning the utopia of a drug capable of freeing human beings from pain without paying the high price of addiction, Pynchon seems to be attempting to reassess the euphoric and affirmative *élan* toward drugs that had characterized a large part of beat literature in the mold of Kerouac. Drugs become a palliative in this case, an attempt, with varying degrees of success, to sidestep the inability or the impossibility, of playing an active role in history. In another conversation, Tchitcherine and Wimpe discuss a particular class of narcotics, "political narcotics":

> Young Tchitcherine was the one who brought up political narcotics. Opiates of the people.
>
> Wimpe smiled back. An old, old smile to chill even the living fire in Earth's core. "Marxist dialectics? That's *not* an opiate, eh?"
>
> "It's the antidote."
>
> "No." . . . "The basic problem" he proposes, "has always been getting other people to die for you. What's worth enough for a man to give up his life? That's where religion had the edge, for centuries. Religion was always about death. . . . But ever since it became impossible to die for death, we have had a secular version—yours. Die to help History grow to its predestined shape. . . . But look: if History's changes *are* inevitable why not *not* die? Vaslav? If it's going to happen anyway, what does it matter?" (Ibid., 831–2)

Religion as the "opiate of the people" is equated by Wimpe to Marxist dialectics, to the incomprehension and vexation of Tchitcherine, the young official of the Red Army. To avoid arguing, the two prefer to skirt the problem by injecting themselves with a dose of Oneirine:

> Shh, shh. A syringe, a number 26 point. Bloods stifling in the brownwood hotel suite. To chase or worry this argument is to become word-enemies, and neither man really wants to. Oneirine theophosphate is one way around the problem. (Tchitcherine: "You mean *thio*phosphate, don't you?" Thinks *indicating the presence of sulfur. . . .* Wimpe: "I mean *theo*phosphate, Vaslav," *indicating the Presence of God.*) They shoot up. . . .

> For 15 minutes the two of them run screaming all over the suite, staggering around in circles, lined up with the rooms' diagonals. There is in Laszlo Jamf's celebrated molecule a particular twist, the so-called "Pökler singularity" . . . responsible for the hallucinations which are unique to this drug. Not only audiovisual, they touch all senses, equally. And they recur. . . . this recurrence phenomenon is known, in the jargon, as "haunting." Whereas other sorts of hallucinations tend to flow by, related in deep ways that aren't accessible to the casual dopefiend, these Oneirine hauntings show a definite narrative continuity. . . . Often they are so ordinary, so conventional . . . that they are only recognized as hauntings through some radical though plausible violations of possibility: the presence of the dead, journeys by the same route. . . .
>
> About the paranoia often noted under the drug, there is nothing remarkable. Like other sorts of paranoia, it is nothing less than the onset, the leading edge, of the discovery that *everything is connected*. . . . (Ibid., 832–3)

The Oneirine overshadows the political component of the discussion, unveiling the twisted and paranoid Weltanschauung of the drug addict.[21] Oneirine theophosphate: the consumption of mind-altering substances is the antechamber to the revelation of the supreme holistic truth which governs Pynchon's narrative universe,[22] liquidating the real in the hallucinatory opaqueness caused by the so-called "Pökler singularity." The conversation between Tchitcherine and Wimpe concludes with the prospect of a paranoid epiphany, in which drugs act as an objective correlative of the holistic ontology of the maximalist novel. Following a line of thought that starts from Antonin Artaud[23] and Aldous Huxley,[24] and continues to the music of The Doors and to Timothy Leary,[25] drugs are understood, in essence, as a possibility for a

[21] The same paranoia which, according to the findings of experiments published in 1967 by the American psychiatrist John Lilly, likewise seemed to dominate the thoughts and behavior of subjects exposed to LSD treatment. See John C. Lilly, *Programming and Metaprogramming in the Human Biocomputer: Theory and Experiments* [1967] (New York: The Julian Press, 1987), ch. 2.

[22] See Ghelli, *Viaggi nel regno dell'illogico*, 137–44.

[23] Antonin Artaud, "Lettres de Rodez" [1945], in Artaud, *Oeuvres completes*, vol. 9. *Les Tarahumara. Lettres de Rodez* (Paris: Gallimard, 1979).

[24] Aldous Huxley, *The Doors of Perception & Heaven and Hell* [1954] (New York: HarperCollins, 2004).

[25] See Timothy Leary and Ralph Metzner, *The Psychedelic Experience* [1967] (New York: Citadel Press, 1995).

mystical expansion of consciousness, as a heightening of perceptions: a way to reach, a truer awareness of existence. And although, at a certain point, their use is presented as an apolitical diversion, it seems that *Gravity's Rainbow* never manages to completely free itself from the influences of the psychedelic experiences of the 1960s' counterculture. The situation is different, instead, in *The Corrections.*

In Franzen's novel, the mystical component linked to the consumption of narcotics is weaker, and addiction makes its appearance. As in *Gravity's Rainbow*, here too drugs have a liberating power, but without hiding any longer their dark side, addiction. Nevertheless, the euphoric moment of the drug habit remains in the foreground, that moment in which the benefits obtained through the use of drugs appear vastly superior to their side effect, addiction. That is to say, we are still in the ascendant phase of drug dependency.

It is Melissa who for the first time offers Aslan, in its Mexican A variant, to Chip:

> "Take this," she told him, closing the door.
>
> "This is? Some kind of Ecstasy?"
>
> "No. Mexican A."
>
> Chip felt culturally anxious. Not long ago, there had been no drugs he hadn't heard of. "What does it do?"
>
> "Nothing and everything," she said, swallowing one herself. "You'll see."
>
> "How much do I owe you for this?"
>
> "Never mind that."
>
> For a while the drug did seem, as promised, to do nothing. But on the industrial outskirts of Norwich, still two or three hours from the Cape, he turned down the trip hop that Melissa was playing on his stereo and said, "We have to stop immediately and fuck."
>
> She laughed. "I guess *so*."
>
> "Why don't I pull over," he said.
>
> She laughed again. "No, let's find a room." (*The Corrections*, 63–4)

After four days of intense sex because of the sexual hyperarousal caused by the Mexican A and having forgotten to take a final caplet before going to sleep,

Chip wakes up on Thanksgiving morning disintoxicated and prey to a mortal shame for having brutalized Melissa:

> . . . he was plunged into shame and self-consciousness. He couldn't bear to stay in bed a moment longer. . . . His problem consisted of a burning wish not to have done the things he'd done. And his body, its chemistry, had a clear, a distinctive understanding of what he had to do to make this burning wish go away. He had to swallow another Mexican A. (Ibid., 66)

Mortified, he rummages through Melissa's things looking for the drug, knowing that only Mexican A could have relieved his pain. The golden pills are over, however, and Chip cannot do anything but submit, without any psychedelic shield, to Melissa's humiliating half confession concerning his meager skills as a lover:

> "I never asked you to get that drug," he said.
>
> "Not in so many words," she said.
>
> "What do you mean by that?"
>
> "Well, a fat lot of fun we were going to have without it."
>
> Chip didn't ask her to explain. He was afraid she meant he'd been a lousy, anxious lover until he took Mexican A. He had, of course, been a lousy, anxious lover; but he'd allowed himself to hope she hadn't noticed. Under the weight of this fresh shame, and with no drug left in the room to alleviate it, he bowed his head and pressed his hands into his face. (Ibid., 69)

A key characteristic of Aslan is that it eliminates shame in whoever takes it. Plagued by insomnia, during her cruise with her husband, Enid turns to the ship's doctor for something to help her sleep. And Dr Hibbard, a grotesque personage between a pusher and a pharmaceutical representative, suggests Aslan, the Cruiser version:

> ". . . The drug exerts a remarkable blocking effect on 'deep' or 'morbid' shame." . . . "This interests you?" he said. "I have your full attention?"
>
> Enid lowered her eyes and wondered if people ever died of sleep loss. Taking her silence for assent, Hibbard continued: ". . . What's happening on

the molecular level, Edna, when you drink those martinis, is that the ethanol interferes with the reception of excess Factor 28A, i.e., the 'deep' or 'morbid' shame factor. But the 28A is not metabolized or properly reabsorbed at the receptor site. . . . So when the ethanol wears off, the receptor is *flooded* with 28A. . . . Aslan's effect on the chemistry of shame is entirely different from a martini's. We're talking complete annihilation of the 28A molecules. Aslan's a fierce predator." (Ibid., 366)

From this moment on, Enid will take Aslan habitually, with the desired effects, but when her supply from the cruise is exhausted, she goes into withdrawal, eventually begging a friend to get some for her in Europe, since in the United States Aslan was not yet available commercially. When the effect of the Aslan ceases, Enid, like Chip, also plunges back into shame. Tormented by the idea of what the other participants on the cruise must have thought after her husband's fall from the ship, Enid, in her insomnia, calls to mind the image of the miraculous pills: "Night after night she lay awake, suffered shame, and pictured the golden caplets. She was ashamed of lusting for these caplets, but she was also convinced that only they could bring relief" (Ibid., 538).

Enid is subject to a fascination for the narcotic substance as a thing, to its deadly sex appeal, trapped in the mechanism of the metaphysical transfiguration of commodity. In this regard, and against the backdrop of the postmodern sexualization of the inorganic theorized by Perniola, Chip expresses himself explicitly: "What made drugs perpetually so sexy was the opportunity to be other. Years after he'd figured out that pot only made him paranoid and sleepless, he still got hard-ons at the thought of smoking it. Still lusted for that jailbreak" (Ibid., 134).

Drugs are sexy because they enable one to become someone else. Drugs are sexy because they allow Enid to escape from the middle-class dreariness of her life with Alfred and Chip from his repeated failures in love and work. In the depersonalizing power of drugs, Enid finds relief from her shame of not being as rich as she would like and of not having a successful husband like those of her friends, while Chip tries to lift himself beyond his impotence and beyond his creative paralysis when facing a screenplay that he has revised over and over again. Aslan seems then to offer itself as a versatile remedy for every sort of bourgeois ailment: a drug with a surefire liberating, if not messianic, potency. It takes its name in fact from the "great benign Lion" (Ibid., 360) in the saga of Narnia. In the description of the passionate reading of *The Chronicles of Narnia: Prince Caspian* by Gary and Caroline's son Jonah, we are told:

> Caroline did not entirely approve of Narnia—C. S. Lewis was a known Catholic propagandist, and the Narnian hero, Aslan, was a furry, four-pawed Christ figure—but Gary had enjoyed reading *The Lion, the Witch and the Wardrobe* as a boy, and he had not, it was safe to say, grown up to be a religious nut. (In fact he was a strict materialist.) (Ibid., 161)

Aslan, a benign Christ-like reincarnation, who, having sacrificed himself for the good of his people and having then arisen to save Narnia from the wicked White Witch, gives his own name to the drug Chip and Enid love passionately, thereby underscoring its grotesque salvific nature. And even if there is an overt irony in presenting Aslan as a panacea for all the small and petty dramas of the American middle class, drugs retain, nonetheless, a consolatory aspect in *The Corrections*. Their effectiveness seem to justify, in the short run, the price of addiction, a cost that not even Franzen is prepared to take all too seriously. Who, instead, has braved the atrocious descent into the hell of drug addiction is Wallace, realizing perhaps the darkest and most tortured portrayal ever of American society at the end of the twentieth century.

If up until this moment the consumption of drugs was directed toward the attainment of a holistic insight or at the overcoming of a bourgeois unease with a marked stress on the euphoric and liberating component of the psychedelic experience, in *Infinite Jest* things change radically. While in *The Corrections*, as was already the case in De Quincey, the use of Aslan was due to the need to overcome a painful condition—the shame of impotence (Chip) and the embarrassment at having a husband terminally ill with Parkinson's disease (Enid)—in Wallace's novel, the use of drugs is an end in itself, without a purpose. We enter into the descendant stage of addiction, in which the subject is forced to turn to substances to counter withdrawal; the stage, that is, in which the subject is now a drug addict. The departure point changes: at the base of the dependency there is no longer a need, or a mystical *élan*, but rather *anhedonia*, a neutral state devoid of emotions in which the subject is.

In his day, William Burroughs, had already pointed out the gratuitous nature of substance abuse:

> You become a narcotics addict because you do not have strong motivations in any other directions. . . . They [most addicts] do not start using drugs for any reason they can remember. They just drift along until they get hooked. . . . You don't decide to be an addict.[26]

But anhedonia is something more than a lack of motivation. It is an emotional incapacity, a *discomfort*—a word that recurs obsessively in all of Wallace's work—an icy intellectual prison. The character in *Infinite Jest* who is oppressed more than anyone else by this condition is Hal, a smart 17-year-old hooked on marijuana, whose reflections on anhedonia transcend the theme of drug addiction in a strict sense to envelop the world of art and, in particular, American fiction at the turn of the century, in an unrelenting recognition of the motivational void into which the younger generations have fallen:

> It's of some interest that the lively arts of the millennial U.S.A. treat anhedonia and internal emptiness as hip and cool. It's maybe the vestiges of the Romantic glorification of *Weltschmerz*, which means world-weariness or hip ennui. . . . The U.S. arts are our guide to inclusion. A how-to. We are shown how to fashion masks of ennui and jaded irony at a young age where the face is fictile enough to assume the shape of whatever it wears. And then it's stuck there, the weary cynicism that saves us from gooey sentiment and unsophisticated naïveté. Sentiment equals naïveté on this continent (at least since the Reconfiguration). . . . Hal, who's empty but not dumb, theorizes privately that what passes for hip cynical transcendence of sentiment is really some kind of fear of being really human, since to be really human (at least as he conceptualizes it) is probably to be unavoidably sentimental and naïve and goo-prone and generally pathetic, is to be in some basic interior way forever infantile, some sort of not-quite-right-looking infant dragging itself anaclitically around the map, with big wet eyes and froggy-soft skin, huge skull, gooey drool. One of the really American things about Hal, probably, is the way he despises what it is he's really lonely for: this hideous internal self, incontinent of sentiment and need, that pules and writhes just under the hip empty mask, anhedonia. (*Infinite Jest*, 694–5)

[26] William S. Burroughs, *Junky* [1952] (Harmondsworth: Penguin, 1977), xv.

Anhedonia is a mask that hides the fear or the impossibility of being truly human. A grand metaphor for American post-metafictional narrative; a metaphor for the emotional and creative season following the era in which it was proclaimed that one could no longer speak "innocently,"[27] when empty intellectual poses were assumed that feebly concealed the greatest intellectual fear of a certain type of postmodernism: ridiculousness.

So then, the question is not why Hal, a rich and extremely gifted youth like so many of his companions at the Enfield Tennis Academy who are addicted to a wide array of substances, abuses marijuana, but why he should *not* do so. Anhedonia deadens the emotional component of the experience of addiction, rendering it equal to any other. The world of anhedonia is undifferentiated, qualitatively neutral, and taking drugs corresponds precisely to the profound discomfort one undergoes in such circumstances. A far-reaching discomfort, which reveals itself in all of its drama at the moment of the onset of addiction, and which propels the addict from dose to dose, driven by a boundless yearning; a yearning in which there no longer remains even the promise of pleasure.[28]

The absence of pleasure is a recurring theme in the narrative of addiction in *Infinite Jest*. In the description of the spasmodic wait by the publicist Ken Erdedy for the delivery of two hundred grams of marijuana, we read:

> He began to grow disgusted with himself for waiting so anxiously for the promised arrival of something that had stopped being fun anyway. He didn't even know why he liked it anymore. . . . He didn't even know what its draw was anymore. He couldn't even be around anyone else if he'd smoked marijuana that same day, it made him so self-conscious. And the dope often gave him a painful case of pleurisy if he smoked it for more than two straight days of heavy continuous smoking in front of the Inter-Lace viewer in his bedroom. . . . He pulled his necktie down smooth while he gathered his intellect, will, self-knowledge, and conviction and determined that when this latest woman came as she surely would this would simply be his very last marijuana debauch. (*Infinite Jest*, 21–2)

[27] Umberto Eco, *Postscript to the Name of the Rose* [1983], trans. William Weaver (San Diego-New York-London: Harcourt Brace Jovanovich, 1984), 67.
[28] See Ghelli, *Viaggi nel regno dell'illogico*, 212–14.

The extraneousness of pleasure in a stage of advanced addiction[29] has been underscored not just by Wallace. As we have already recalled, De Quincy too had spoken of his daily need for opium to prevent the onset of severe crises of withdrawal. In De Quincey, the course of addiction can be schematized into the elementary phenomenological chain pain-pleasure-pain, in which, through drugs, one escapes from a situation of suffering and attains an intense pleasure which then gives way to the pain of withdrawal. In Wallace, on the other hand, one starts with an initial anhedonia which, thanks to drugs, is followed by a momentary relief from "Discomfort"; a relief which, however, completely disappears very quickly, giving way to an even greater discomfort and to the tremendous sufferings of drug addiction, in accordance with the uncompromising progression anhedonia (discomfort)-relief-greater discomfort-pain.

In the quarter of a century separating *Gravity's Rainbow* from *Infinite Jest*, the perception of the psychedelic experience has changed, for if, in the 1950s and 1960s, the latter was connoted by a strong novelty, at the end of the century it seems, instead, to have completely exhausted its attraction, inaugurating an always-identical of drugs which has ended up turning it into a common experience.[30] Whence the search by Pemulis, Hal, and their friends for ever more sophisticated and dangerous drugs such as the devastating and unobtainable Dmz, the most potent synthetic hallucinogen ever created by man. Ghelli writes:

> The idea of drugs falls away [in the postmodern] as an experience of novelty, a perceptive and cognitive shock, a radical alteration of the continuity of experience. But what also seems to exhaust itself is the association between drugs and the individual productivity of the imagination, the idea that they can stimulate and increase the potentiality of the subject.[31]

However, as the examples of *Gravity's Rainbow* and *The Corrections* demonstrate, more than speaking of a complete decline of the traditional psychedelic

[29] An extraneousness theorized by Perniola also in reference to the neutral sexuality of the "thing that feels." See Perniola, *The Sex Appeal of the Inorganic*, 132–41.

[30] See Theodor W. Adorno, *Minima Moralia: Reflections from Damaged Life* [1951], trans. E. F. N. Jephcott (London-New York: Verso, 1978), 235.

[31] Ghelli, *Viaggi nel regno dell'illogico*, 240.

experience in the postmodern because of a sort of scattered psychedelia,[32] we might conceive of it rather as a weakening, as a nongeneralized tendency in the direction of its normalization, as an experience based on a commodity which, at bottom, is identical to all others; a commodity that has by now lost its characteristic of newness and, hence, in accordance with Benjamin, its sex appeal.[33]

The icy abode of anhendonia is not sufficiently large enough, however, to hold the innumerable forms of addiction contemplated in *Infinite Jest*. The abuse of narcotic substances is often closely tied to true illnesses such as depression; a malady which, even if kept separate by Wallace from anhedonia, of which the latter nevertheless is generally a symptom, is associated with addiction in dysphoric terms:

> Hal isn't old enough yet to know that this is because numb emptiness isn't the worst kind of depression. That dead-eyed anhedonia is but a remora on the ventral flank of the true predator, the Great White Shark of pain. Authorities term this condition *clinical depression* or *involutional depression* or *unipolar dysphoria*. . . . It goes by many names . . . but Kate Gompert, down in the trenches with the thing itself, knows it simply as *It*.
>
> *It* is a level of psychic pain wholly incompatible with human life as we know it. *It* is a sense of radical and thoroughgoing evil not just as a feature but as the essence of conscious existence. *It* is a sense of poisoning that pervades the self at the self's most elementary levels. *It* is a nausea of the cells and soul. . . . *Its* emotional character, the feeling Gompert describes It as, is probably mostly indescribable except as a sort of double bind in which any/all of the alternatives we associate with human agency—sitting or standing, doing or resting, speaking or keeping silent, living or dying—are not just unpleasant but literally horrible. (*Infinite Jest*, 695–6)

Even if the initial condition of departure is not constituted by a neutral state such as anhedonia, but by a depressive one, drug addiction always appears as

32 Ibid., 259–64.

33 "Newness is a quality independent of the use value of the commodity. It is the origin of the illusory appearance that belongs inalienably to images produced by the collective unconscious. It is the quintessence of that false consciousness whose indefatigable agent is fashion. The semblance of the new is reflected, like one mirror in another, in the semblance of the ever recurrent. The product of this reflection is the phantasmagoria of 'cultural history,' in which the bourgeoisie enjoys its false consciousness to the full." Benjamin, "Paris, the Capital of the Nineteenth Century," 11.

an experience devoid of any attraction or promise of happiness; indeed, as a condition in which both Hal's discomfort and Kate's *It* reveal their tremendous concreteness and omnipotence.

In the "chemically troubled" times narrated by Wallace in *Infinite Jest* (151), addiction assumes its supreme form in the fatal entertainment created by James Incandenza. It is a film with a mysterious content,[34] but so engrossing that whoever watches it cannot stop doing so, in an infinite repetition compulsion that leads to death by starvation and dehydration in front of the teleputer. Via a new and unsettling reworking of the longstanding *topos* of the "killing vision"—from the myths of Actaeon, Medusa, Narcissus, Orpheus, Pentheus, and Semele, including Michael Powell's *Peeping Tom*, David Cronenberg's *Videodrome*, Alejandro Amenábar's *Tesis*, Hideo Nakata's *The Ring* and *The Ring 2* (the sequel of Verbinski's *The Ring*), Norio Tsuruta's *Ring 0: Birthday*, Gore Verbinski's *The Ring*, Shinya Tsukamoto's *A Snake of June*, Jonathan Liebesman's *Darkness Falls*, Werner Herzog's documentary film *The White Diamond*,[35] Takashi Shimizu's *Marebito*, John Carpenter's *Cigarette Burns*, and Scott Derrickson's *Sinister*—Wallace does partially reintegrate pleasure into addiction, but always under the sign of death and self-destruction. In fact, it is precisely the immense pleasure generated by viewing *Infinite Jest* that constitutes the lethal component of the entertainment, which is the reason why the Wheelchair Assassins are constantly trying to obtain the master cartridge so that they can make an indefinite number of copies to exterminate the American people. The deep-seated conviction of the A. F. R. is in fact that Americans will not have the moral strength to resist the "recreational" power of *Infinite Jest*. In the lengthy conversation between Marathe and Steeply on the night of 30 April–1 May of the YDAU we read:

> "'Again you pass over what is important. Why B.S.S. cannot understand us. You cannot kill what is already dead.'
>
> 'Just you wait and see if we're dead, paisano.'

[34] For convincing conjectures as to the content of the film *Infinite Jest*, see Boswell, *Understanding David Foster Wallace*, 126–34.

[35] See Stefano Ercolino, "The Killing Vision: David Foster Wallace's *Infinite Jest*," in *Fictional Cinema: How Literature Describes Imaginary Films*, eds. Ercolino et al. (Göttingen: Vandenhoeck and Ruprecht Unipress, 2014), forthcoming.

> Marathe made a gesture as if striking his own head. 'Again passing over the important. This appetite to choose death by pleasure if it is available to choose—this *appetite* of your people unable to choose appetites, *this* is the death. What you call the death, the collapsing: this will be the formality only. Do you not see?'" (*Infinite Jest*, 319)

Marathe maintains that Americans will not survive the terrible entertainment because they lack any sense of responsibility and because they are incapable of making sacrifices, governed as they are by the most superficial and infantile instincts, victims of the myth of happiness at all costs, of happiness here and now:

> "'Ah, yes, but then you say: No?' Steeply said. 'No? you say, not children? You say: What is the difference, please, if you make a recorded pleasure so entertaining and diverting it is lethal to persons you find a Copy-Capable copy and copy it and disseminate it for us to choose to see or turn off, and if we cannot choose to resist it, the pleasure, and cannot choose instead to live? You say what your Fortier believes, that we *are* children, not human adults like the noble Québecers, we are children, bullies but still children inside, and will kill ourselves for you if you put the candy within the arms' reach.'" (*Infinite Jest*, 321)

A tendency seems, then, to materialize in the new and refined addiction generated by *Infinite Jest*, which Burroughs had already pointed to in his day,[36] that of equalizing drugs and image, in the direction of an extrinsication of the psychedelic experience.[37] The *drug-image* is thus transformed into an instrument for fueling the apocalyptic fantasies that envelop the maximalist novel and *Infinite Jest* in particular, hypostatizing in negative the enormous conditioning power images hold in our lives. Ghelli:

> . . . the metaphor of the drug-image implies a new conception of the subject as well as of drugs. Drugs are no longer (an aid to) imagination but already the image itself, no longer linked to a production, but already a finished product. The movement is no longer from the internal to the external, from interiority to expression, it proceeds instead from the external to the internal,

[36] "Since junk *is* the image the effects of junk can easily be produced and concentrated in a sound and image track." William S. Burroughs, *Nova Express* [1964] (New York: Grove Press, 1992), 63.

[37] See Ghelli, *Viaggi nel regno dell'illogico*, 252–8.

> toward a psyche that is a *tabula rasa* (or almost). The subject, in short, is not a fullness but an emptiness, not an origin but a target.[38]

The addicted subject is revealed then to be a void that the drug-image is free to destroy because nothing is left to oppose it; nothing which enables one to look beyond the categorical imperative of pleasure that seems to dominate the ethical dimension of that sad portion of the West described by Wallace.

[38] Ghelli, *Viaggi nel regno dell'illogico*, 256.

10

Hybrid Realism

The twentieth century was continually traversed by strong antirealist impulses. From the historical avant-gardes to the neo-avant-gardes, from structuralism to post-structuralism, realism was variously contested as illusion, ideology, or convention.[1] Within the postmodern cultural horizon, there emerged a revival of romance, from J. R. R. Tolkien to John Fowles, from Antonia Byatt to David Lodge, and Jonathan Coe.[2] While from the South America of Gabriel García Marquéz and Julio Cortázar to the India of Salman Rushdie, there took place the prodigious irruption of magical realism into the Western literary canon. Federico Bertoni writes:

> Anti-referential fury, linguistic extremism, new avant-gardes, postmodern irony, meta-literary drift, the revival of romance and magical realism, *real-maravilloso* or the neo-fantastic: very different artistic tendencies, founded on extremely heterogeneous epistemological and cultural assumptions, but which seem allied nevertheless in the struggle against a common enemy, and in a tension towards the same objective: to finally escape from the squalid "prison-house of realism."[3]

To imagine, however, the second half of the twentieth century or, worse still, the entire century as a wholly antirealist era is surely misleading, all the more because in American fiction, for instance, over the last 30 years, there have been various attempts, some more convincing than others, to link back to the most illustrious tradition of the North American realist novel, from the

1 Federico Bertoni, *Realismo e letteratura: Una storia possibile* (Turin: Einaudi, 2007), 299–307.
2 Diane Elam, *Romancing the Postmodern* (London: Routledge, 1992), 1–25.
3 Bertoni, *Realismo e letteratura*, 305–6.

"New Realism" discussed by Frederick Karl,[4] to the "catatonic realism" and "midfiction" theorized by Alan Wilde.[5] Nevertheless, a conspicuous tendency aiming in the direction of an elimination of the referential dimension of the literary word is certainly identifiable within the postmodern literary system. And it is precisely this antireferential tendency, proper to a consistent portion of the narrative of the last decades, which we will take as our starting point in order to understand the particular form that realism assumes in the maximalist novel.

Taking DeLillo's *Underworld* as an example of literary realism, and pointing to it as a possible way out from the epistemological uncertainties of postmodernism, Bertoni draws the maximalist novel directly into the debate.[6] After having resisted the temptation to offer yet another dogmatic and inevitably partial definition of realism, Bertoni proposes a persuasive model articulated on the basis of four distinct levels, (1) thematic-referential, (2) formal-stylistic, (3) semiotic, and (4) cognitive, by means of which it would be possible to analyze any type of realist writing,[7] and he tries to verify its efficaciousness on a sample text, *Underworld*, a text, which according to Bertoni, "more than most manages to operate in an integral way across the four levels of mimesis."[8] Although Bertoni praises DeLillo's intersemiotic writing as an

[4] Karl refers to the narrative of authors such as Richard Ford, Saul Bellow, Ethan Canin, Cynthia Ozick, Robert Stone, Kathy Acker, Russell Banks, Joyce Carol Oates, Nicholson Baker, Peter Matthiessen, and Annie Proulx in terms of "New Realism," identifying the immediate historico-literary backdrop of the latter in the works of Theodore Dreiser, Sinclair Lewis, Richard Wright, Edith Wharton, and Ernest Hemingway. For "New Realism," he intends a type of "expanded" realism that does not spurn soft forms of linguistic experimentalism, or incursions into the fantastic. Beyond the problem of how much this form of realism can truly be called new—a problem which Karl himself poses—various doubts remain concerning the very hypothesis of its being a tendency of some sort. The idea, for instance, that "New Realism" opens up a broader space for linguistic experimentalism as opposed to what occurs in the traditional realist novel smacks of the prejudice that there exists a natural incompatibility between realism and experimentalism. See Karl, *American Fictions: 1980-2000*, 226–68.

[5] Alan Wilde speaks of "midfiction" primarily in reference to writers such as Max Apple, Thomas Berger, Donald Barthelme, Joan Didion, Ann Beattie, and Raymond Carver; writers who, according to Wilde, can be located in an intermediary position between an experimentalism with new expressive means and a rootedness in a certain "moribund humanism." In this way, they would distinguish themselves from more radical postmodernist writers, by remaining anchored, in a certain sense, to a traditional literary realism, even if in their case it would be a "catatonic" realism. See Alan Wilde, *Middle Grounds: Studies in Contemporary American Fiction* (Philadelphia: University of Pennsylvania Press, 1987).

[6] Bertoni, *Realismo e letteratura*, 318–66.

[7] Ibid., 315–16.

[8] Ibid., 316.

example of transmedial realism, well-adapted to the representation of the multiplicity of the aesthetic and perceptive experiences of the contemporary world,[9] it is not simple to reconcile such a transmedial opening with the revindication of a new realist impulse and a renewed idea of literature—which are instances that, to say the least, can be certainly shared—in the name of the modeling and heuristic power of the word. Bertoni maintains, indeed, that literature will never renounce realism:

> Because this force will never be able to fully exhaust itself, at least as long as there will be the need for explanations of the world and of those things—few but irreplaceable—that only literature can seek out and teach. In a historical phase of the overwhelming invasion of the media, informational hypertrophy, the extreme power of the image, ideological ambiguity and triumphant irrationalism, it is still the proper moment—perhaps more than ever—to launch the challenge to the labyrinth, to revindicate a new realist impulse and an idea of literature founded on the indispensable power of the word as an instrument for constructing and interpreting the world.[10]

A conviction that seems to reveal somehow a logocentrism that we have seen put into question by the maximalist novel, under the sign of the intrinsic transmedial nature of artistic languages. Like all maximalist novelists, DeLillo is deeply fascinated by images, and, even if he maintains an ambivalent relationship with them between attraction and repulsion—a fact attested to, for example, by Edgar Hoover's morbid obsession with Bruegel's *The Triumph of Death*—we are well aware of the extent to which visuality permeates his work, playing a decisive role both in the production of meaning and in suggesting pictorial *mises en abyme* (*Kinderspielen*) for the perspective strategies enacted in the novel.

A significant indicator of the intersemiotic openness of DeLillo's novel and of the systematic transmedial hybridization practiced by the maximalist novel is constituted by the word "Peace" which appears on a computer screen after a virtual nuclear apocalypse. A word which Bertoni rightly aligns to the celebrated endings of two of the cornerstones of literary modernism: the "Yes"

[9] Ibid., 345. See Stefania Consonni, "Disegni e realtà: Le finzioni di Don DeLillo," *Paragrafo* 1 (2006): 9–30.

[10] Bertoni, *Realismo e letteratura*, 306–7.

of *Ulysses* and the "Shantih shantih shantih" of *The Waste Land*. The ending of *Underworld* might not represent, however, "a last modernist gasp," at least not in the sense that DeLillo himself referred to it in expressing his reservations toward those who defined his novel as postmodern.[11] The conclusion of *Underworld* does refer back, in an almost automatic way, to the masterpieces of Joyce and Eliot, yes, but as an attempt, perhaps, to overcome their logocentrism, in the direction, that is, of a hybrid view of literature, arising from the systematic contaminations between different media in the postmodern aesthetic sphere. After all, the word "Peace" is displayed by a computer screen. But let us take a step forward.

Underworld's realism cannot be included within the framework of traditional realist writings. In the maximalist novel, we find ourselves face-to-face with a particular form of realism, one which is heavily conditioned by the powerful antireferential and tautological friction of the artistic act running throughout the entire system of the arts in the twentieth century, which we will call *hybrid realism*.

James Wood has coined the term "hysterical realism" to describe the grand, ambitious novels written by authors such as Pynchon, DeLillo, Rushdie, Wallace, and Smith. The deep-rooted grammar of this genre, according to Wood, consists in an unrestrained "storytelling," the fundamental goal of which is to guarantee "the pursuit of vitality at all costs":

> The big contemporary novel is a perpetual-motion machine that appears to have been embarrassed into velocity. It seems to want to abolish stillness, as if ashamed of silence. Stories and substories sprout on every page, and these novels continually flourish their glamorous congestion. Inseparable from this culture of permanent storytelling is the pursuit of vitality at all costs.[12]

In these novels we find:

> . . . a nun called Sister Edgar who is obsessed with germs and who may be a reincarnation of J. Edgar Hoover, and a conceptual artist who is painting retired B-52 bombers in the New Mexican desert (DeLillo); a terrorist group

11 See Richard Williams, "Everything under the Bomb," *The Guardian*, 10 January 1998.
12 Wood, *The Irresponsible Self*, 178.

> devoted to the liberation of Quebec called the Wheelchair Assassins, and a film so compelling that anyone who sees it dies (Wallace). And Zadie Smith's novel features, among other things: a terrorist Islamic group based in North London with a silly acronym (KEVIN), an animal rights group called FATE, a Jewish scientist who is genetically engineering a mouse, a woman born during an earthquake in Kingston, Jamaica, in 1907, a group of Jehovah's Witnesses who think that the world is ending on December 31, 1992, and twins, one in Bangladesh and one in London, who both break their noses at about the same time.[13]

And the list could go on: an American army lieutenant, Tyron Slothrop, able with the erection of his penis to predict the exact spot in London where the V-2 rockets launched by the Germans will fall (Pynchon); a Lithuanian political party with the absurd acronym VIPPPAKJRIINPB17, originator of the for-profit nation-state (Franzen); a desecrator of churches, called the "Demon Penitent" and endowed with a bladder of abnormal dimensions (Bolaño); a trendy television host, Quentin Savona, who engages in lengthy mental conversations with an imaginary audience (Babette Factory).

In all of the above cases, we are not dealing with impossible stories, stories that is, which could never come true in the real world, because none of them violates any law of physics. What seems to be lacking instead are the "laws of persuasion":

> This is what Aristotle means when he says that in storytelling "a convincing impossibility" (a man levitating, say) is always preferable to "an unconvincing possibility" (say, the possibility that a fundamentalist group in London would continue to call itself KEVIN). And what above all makes these stories unconvincing is their very profusion, their relatedness. One cult is convincing; three are not.[14]

To a greater or lesser degree, many of the stories and characters we encounter in maximalist novels are implausible, grotesque, and bordering on the ridiculous. According to Wood, the storytelling of hysterical realism is a cover for a rampant "lack of humanity," characteristic of much Anglo-American literature of the

[13] Ibid., 179.
[14] Ibid., 180–1.

last decades, due to a progressive marginalization of the traditional character in favor of a new and inhuman centrality acquired by information:

> . . . some of the more impressive novelistic minds of our age do not think that language and the representation of consciousness are the novelist's quarries anymore. Information has become the new character. It is this, and the use made of Dickens, that connects DeLillo and the reportorial Tom Wolfe, despite the literary distinction of the former and the cinematic vulgarity of the latter.[15]

Arguing against a statement made by Zadie Smith in an interview in which she maintained that the task of the writer was not to speak of the feelings of an individual regarding something or someone, but rather to show "how the world works,"[16] and branding the "social news" that abounds in Franzen's *The Corrections* and in the novels of "hysterical realists" in general as useless and lacking in any aesthetic merit whatsoever,[17] Wood has criticized the obsession with information typical of hysterical realism, an obsession which has emptied many products of contemporary fiction of humanity, rendering their stories "inhuman" and their characters "unconvincing."[18]

Wood is not entirely wrong in lamenting a generic decline of the human in a certain type of contemporary literature, but he is probably mistaken in ascribing its cause to the centrality that information has acquired in that literature. The realism of novels such as *Gravity's Rainbow*, *Infinite Jest*, *Underworld*, *White Teeth*, *The Corrections*, *2666*, and *2005 dopo Cristo* is heavily influenced by the antirealist impulse that has characterized a large part of twentieth-century literature, and which has undergone a fundamental development in the postmodern aesthetic realm. And it is to this impulse that we might ascribe the abundance of "inhuman" and "non-convincing" stories in maximalist novels; an impulse, however, which has certainly not extinguished important aspects of maximalist literary representation that take recourse to the finest traditions of realism. From the social frescos of *Underworld*, *White Teeth*, and

15 Ibid., 185.

16 Quoted in Wood, *The Irresponsible Self*, 186. See James Wood, "Tell Me How Does It Feel?," *The Guardian*, 6 October 2001, and Zadie Smith's response, "This is How It Feels To Me," *The Guardian*, 13 October 2001.

17 Wood, *The Irresponsible Self*, 209.

18 Ibid., 180–3.

2005 dopo Cristo, to the subtle psychological realism of *Infinite Jest*; from the novel of manners of *The Corrections*, to the historical narratives of *Gravity's Rainbow* and *2666*: the maximalist novel contemplates the quasi-totality of the configurations assumed by realism in literature over nearly two centuries of history. The intertwining of realism and antirealism gives life to what we could call a *hybrid* realism, a particular fictional dimension of the representation in which mimesis and anti-mimesis are inextricably fused. This condition is confirmed also at the level of the contaminations between genres, with the co-presence in the diegesis of types of writing developed at the margins of reportage and the novel, such as the nonfiction novel, and types of writing which instead reinvent fiction in that ambiguity between the real and the fantastic, typical of magical realism[19]—a supreme and prodigious synthesis realized by Roberto Bolaño in *2666*.

Realism and postmodern, in fact, are not incompatible.[20] If Walker Evans and James Agee's photographical book *Let Us Now Praise Famous Men* had already elicited comments, and rightfully, of "postmodern realism,"[21] maximalist novels reveal a simultaneous and complex rethinking of both the limits and the potentialities of realist representation in the attempt to arrive at hybrid forms of realism in which the immediate referentiality of the word is partially sacrificed for the sake of a greater critical impact on the readers' conscience, not to mention for the sake of an aesthetic refoundation of mimesis itself. The maximalist author who more than any other has demonstrated awareness of this issue is David Foster Wallace, who, in *Infinite Jest*, elaborates a very personal mimetic theory, baptized as *radical realism*.

After the shootout at the Ennet House, the wraith of James Incandenza appears to Don Gately, immobilized in his hospital bed, inflicting irritating

19 Ato Quayson, "Fecundities of the Unexpected: Magical Realism, Narrative, and History [2002]," in *The Novel*, ed. Moretti, vol. I, 728.

20 Raffaele Donnarumma is of a contrary opinion, and in the return of a certain interest in the real together with a revival of realist types of writing he has seen an attempt to break away from the postmodern. See Raffaele Donnarumma, "Nuovi realismi e persistenze postmoderne: Narratori italiani di oggi," *Allegoria* XX, 57 (2008): 26–54. More nuanced instead is Gianluigi Simonetti's position in "I nuovi assetti della narrativa italiana (1996-2006)," *Allegoria* XX, 57 (2008): 95–136.

21 See T. V. Reed, "Unimagined Experience and the Fiction of the Real: Postmodernist Realism in *Let Us Now Praise Famous Men*," *Representations* 24 (1988): 156–76; Idem, *Fifteen Jugglers, Five Believers: Literary Politics and the Poetics of American Social Movements* (Berkeley-Los Angeles: University of California Press, 1992), 18–21. See also Fusillo, *Estetica della letteratura*, 104.

monologues on him, among which a long reflection on cinematographic realism:

> And the wraith on the heart monitor looks pensively down at Gately from upside-down and asks does Gately remember the myriad thespian extras on for example his beloved "Cheers!," not the center-stage Sam and Carla and Nom, but the nameless patrons always at tables, filling out the bar's crowd, concessions to realism, always relegated to back- and foreground; and always having utterly silent conversations: their faces would animate and mouths move realistically, but without sound; only the name-stars at the bar itself could audibilize. The wraith says these fractional actors, human scenery, could be seen (but not heard) in most pieces of filmed entertainment. (*Infinite Jest*, 834)

Crowds of characters, who can "be seen, but not heard." The wraith continues:

> The wraith says that he himself, the wraith, when animate, had dabbled in filmed entertainments, as in making them, cartridges, for Gately's info to either believe or not, and but in the entertainments the wraith himself made, he says he goddamn bloody well made sure that either the whole entertainment was silent or else if it wasn't silent that you could bloody well hear every single performer's voice, no matter how far out on the cinematographic or narrative periphery they were; and that it wasn't just the self-conscious overlapping dialogue of a poseur like Schwulst or Altman, i.e. it wasn't just the crafted imitation of aural chaos: it was real life's real egalitarian babble of figurantless crowds, of the animate world's real agora, the babble of crowds every member of which was the central and articulate protagonist of his own entertainment. (Ibid., 835–6)

This is an effective *mise en abyme* of the compositional procedures and of the guiding mimetic criterion adopted by Wallace in *Infinite Jest*. The choral extremism of the entertainments created by James leads to a new "aural realism": an egalitarian realism, more democratic than the usual one in which the mass of figurants was silenced to foreground the protagonists. A realism in which the enunciative hierarchies of mimesis no longer exist, but only the uninterrupted babble of the crowd; a realism in which each character becomes the protagonist of a mini-narrative universe created specifically for her by the author. It is a matter, in brief, of a *radical realism*:

> Which was why, the wraith is continuing, the complete unfiguranted egalitarian aural realism was why party-line entertainment-critics always complained that the wraith's entertainments' public-area scenes were always incredibly dull and self-conscious and irritating, that they could never hear the really meaningful central narrative conversations for all the unaltered babble of the peripheral crowd, which they assumed the babble (/babel) was some self-conscious viewer-hostile heavy-art directorial pose, instead of radical realism. (Ibid., 836)

A mimetic project corresponding to a peremptory aesthetic and ethical urgency felt by Wallace. In a 1993 interview with Larry McCaffery,[22] Wallace confronted the theme of realism, taking his distance from what he defines as "big-Realism." In his view, classic mimesis has, for some time now, been without impact on the reader, from the moment that its language was progressively absorbed and exhausted by television and advertising, acquiring, negatively, an anesthetic character:

> This might be my best response to your claim that my stuff's not "realistic." I'm not much interested in trying for classical, big-R Realism, not because the big-R's form has now been absorbed and suborned by commercial entertainment. The classical Realist form is soothing, familiar and anesthetic; it drops right into spectation. It doesn't set up the sort of expectations serious 1990s fiction ought to be setting up in readers.[23]

The task of the engaged writer, then, is to recuperate for mimesis zones of the real, hitherto unexplored by classical realism, in the hope of producing an estrangement effect on the reader. This new realism, a critical realism, should aim, paradoxically, at a *defamiliarization* of the real, at the same time exploring its hidden folds, in an ethical impetus without precedent. The movement, characteristic of traditional realism, toward the familiarization of reality is abruptly inverted into an operation which no longer has much

22 Larry McCaffery, "An Interview with David Foster Wallace," *Review of Contemporary Fiction* 13, 2 (1993): 127–50.
23 Ibid., 138.

to do with realism as commonly understood; an operation imbued with the antirealism permeating twentieth-century literature and which marked the birth of the great American narrative[24]:

> L.M: . . . I noticed you didn't take off down the hall when I said earlier that your work didn't seem "realistic." Do you agree with that?
>
> D.F.W.: Well, it depends whether you're talking little-r realistic or big-R. If you mean is my stuff in the Howells/Wharton/Updike school of U.S. Realism, clearly not. But to me the whole binary of realistic vs. unrealistic fiction is a canonical distinction set up by people with a vested interest in the big-R tradition. A way to marginalize stuff that isn't soothing and conservative. Even the goofiest avant-garde agenda, if it's got integrity, is never, "Let's eschew all realism," but more, "Let's try to countenance and render real aspects of real experiences that have previously been excluded from art." The result often seems "unrealistic" to the big-R devotees because it's not a recognizable part of the "ordinary experience" they're used to countenancing. I guess my point is that "realistic" doesn't have a univocal definition. . . . For our generation, the entire world seems to present itself as "familiar," but since that's of course an illusion in terms of anything really important about people, maybe any "realistic" fiction's job is opposite what it used to be—no longer making the strange familiar but making the familiar strange again. It seems important to find ways of reminding ourselves that most "familiarity" is meditated and delusive.[25]

Straddling alternative hypotheses of realism, the maximalist novel has issued new aesthetic challenges to the postmodern literary system, in the bitter awareness that to relate today's world, one probably has to render it unrecognizable. A high price, imposed by an era of widespread unreality but one which the authors discussed in this study seem, for their part, prepared to pay, sustained by a profound faith in the critical and universalizing power of maximalist writing.

[24] Classics, although somewhat dated and debated, are: Richard V. Chase, *The American Novel and Its Tradition* [1957] (Baltimore-London: The Johns Hopkins University Press, 1980), and Leslie A. Fiedler, *Love and Death in American Novel* [1960] (Urbana-Champaign: Dalkey Archive Press, 1998). See Robert Glen Deamer, "The American Dream and the Romance Tradition in American Fiction: A Literary Study of Society and Success in America," *The Journal of American Culture* 2, 1 (1979): 5–16.

[25] McCaffery, *An Interview*, 139–41.

Bibliography

Primary texts

Babette Factory. *2005 dopo Cristo*. Turin: Einaudi, 2005.

Bolaño, Roberto. *2666* [2004]. Barcelona: Anagrama, 2008. Translated as *2666* by Natasha Wimmer. New York: Farrar, Straus and Giroux, 2008.

DeLillo, Don. *Underworld*. New York: Scribner, 1997.

Franzen, Jonathan. *The Corrections* [2001]. New York: Harper Perennial, 2007.

Pynchon, Thomas. *Gravity's Rainbow* [1973]. New York: Vintage, 1998.

Smith, Zadie. *White Teeth*. New York: Vintage, 2000.

Wallace, David Foster. *Infinite Jest* [1996]. Forward by Dave Eggers. New York: Back Bay Books/Little, 2006.

Essays

Abadi-Nàgy, Zoltan. "Minimalism vs. Postmodernism in Contemporary American Fiction." *Nohelicon* 28, 1 (2001): 129–44.

Adams Sitney, P. *Modernist Montage: The Obscurity of Vision in Cinema and Literature*. New York: Columbia University Press, 1990.

Adorno, Theodor W. *Minima Moralia: Reflections from Damaged Life* [1951]. Translated by E. F. N. Jephcott. London-New York: Verso, 1978.

Allegretti, Pietro, ed. *Brueghel*. Milan: Rizzoli/Skira, 2003.

Anceschi, Giovanni. *Il progetto delle interfacce: Oggetti colloquiali e protesi virtuali*. Milan: Domus Academy, 1992.

Arnao, Giancarlo. *Proibizionismo, antiproibizionismo e droghe*. Rome: Stampa alternativa, 1992.

Arnheim, Rudolf. *Film As Art*. Berkeley-Los Angeles: University of California Press, 1969.

—. "A New Laocoön: Artistic Composites and the Talking Film" [1938]. In Arnheim, *Film As Art*, 199–230.

Babbit, Irving. *The New Laokoon: An Essay on the Confusion of the Arts*. Boston: Houghton Mifflin, 1910.

Bakhtin, Mikhail. *The Dialogic Imagination.* Edited by Michael Holquist. Translated by Caryl Emerson and Michael Holquist. Austin: University of Texas Press, 1981.

—. "Discourse in the Novel" [1934-1935]. In Bakhtin, *The Dialogic Imagination*, 259–422.

Barth, John. "A Few Words about Minimalism." *The New York Times*. 28 December 1986.

—. *The Friday Book: Essays and Other Non-fiction* [1984]. Baltimore-London: The Johns Hopkins University Press, 1997.

—. "The Literature of Exhaustion" [1967]. In Barth, *The Friday Book*, 166–71.

Barthelme, Frederick. "On Being Wrong: Convicted Minimalist Spills Beans." *The New York Times*. 3 April 1988.

Barthes, Roland. *Arcimboldo* [1978]. Introduction by Achille Bonito Oliva. Milan: F. M. Ricci, 1980.

—. "The Death of the Author" [1968]. In Barthes, *The Rustle of Language*, 49–55.

—. "The Rustle of Language" [1975]. In Barthes, *The Rustle of Language*, 76–9.

—. *The Rustle of Language* [1984]. Translated by Richard Howard. New York: Hill and Wang, 1986.

Baudrillard, Jean. *Simulacra and Simulation* [1980]. Translated by Sheila Faria Glaser. Ann Arbor: University of Michigan Press, 1995.

Beissinger, Margaret, et al., eds. *Epic Traditions in the Contemporary World: The Poetics of Community*. Berkeley-Los Angeles: University of California Press, 1999.

Bell, Madison Smartt. "Less Is Less: The Dwindling of the American Short Story." *Harper's*. April 1986, 64–9.

Benedetti, Carla. *The Empty Cage: Inquiry into the Mysterious Disappearance of the Author* [1999]. Ithaca-London: Cornell University Press, 2005.

Benjamin, Walter. *The Arcades Project* [*Das Passagen-Werk* (1927-1940). Edited by Rolf Tiedemann]. Translated by Howard Eiland and Kevin McLaughlin. Cambridge, MA: Belknap Press of Harvard University Press, 1999.

—. "Paris, the Capital of the Nineteenth Century" [1935]. In Benjamin, *The Arcades Project*, 3–13.

Bernstein, Michael A. "Making Modernist Masterpieces." *Modernism/Modernity* 5, 3 (1998): 1–17.

Bertalanffy, Ludwig von. *General Systems Theory: Foundations, Developments, Applications*. New York: G. Braziller, 1969.

Bertoni, Clotide. *Percorsi europei dell'eroicomico*. Pisa: Nistri Lischi, 1997.

Bertoni, Federico. *Realismo e letteratura: Una storia possibile*. Turin: Einaudi, 2007.

Best, Steven. "Jameson, Totality, and the Poststructuralist Critique." In Kellner (ed.), *Postmodernism. Jameson. Critique*, 333–68.

Bhabha, Homi K. *The Location of Culture* [1994]. New York: Routledge, 2005.

Bibbò, Antonio. "'There can't be two Jameses can there?': Il montaggio di *Manhattan Transfer* e l'indeterminatezza." In Lombardi (ed.), *Il personaggio*, 323–35.

Blumenberg, Hans. *The Legitimacy of the Modern Age* [1966]. Translated by Robert M. Wallace. Cambridge, MA: MIT Press, 1983.

Boisseau, Denis. "De l''inexistance' du detail." In Louvel (ed.), *Le détail*, 15–33.

Booth, Wayne C. *The Company We Keep: An Ethics of Fiction*. Berkeley-Los Angeles: University of California Press, 1988.

—. *The Rhetoric of Fiction* [1961]. Chicago-London: The University of Chicago Press, 1983.

Borsato, Battista. *L'alterità come etica: Una lettura di Emmanuel Lévinas*. Milan: EDB, 1996.

Boswell, Marshall. *Understanding David Foster Wallace*. Columbia: University of South Carolina Press, 2003.

Braudel, Fernand. "History and the Social Sciences: The *Longue Durée*" [1958]. In Braudel, *On History*, 25–54.

—. *On History*. Translated by Sarah Matthews. Chicago: University of Chicago Press, 1980.

Bruni, Frank. "The Grunge American Novel." *New York Times Magazine*. 24 March 1996.

Budgen, Frank. *James Joyce and the Making of "Ulysses" and Other Writings*. London: Oxford University Press, 1972.

Burn, Stephen J. "The Collapse of Everything: William Gaddis and the Encyclopedic Novel." In Tabbi and Shavers (eds), *Paper Empire*, 46–62.

—. *David Foster Wallace's "Infinite Jest": A Reader's Guide*. New York-London: Continuum, 2003.

Butler, Judith. "Values of Difficulty." In Culler and Lamb (eds), *Just Being Difficult?*, 199–215.

Calvino, Italo. *Six Memos for the Next Millennium*. Cambridge, MA: Harvard University Press, 1988.

Carboni, Massimo. *Il sublime è ora: Saggio sulle estetiche contemporanee*. Rome: Calstelvecchi, 2003.

Carver, Raymond. *Fires: Essays, Poems, Stories*. New York: Vintage, 1989.

—. "*On Writing*" [1981]. In Carver, *Fires*, 22–7.

Caserio, Robert L., ed. *The Cambridge Companion to the 20th Century English Novel*. New York: Cambridge University Press, 2009.

Ceserani, Remo, "L'immaginazione cospiratoria." In Micali (ed.), *Cospirazioni, trame: Quaderni di Synapsis II*, 7–20.

Chase, Richard V. *The American Novel and Its Tradition* [1957]. Baltimore-London: The Johns Hopkins University Press, 1980.

Christ, Birte, et al. *American Studies/Shifting Gears*. Heidelberg: Universitätverlag Winter, 2010.

Clark, Hillary. *The Fictional Encyclopaedia: Joyce, Pound, Sollers*. New York: Garland, 1990.

Coale, Samuel Chase. *Paradigms of Paranoia: The Culture of Conspiracy in Contemporary American Fiction*. Tuscaloosa: University of Alabama Press, 2005.

Cohen, Keith. *Film and Fiction: The Dynamics of Exchange*. New Haven: Yale University Press, 1979.

Cohn, Norman. *Cosmos, Chaos, and the World to Come: The Ancient Roots of Apocalyptic Faith*. New Haven: Yale University Press, 1993.

Cometa, Michele. "Letteratura e arti figurative: Un catalogo." In Fusillo and Polacco (eds), *La letteratura e le altre arti*, 15–29.

—. *Visioni della fine: Apocalissi, catastrofi, estinzioni*. Palermo: :duepunti Edizioni, 2004.

Compagnon, Antoine. *Literature, Theory, and Common Sense* [1998]. Translated by Carol Cosman. Princeton: Princeton University Press, 2004.

Consonni, Stefania. "Disegni e realtà: Le finzioni di Don DeLillo." *Paragrafo* 1 (2006): 9–30.

Costa, Antonio. "Nel corpo della parola, l'immagine: Quando la letteratura cita il cinema." In Fusillo and Polacco (eds), *La letteratura e le altre arti*, 59–67.

—. *Saper vedere il cinema* [1985]. Milan: Bompiani, 2004.

Couégnas, Daniel. *Introduction à la paralittérature*. Paris: Seuil, 1992.

Coupe, Laurence. *Myth (The New Critical Idiom)* [1997]. 2nd Edition. New York: Routledge, 2009.

Culler, Jonathan and Kevin Lamb, eds. *Just Being Difficult? Academic Writing in the Public Arena*. Stanford: Stanford University Press, 2003.

Curry, Richard O. and Thomas M. Brown, eds. *Conspiracy: The Fear of Subversion in American History*. New York: Holt, 1972.

D'Alembert, Jean-Baptiste Le Rond. *Preliminary Discourse to the Encyclopedia of Diderot* [1751]. Translation by Richard N. Schwab and Walter E. Rex. Introduction by Richard Schwab. Indianapolis: Bobbs-Sams, 1963.

Dalle Vacche, Angela, ed. *The Visual Turn: Classical Film Theory and Art History.* Piscataway: Rutgers University Press, 2003.

Davidson, Donald. *Inquiries into Truth and Interpretation.* Oxford: Clarendon Press, 1984.

—. "Truth and Meaning" [1967]. In Davidson, *Inquiries into Truth and Interpretation,* 17–36.

Davis, Todd F. and Kenneth Womack, eds. *Mapping the Ethical Turn: A Reader in Ethics, Culture and Literary Theory.* Charlottesville: University of Virginia Press, 2001.

Deamer, Robert Glen. "The American Dream and the Romance Tradition in American Fiction: A Literary Study of Society and Success in America." *The Journal of American Culture* 2, 1 (1979): 5–16.

Debenedetti, Giacomo. "Commemorazione provvisoria del personaggio-uomo" [1965]. In Benedetti, *Saggi,* 1280–322.

—. *Saggi.* Edited by Alfonso Berardinelli. Milan: Mondadori, 1999.

De Jong, Irene. *Narrators and Focalizers: The Presentation of the Story in the "Iliad."* Amsterdam: Grüner, 1987.

Deleuze, Gilles and Félix Guattari. *Anti-Oedipus: Capitalism and Schizophrenia* [1980]. Preface by Michel Foucault. Translated by Robert Hurley, Mark Seem, and Helen R. Lane. Minneapolis: University of Minnesota Press, 1983.

DeLillo, Don. "The Power of History." *New York Times Magazine.* 7 September 1997.

Dellamora, Richard. *Postmodern Apocalypse: Theory and Cultural Practice at the End.* Philadelphia: University of Pennsylvania Press, 1995.

Della Volpe, Galvano. *Critica del gusto* [1960]. Milan: Feltrinelli, 1996.

Deming, Robert, ed. *James Joyce 1907-27: The Critical Heritage,* Vol. I. London: Routledge & Kegan Paul, 1970.

DePietro, Thomas, ed. *Conversations with Don DeLillo.* Jackson: University Press of Mississippi, 2005.

Derrida, Jacques. "The Rhetoric of Drugs" [1988]. Translated by Michael Israel. In Derrida, *Points . . .: Interviews, 1974-1994,* 228–54.

—. *Specters of Marx: The State of the Debt, the Work of Mourning, and the New International* [1993]. Translated by Peggy Kamuf. New York: Routledge, 1994.

—. *Points . . .: Interviews, 1974-1994.* Edited by Elisabeth Weber. Translated by Peggy Kamuf, et al. Stanford: Stanford University Press, 1995.

Didi-Huberman, Georges. *Devant le Temps: Histoire de l'art et anachronism des images.* Paris: Éditions de Minuit, 2000.

—. *L'Image survivante: Histoire de l'art et temps des fantômes selon Aby Warburg.* Paris: Éditions de Minuit, 2004.

Donnarumma, Raffaele. "Nuovi realismi e persistenze postmoderne: Narratori italiani di oggi." *Allegoria* XX, 57 (2008): 26–54.

Eaglestone, Robert. *Ethical Criticism: Reading After Lévinas*. Edinburgh: Edinburgh University Press, 1997.

Eco, Umberto. *Postscript to the Name of the Rose* [1983]. Translated by William Weaver. San Diego-New York-London: Harcourt Brace Jovanovich, 1984.

Eisenstein, Sergei. *The Eisenstein Reader*. Edited by Bruce Taylor. Translated by Richard Taylor and William Powell. London: British Film Institute, 1998.

—. "The Montage of Attractions" [1923]. In Taylor (ed.), *The Eisenstein Reader*, 29–34.

Elam, Diane. *Romancing the Postmodern*. London: Routledge, 1992.

Eliot, T. S. *Selected Prose*, Hammondsworth, Penguin, 1951.

—. "The Metaphysical Poets" [1921]. In Eliot, *Selected Prose*, 59–67.

—. "'Ulysses,' Order and Myth." *The Dial* LXXV (November 1923): 480–3.

Ercolino, Stefano. "Il difficile ritorno dell'autore." In Pontuale (ed.), *Lezioni di dottorato 2009*, 253–72.

—. "Per un'estetica dell'irrappresentabile: Le immagini della Shoah in *Austerlitz* di W. G. Sebald." *Contemporanea* 9 (2011): 93–107.

—. "The Killing Vision: David Foster Wallace's *Infinite Jest*." In Ercolino et al. (eds), *Fictional Cinema: How Literature Describes Imaginary Films*. Göttingen: Vandenhoeck and Ruprecht Unipress, 2014. Forthcoming.

Ercolino, Stefano, et al., eds. *Fictional Cinema: How Literature Describes Imaginary Films*. Göttingen: Vandenhoeck and Ruprecht Unipress, 2014. Forthcoming.

Escohotado, Antonio. *A Brief History of Drugs: From the Stone Age to the Stoned Age* [1996]. Rochester, VT: Park Street Press, 1999.

Farrel, Thomas J., ed. *Bakhtin and Medieval Voices*. Gainesville: University Press of Florida, 1995.

Fenster, Mark. *Conspiracy Theories: Secrecy and Power in American Culture*. Minneapolis: University of Minnesota Press, 1999.

Fiedler, Leslie A. *Love and Death in American Novel* [1960]. Urbana-Champaign: Dalkey Archive Press, 1998.

Flaubert, Gustave. *The Letters of Gustave Flaubert (1830-1857)*. Edited and translated by Francis Steegmuller. Cambridge, MA-London: Belknap Press, 1979.

Fludernik, Monika. "Hänsel und Gretel, and Dante: The Coordinates of Hope in Pynchon's *Gravity's Rainbow*." *Arbeiten aus Anglistik und Amerikanistik* 14, 1 (1989): 39–55.

Foster, Hal. *The Anti-Aesthetic: Essays on Postmodern Culture* [1983]. New York: New Press, 1998.

Foucault, Michel, et al. *Tel Quel: Théorie d'ensemble*. Paris: Seuil, 1968.

Fowler, Dan. "Second Thoughts on Closure." In Roberts et al. (eds), *Classical Closure*, 3–22.

Francalanci, Ernesto L. *Estetica degli oggetti*. Bologna: Il Mulino, 2006.

Franz, Michael, et al., eds. *Electric Laokoon: Zeiche und Mieden, von der Lochkarte zur Grammatologie*. Berlin: Akademie, 2007.

Frazer, James. *The Golden Bough: A Study in Magic and Religion* [1890-1922]. London: Oxford University Press, 1994.

Frege, Gottlob. *The Foundations of Arithmetic: A Logico-Mathematical Enquiry into the Concept of Number* [1884]. Translated by J. L. Austin. Oxford: Basil Blackwell, 1959.

Freud, Sigmund. "The Fetish" [1927]. In *The Standard Edition of the Complete Psychological Works of Sigmund Freud*, vol. XXI, 152–7.

—. *The Standard Edition of the Complete Psychological Works of Sigmund Freud*. Edited and translated by James Strachey et al., vol. XXI. London: The Hogarth Press, 1961.

Friedman, Norman. "Point of View in Fiction: The Development of a Critical Concept." In Stevick (ed.), *The Theory of the Novel*, 108–36.

Frye, Northrop. *Anatomy of Criticism: Four Essays* [1957]. Preface by Harold Bloom. Princeton-Oxford: Princeton University Press, 2000.

Fusillo, Massimo. "Comparare la letteratura con le altre arti oggi: Per una visione 'impura.'" In Fusillo and Polacco (eds), *La letteratura e le alte arti*, 9–10.

—. "Epic, Novel" [2002]. Translated by Michael F. Moore. In Moretti (ed.), *The Novel*, vol. II, 32–63.

—. *Estetica della letteratura*. Bologna: Il Mulino, 2009.

—. *Feticci: Letteratura, cinema, arti visive*. Bologna: Il Mulino, 2012.

—. *Il romanzo Greco: Polifonia ed Eros*. Venice: Marsilio, 1989.

Fusillo, Massimo and Marina Polacco, eds. "La letteratura e le altre arti: Atti del convegno annuale dell'Associazione di teoria e studi di Letteratura comparata – L'Aquila, Febbraio 2004." *Contemporanea* 3 (2005).

Genette, Gerard. *Narrative Discourse: An Essay in Method* [1972]. Translated by Jane E. Lewin. Foreward by Jonathan Culler. Ithaca: Cornell University Press, 1980.

—. *Palimpsests: Literature in the Second Degree* [1982]. Translated by Channa Newmann and Claude Doubinsky. Foreword by Gerald Prince. Lincoln: University of Nebraska Press, 1997.

Gentry, Marshall Bruce and William L. Stull. *Conversations with Raymond Carver*. Jackson: University of Mississippi Press, 1990.

Ghelli, Francesco. *Viaggi nel regno dell'illogico: Letteratura e droga da De Quincey ai giorni nostri*. Naples: Liguori, 2003.

Gibson, Andrew. *Postmodernity, Ethics and the Novel: From Leavis to Lévinas*. London-New York: Routledge, 1999.

Goethe, Johann Wolfgang and Friedrich Schiller. *Correspondence between Goethe and Schiller 1794-1805*. Translated by Liselotte Dieckmann. New York: Peter Lang, 1994.

Goldberg, Robert Alan. *Enemies Within: The Culture of Conspiracy in Modern America*. New Haven: Yale University Press, 2001.

Greenberg, Clement. "Toward a Newer Laocoon." *Partisan Review* 7, 4 (1940): 296–310.

Hagen, Rose-Marie and Rainer Hagen. *Pieter Bruegel the Elder, c. 1525-1569: Peasants, Fools, and Demons*. Cologne: Benedikt Taschen, 1994.

Hale, Dorothy J. "Aesthetics and the New Ethics: Theorizing the Novel in the Twenty-First Century." *PMLA* 124 (2009): 896–905.

—. "*An Aesthetics of Alterity: The Art of English Fiction in the 20th Century*." In Caserio (ed.), *The Cambridge Companion to the 20th Century English Novel*, 10–22.

—. "Fiction as Restriction: Self-Binding in New Ethical Theories of the Novel." *Narrative* 15, 2 (2007): 187–206.

—. "*On Beauty* as Beautiful? The Problem of Novelistic Aesthetics by Way of Zadie Smith." *Contemporary Literature* 53, 4 (2012): 814–44.

Hartley, George. *The Abyss of Representation: Marxism and the Postmodern Sublime*. Durham: Duke University Press, 2003.

Hayles, Katherine N., ed. *Chaos and Order: Complex Dynamics in Literature and Science*. Chicago: The University of Chicago Press, 1991.

Heffernan, James A. W. *Museum of Words: The Poetics of Ekphrasis from Homer to Ashbery*. Chicago-London: The University of Chicago Press, 1993.

Hegel, Georg Wilhelm Friedrich. *Aesthetics* [1836-38], vol. II. Translated by T. M. Knox. Oxford: Clarendon Press, 1975.

Heise, Ursula K. *Chronoschisms: Time, Narrative, and Postmodernism*. Cambridge: Cambridge University Press, 1997.

Hite, Molly. *Ideas of Order in the Novels of Thomas Pynchon*. Columbus: Ohio State University Press, 1983.

Hoffmann, Gerhard. *From Modernism to Postmodernism: Concepts and Strategies of Postmodern American Fiction*. Amsterdam-New York: Rodopi, 2005.

Hofstadter, Richard. *The Paranoid Style in American Politics*. New York: Knopf, 1946.

Hölscher, Uvo. *Die "Odyssee": Epos zwischen Märchen und Roman*. Munich: C. H. Beck, 1988.

Hume, Katherine. *Pynchon's Mythography: An Approach to "Gravity's Rainbow."* Carbondale: Southern Illinois University Press, 1987.

Huyssen, Andreas. *After the Great Divide: Modernism, Mass Culture, Postmodernism* [1986]. Basingstoke: Macmillan, 1988.

Iacono, Alfonso Maria. *Teorie del feticismo: Il problema filosofico e storico di un "immenso malinteso."* Milan: Giuffré, 1985.

Jacob, François. "Evolution and Tinkering." *Science* 196 (10 June 1977): 1161–6.

Jacobs, Timothy. "The Brothers Incandenza: Translating Ideology in Fyodor Dostoevsky's *The Brothers Karamazov* and David Foster Wallace's *Infinite Jest*." *Texas Studies in Literature and Language* 9, 3 (2007): 265–92.

Jameson, Fredric. *The Political Unconscious: Narrative as a Socially Symbolic Act*. Ithaca: Cornell University Press, 1981.

—. *Postmodernism, or the Cultural Logic of Late Capitalism*. Durham: Duke University Press, 1991.

Jannidis, Fotis, et al., eds. *Rückkehr des Autors: Zur Erneuerung eines umstrittenen Begriffs*. Tübingen: Niemeyer, 1999.

Jay, Martin. *Downcasts Eyes: The Denigration of Vision in Twentieth-Century French Thought*. Berkeley-Los Angeles: University of California Press, 1994.

—. *Marxism and Totality: The Adventures of a Concept from Lukács to Habermas*. Berkeley-Los Angeles: University of California Press, 1984.

Johnston, John. *Information Multiplicity: American Fiction in the Age of Media Saturation*. Baltimore-London: The Johns Hopkins University Press, 1998.

Joyce, James. *Selected Letters of James Joyce*. Edited by Richard Ellmann. London: Faber, 1975.

—. *The Critical Writings of James Joyce*. Edited by Ellsworth Mason and Richard Ellmann. New York: Viking Press, 1964.

Karl, Frederick R. *American Fictions: 1940-1980: A Comprehensive History and Critical Evaluation*. New York: Harper and Row, 1983.

—. *American Fictions: 1980-2000: Whose America Is It Anyway?* Bloomington: Xlibris, 2001.

Kellner, Douglas, ed. *Postmodernism. Jameson. Critique*. Washington: Maisonneuve Press, 1989.

Knight, Peter, ed. *Conspiracy Nation: The Politics of Paranoia in Postwar America*. New York: New York University Press, 2002.

—. "Everything is Connected: "*Underworld*'s Secret History of Paranoia." *Modern Fiction Studies* XLV, 3 (1999): 811–36.

Komar, Kathleen L. *Pattern and Chaos: Multilinear Novels by Dos Passos, Faulkner, Döblin, and Koeppen*. Columbia: Camden House, 1983.

Kramer, Jane. *Lone Patriot*. New York: Pantheon, 2002.

Krieger, Murray. *EKPHRASIS: The Illusion of the Natural Sign*. Baltimore-London: The Johns Hopkins University Press, 1992.

Landowski, Eric and Gianfranco Marrone, eds. *La società degli oggetti: Problemi di intersoggettività*. Rome: Meltemi, 2002.

Lavagetto, Mario. *Lavorare con piccoli indizi*. Turin: Bollati Boringhieri, 2003.

Leary, Timothy and Ralph Metzner. *The Psychedelic Experience* [1967]. New York: Citadel Press, 1995.

LeClair, Tom. *The Art of Excess: Mastery in Contemporary American Fiction*. Urbana: University of Illinois Press, 1989.

—. "The Prodigious Fiction of Richard Powers, William Vollmann, and David Foster Wallace." *Critique* 38, 1 (1996): 12–37.

Lentricchia, Frank, ed. *Introducing Don DeLillo* [1991]. Durham: Duke University Press, 1999.

Lévinas, Emmanuel. *Otherwise than Being or Beyond Essence* [1978]. Pittsburgh: Duquesne University Press, 1998.

Levine, George and David Leverence, eds. *Mindful Pleasures: Essays on Thomas Pynchon*. Boston: Little, 1976.

Lewis, Barry. "Postmodernism and Fiction." In Sim (ed.), *The Routledge Companion to Postmodernism*, 111–21.

Lilly, John C. *Programming and Metaprogramming in the Human Biocomputer: Theory and Experiments* [1967]. New York: The Julian Press, 1987.

Lino, Mirko. *L'apocalisse postmoderna tra letteratura e cinema: Catastrofi, oggetti, metropoli, corpi*. Florence: Le Lettere, 2014. Forthcoming.

Lombardi, Chiara, ed. *Il personaggio: Figure della dissolvenza e della permanenza*. Turin: Edizioni dell'orso, 2008.

Louvel, Liliane, ed. *Le détail*. Poitiers: la Licorne, 1999.

Lovelock, James. *Gaia: A New Look at Life on Earth*. New York: Oxford University Press, 1979.

—. *The Revenge of Gaia: Earth's Climate Crisis and the Fate of Humanity* [2006]. New York: Basic Books, 2007.

Lukács, Georg. *The Theory of the Novel* [1919]. Translated by Anna Bostock. Cambridge, MA: MIT Press, 1971.

Luperini, Romano. *L'incontro e il caso: Narrazioni moderne e destino dell'uomo occidentale*. Rome-Bari: Laterza, 2007.

Lyotard, Jean-François. *The Postmodern Condition: A Report on Knowledge* [1979]. Translation by Geoff Bennington and Brian Massumi. Foreward by Fredric Jameson. Minneapolis: University of Minnesota Press, 1984.

Madelenat, Daniel. *L'épopée*. Paris: Presses Universitaires de France, 1986.

Maggitti, Vincenzo. *Lo schermo fra le righe: Cinema e letteratura del Novecento*. Naples: Liguori, 2007.

Margaron, Henri. *Le stagioni degli dei: Storia medica e sociale delle droghe*. Milan: Raffaello Cortina, 2001.

Marx, Karl. *Capital: A Critical Analysis of Capitalist Production* [1867], vol. I. Introduction by Ernest Mandel. Translation by Ben Fowles. New York: Vintage, 1977.

McCaffery, Larry. "An Interview with David Foster Wallace." *Review of Contemporary Fiction* 13, 2 (1993): 127–50.

McClure, John. "Postmodern Romance: Don DeLillo and the Age of Conspiracy." In Lentricchia (ed.), *Introducing Don DeLillo*, 99–115.

Melley, Timothy. *Empire of Conspiracy: The Culture of Paranoia in Postwar America*. Ithaca: Cornell University Press, 2000.

Memmi, Albert. *Le Buveur et l'amoureux: Le Prix de la dependence*. Paris: Arléa, 1998.

Mendelson, Edward. "Encyclopedic Narrative: From Dante to Pynchon." *Modern Language Notes* 91 (1976): 1267–75.

—. "Gravity's Encyclopedia." In Levine and Leverence (eds), *Mindful Pleasures*, 161–95.

Metz, Christian. *Film Language: A Semiotics of Cinema*. Translated by Michael Taylor. New York: Oxford University Press, 1974.

Micali, Simona, ed. *Cospirazioni, trame: Quaderni di Synapsis II*. Florence: Le Monnier, 2003.

Miconi, Andrea. "Dal 'real meravilloso' al realismo magico: Approccio evolutivo alla formazione di un genere." *Paragrafo* II (2006): 7–48.

Miller, J. Hillis. *The Ethics of Reading: Kant, de Man, Eliot, Trollope, James, and Benjamin*. New York: Columbia University Press, 1987.

Mistura, Stefano. *Figure del feticismo*. Turin: Einaudi, 2001.

Mitchell, W. J. T. *Iconology: Image, Text, Ideology*. Chicago-London: The University of Chicago Press, 1986.

—. *Picture Theory: Essays on Verbal and Visual Representation*. Chicago-London: The University of Chicago Press, 1994.

Moore, Thomas. *The Style of Connectedness: "Gravity's Rainbow" and Thomas Pynchon*. Columbia: University of Missouri Press, 1987.

Moretti, Franco. *Graphs, Maps and Trees: Abstract Models for Literary History*. Afterword by Alberto Piazza. London: Verso, 2005.

—. *Modern Epic: The World System from Goethe to García Marquez* [1994]. Translated by Quintin Hoare. London: Verso, 1996.

—, ed. *The Novel*, vols. I and II. Princeton: Princeton University Press, 2006.

Murnaghan, Sheila. "Equal Honor and Future Glory: The Plan of Zeus in the *Iliad*." In Roberts, et al. (eds), *Classical Closure*, 23–42.

Newman, Charles. *The Post-Modern Aura: The Act of Fiction in an Age of Inflation*. Evanston: Northwestern University Press, 1985.

Nichols, Catherine. "Dialogizing Postmodern Carnival: David Foster Wallace's *Infinite Jest*." *Critique* 43 (2001): 3–16.

Nussbaum, Martha C. *Love's Knowledge: Essays on Philosophy and Literature*. New York: Oxford University Press, 1990.

O'Donnell, Patrick. *Latent Destinies: Cultural Paranoia and Contemporary United States Narrative*. Durham: Duke University Press, 2000.

Paduano, Guido. "Le scelte di Achille." In Homer, *Iliade*, edited by Guido Paduano. Turin: Einaudi, 1997.

Panofsky, Erwin. "Iconography and Iconology: An Introduction to the Study of Renaissance Art." In Panofsky, *Meaning in the Visual Arts*, 26–54.

—. *Meaning in the Visual Arts*. Garden City: Doubleday, 1955.

—. *Studies in Iconology*. Oxford: Oxford University Press, 1939.

Parker, David. *Ethics, Theory and the Novel*. Cambridge: Cambridge University Press, 1994.

Parrish, Timothy L. "From Hoover's FBI to Eisenstein's *Unterwelt*: DeLillo Directs the Postmodern Novel." *Modern Fiction Studies* XLV, 3 (1999): 696–723.

—. *From the Civil War to the Apocalypse: Postmodern History and American Fiction*. Amherst: University of Massachusetts Press, 2008.

Penco, Carlo. *Introduzione alla filosofia del linguaggio*. Rome-Bari: Laterza, 2004.

Perniola, Mario. *The Sex Appeal of the Inorganic: Philsophies of Desire in the Modern World* [1994]. Translated by Massimo Verdicchio. New York: Bloomsbury, 2004.

Piccone Stella, Simonetta. *Droghe e tossicodipendenza*. Bologna: Il Mulino, 1999.

Pontuale, Francesco, ed. *Lezioni di dottorato 2009*. Rome: Palombi Editori, 2011.

Ponzio, Augusto. *Tra Bachtin e Lévinas: Scritture, dialogo, alterità*. Bari: Palomar, 2008.

Portelli, Alessandro. *The Text and the Voice: Writing, Speaking and Democracy in American Literature* [1992]. New York: Columbia University Press, 1994.

Pouillon, Jean. *Temps et roman*. Paris: Gallimard, 1946.

Pugliatti, Paola. *Lo sguardo nel racconto: Teorie e prassi del punto di vista*. Bologna: Zanichelli, 1985.

Purdy, Strother. "*Gravity's Rainbow* and the Culture of Childhood." *Pynchon Notes* 22–23 (1988): 7–24.

Pynchon, Thomas. "Is It O. K. to Be a Luddite?" *New York Times Book Review*. 28 October 1984.

Quayson, Ato. "Fecundities of the Unexpected: Magical Realism, Narrative, and History" [2002]. In Moretti (ed.), *The Novel*, vol. I, 726–56.

Quine, Willard Van Orman. *From a Logical Point of View: 9 Logico-Philosophical Essays*. Cambridge, MA: Harvard University Press, 1953.

—. "Two Dogmas of Empiricism" [1951]. In Quine, *From a Logical Point of View: 9 Logico-Philosophical Essays*, 20–46.

Rabel, Robert J. *Plot and Point of View in the "Iliad."* Ann Arbor: University of Michigan Press, 1997.

Rebein, Robert. *Hicks, Tribes, and Dirty Realists: American Fiction after Postmodernism*. Lexington: The University Press of Kentucky, 2001.

Reed, T. V. *Fifteen Jugglers, Five Believers: Literary Politics and the Poetics of American Social Movements*. Berkeley-Los Angeles: University of California Press, 1992.

—. "Unimagined Experience and the Fiction of the Real: Postmodernist Realism in *Let Us Now Praise Famous Men*." *Representations* 24 (1988): 156–76.

Remnick, David. "Exile on Main Street: Don DeLillo's Undisclosed Underworld" [1997]. In DePietro (ed.), *Conversations with Don DeLillo*, 131–44.

Roberts, Deborah H., et al., eds. *Classical Closure: Reading the End in Greek and Latin Literature*. Princeton: Princeton University Press, 1997.

Robinson, Douglas. *American Apocalypses: The Image of the End of the World in American Literature*. Baltimore-London: The Johns Hopkins University Press, 1985.

Rosen, Elizabeth K. *Apocalyptic Transformation: Apocalypse and the Postmodern Imagination*. Lanham: Lexington, 2008.

Saint Girons, Baldine. *Le sublime de l'Antiquité à nos jours*. Paris: Desjonquères, 2005.

Scanlan, Margaret. *Plotting Terror: Novelists and Terrorists in Contemporary Fiction*. Charlottesville: University Press of Virginia, 2001.

Schleifer, Ronald. *Modernism and Time: The Logic of Abundance in Literature, Science, and Culture, 1880-1930*. Cambridge: Cambridge University Press, 2000.

Serres, Michel. *The Parasite* [1997]. Translation by Lawrence R. Schehr. Introduction by Cary Wolfe. Minneapolis: University of Minnesota Press, 2007.

Sesta, Luciano. *La legge dell'altro: La fondazione dell'etica in Lévinas e Kant*. Pisa: ETS, 2005.

Sherman, Mark A. "Problems of Bakhtin's Epic: Capitalism and the Image of History." In Farrel (ed.), *Bakhtin and Medieval Voices*, 180–95.

Siegel, Mark Richard. *Pynchon: Creative Paranoia in "Gravity's Rainbow."* Port Washington: Kennikat Press, 1978.

Sim, Stuart, ed. *The Routledge Companion to Postmodernism* [2001]. London-New York: Routledge, 2005.

Simonetti, Gianluigi. "I nuovi assetti della narrativa italiana (1996-2006)." *Allegoria* XX, 57 (2008): 95–136.

Simmel, Georg. *The Conflict in Modern Culture and Other Essays*. Translated and introduced by K. Peter Etzkorn. New York: Teachers College Press, 1968.

—. "On the Concept and Tragedy of Culture" [1911]. In Simmel, *The Conflict in Modern Culture and Other Essays*, 27–46.

Shlovsky, Viktor. *Material i stil v romane L. N. Tolstogo "Vojna i mir."* Moscow: Federatsiia, 1928.

—. *Theory of Prose* [1929]. Elmwood Park: Dalkey Archive Press, 1990.

Slethaug, Gordon E. *Beautiful Chaos: Chaos Theory and Metachaotics in Recent American Fiction*. Albany: State University of New York Press, 2000.

Smith, Zadie. "This Is How It Feels To Me." *The Guardian*. 13 October 2001.

Sontag, Susan. "Fascinating Fascism" [1975]. In Sontag, *Under the Sign of Saturn*, 73–108.

—. *Under the Sign of Saturn: Essays*. New York: Picador, 2002.

Spivak, Gayatri C. "Ethics and Politics in Tagore, Coetzee, and Certain Scenes of Teaching." *Diacritics* 32, 3–4 (2002): 17–31.

Staiger, Emil. *Basic Concepts of Poetics* [1946]. Translated by Janette C. Hudson and Luanne T. Frank. University Park: The Pennsylvania State University Press, 1991.

Steele, Valerie. *Fetish: Fashion, Sex, and Power* [1996]. New York: Oxford University Press, 1997.

Stephanson, Anders. "Regarding Postmodernism: A Conversation with Fredric Jameson" [1986]. In Kellner (ed.), *Postmodernism. Jameson. Critique*, 43–74.

Stevick, Philip, ed. *The Theory of the Novel*. New York: The Free Press, 1967.

Swedenberg, Hugh Thomas Jr., *The Theory of Epic in England 1650-1800*. Berkeley-Los Angeles: University of California Press, 1944.

Szasz, Thomas. *Ceremonial Chemistry: The Ritual Persecution of Drugs, Addicts, and Pushers*. Garden City: Anchor Press/Doubleday, 1974.

Tabbi, Joseph. *Postmodern Sublime: Technology and American Writing from Mailer to Cyberpunk*. Ithaca: Cornell University Press, 1995.

—. "American World-Fiction in the Longue Durée." In Christ et al. (eds), *American Studies/Shifting Gears*, 117–42.

—. "William Gaddis and the Autopoiesis of American Fiction." In Tabbi and Shavers (eds), *Paper Empire*, 90–117.

Tabbi, Joseph and Rone Shavers, eds. *Paper Empire: William Gaddis and the World System*. Introduction by Joseph Tabbi. Tuscaloosa: University of Alabama Press, 2007.

Todorov, Tzvetan. "Les catégories du récit littéraire." *Communications* 8, 1 (1966): 125–51.

Vargas Llosa, Mario. *García Márquez: Historia de un deicidio*. Barcelona: Barral Editores, 1971.

Vassallo, Nicla. *La naturalizzazione dell'epistemologia: Contro la soluzione quineana*. Milan: Franco Angeli, 1997.

Venturi, Robert, et al., eds. *Learning from Las Vegas: The Forgotten Symbolism of Architectural Form* [1972]. Cambridge, MA: MIT Press, 2001.

Wagner, Peter, ed. *Icons – Texts – Iconotexts: Essays on Ekphrasis and Intermediality*: Berlin-New York: Walter de Gruyter, 1996.

Wallace, David Foster. *A Supposedly Fun Thing I'll Never Do Again: Essays and Arguments*. New York-Boston: Little, 1997.

—. "David Foster Wallace Interviewd by Dave Eggers." *The Believer*. November 2003.

—. "E Unibus Pluram: Television and U. S. Fiction" [1990]. In Wallace, *A Supposedly Fun Thing I'll Never Do Again*, 21–82.

—. *Everything and More: A Compact History of Infinity*. New York: Norton, 2004.

Watt, Ian P. *The Rise of the Novel: Studies in Defoe, Richardson, and Fielding* [1957]. Afterword by W. B. Carnochan. Berkeley-Los Angeles: University of California Press, 2001.

Waugh, Patricia. *Metafiction: The Theory and Practice of Self-Conscious Fiction*. London-New York: Routledge, 1984.

Weber, Eugen. *Apocalypses: Prophecies, Cults, and Millennial Beliefs through the Ages*. Cambridge, MA: Harvard University Press, 1999.

Weber, Max. *Economy and Society: An Outline of Interpretive Sociology* [1922], vol. I. Edited by Geunther Roth and Claus Wittich. Translated by Ephraim Fischoff et al. Berkeley-Los Angeles: University of California Press, 1978.

West, William N. *Theatres and Encyclopedias in Early Modern Europe*. Cambridge: Cambridge University Press, 2002.

Wilde, Alan. *Middle Grounds: Studies in Contemporary American Fiction*. Philadelphia: University of Pennsylvania Press, 1987.

Wilden, Anthony. *Systems and Structure: Essays in Communication and Exchange*. New York: Tavistock, 1980.

Williams, Raymond L. *Drama from Ibsen to Brecht* [1968]. Harmondsworth: Penguin, 1973.

Williams, Richard. "Everything under the Bomb." *The Guardian*. 10 January 1998.

Wittgenstein, Ludwig. *Philosophical Investigations* [1953]. Oxford: Basil Blackwell, 1968.

Wójcik, Daniel. *The End of the World as We Know It: Faith, Fatalism, and Apocalypse in America*. New York: New York University Press, 1997.

Wood, James. *How Fiction Works*. New York: Farrar, 2008.

—. *The Irresponsible Self: On Laughter and the Novel*. New York: Picador, 2004.

—. "Tell Me How Does It Feel?" *The Guardian*. 6 October 2001.

Yeo, Richard. *Encyclopaedic Visions: Scientific Dictionaries and Enlightenment Culture*. Cambridge: Cambridge University Press, 2001.

Index